The AZTECS

Richard F. Townsend

The AZTECS

WITH 143 ILLUSTRATIONS

THAMES AND HUDSON

Ancient Peoples and Places
FOUNDING EDITOR: GLYN DANIEL

For Pala

Author's note

The Aztecs spoke Nahuatl, a language that was transcribed into Roman script by the Conquistadors during the early colonial period. Thus the vowels and most consonants are generally pronounced as they would be in modern Spanish. Exceptions are the Nahuatl *x*, pronounced with the sound of the English *sh*; and the voiceless consonant *tl*, pronounced much like the Welsh *ll*. In Nahuatl, word stress always falls on the penultimate syllable. Accents denoting this have been omitted in the following pages. The correct Nahuatl form "Motecuhzoma" has been adopted for the third and seventh Aztec kings, in preference to inaccurate variants such as "Montezuma" and "Moctezuma."

In the preparation of this book, I must first express my appreciation to Professor Michael Coe and Professor Mary Miller of Yale University, who kindly recommended me to Thames and Hudson. I am doubly indebted to Professor Coe for his invaluable comments on the manuscript. Warmest thanks are due to my friend Dr Felipe Solís, Head of the Archaeology Department at the National Museum of Anthropology in Mexico City, whose unequaled knowledge of Aztec sculpture has always been generously shared. And I am most grateful to Dr Eduardo Matos Moctezuma, who has always been very forthcoming with ideas and information on his ongoing excavations in Mexico City. Special thanks are due to members of my staff at The Art Institute of Chicago: to Linda Morimoto and Anne King whose assistance in preparing the manuscript was indispensable; and to Norma Rosso, Colin McEwan, and Jacqueline Johnson for their support. My wife, Pala, to whom this volume is dedicated, has always been my closest source of strength, and her wise counsel and clear perceptions have helped to shape and inspire many pages of this book.

First published in the United States in 1992 by
Thames and Hudson Inc., 500 Fifth Avenue,
New York, New York 10110

Library of Congress Catalog Card Number 91-67301

Printed and bound in Yugoslavia.

Contents

PART IV AZTEC RELIGION AND BELIEFS

PART V THE AZTEC WAY OF LIFE

Introduction:
The Search for the Aztecs

On 10 February 1519, a Spanish expedition of eleven vessels sailed around the Yucatan Peninsula and along the Gulf of Mexico. Hernán Cortés, the captain of this force, was following a course charted by two earlier voyages of exploration led by Hernández de Córdoba in 1517 and Juan de Grijalva in 1518. These men had returned to the Spanish colony in Cuba with extraordinary descriptions of splendid masonry towns, large populations, powerful rulers leading well-armed warriors, and prodigious quantities of gold. The Spaniards had also heard stories of a rich kingdom beyond the mountains to the west, and it was in quest of this unknown domain that Cortés was now embarked.

The landing on the dunes near the place where Veracruz was founded, the meeting with an embassy from the Aztec emperor Motecuhzoma, and the march across the mountains to the Aztec capital of Tenochtitlan, are vividly described in Cortés' *Letters to Charles V* and the *True History of the Conquest of New Spain* by Bernal Diaz del Castillo.[1] These narratives portray the strange sights of Tenochtitlan, built upon an island in a highland lake, with pyramid temples, palaces, and marketplaces. They also describe the spectacular ceremonies and fearsome sacrifices of an unknown and alien religion. The accounts continue with the capture and death of Motecuhzoma, the outbreak of battle, and the Spaniards' dramatic escape from Tenochtitlan by night, when they and their Tlaxcalan Indian allies met almost complete disaster. The recuperation of the army and the long campaign that followed culminated in the siege of Tenochtitlan. The final assaults across the causeways to the city met fierce resistance, but methodical siegecraft and the decimation caused by disease and starvation within the blockaded city inexorably reduced the defenders. In August 1521 the last Aztec emperor Cuauhtemoc was captured and surrendered in the charred and desolate rubble of what had once been the powerful and brilliant capital of the largest empire in Mexico. The destruction of Tenochtitlan and the collapse of the Aztec empire brought to an end the last – and one of the most remarkable – states in the long history of autonomous Mesoamerican* civilization.

The Conquest was a major turning point in American history, not simply because it marked the defeat of the Aztecs and the victory of the Spaniards, but because their violent encounter set in motion a new process which profoundly and permanently changed a whole cultural frame of existence. Mexico was the first and most systematically colonized of all

---

* Mesoamerica is the term used by archaeologists to mean central and southern Mexico including the Gulf Coast and Yucatan Peninsula, Guatemala, and parts of El Salvador and Honduras. This is the general area where high civilizations flourished between *c.* 1000 BC and AD 1521.

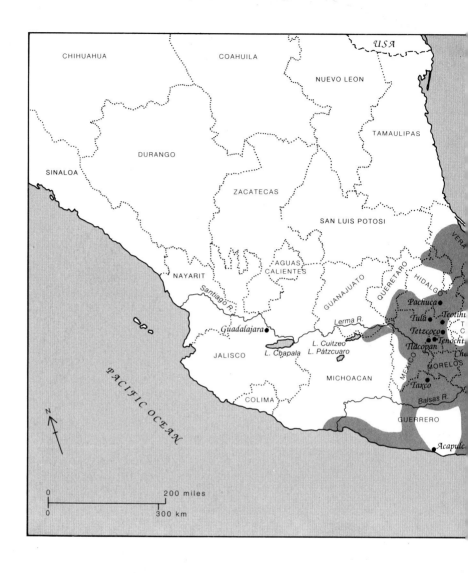

the Spanish possessions in the New World. With surprising rapidity new forms of economy, religion, and government were imposed on Mexico in the image and ideals of Spain. The idea of conquest was charged with a medieval crusading spirit, and the construction of a new social edifice on the ruins of the old was tied to the prospect of bringing the new dominion into the sphere of Christendom. Even as the remains of Tenochtitlan were being razed to build colonial Mexico City, a group of Franciscan friars arrived at Cortés' request. These men, and others who followed, were highly trained and motivated religious radicals, who represented an idealistic movement toward reform and utopian social vision within the Catholic Church in Spain. In Mexico, the first phase of their mission was

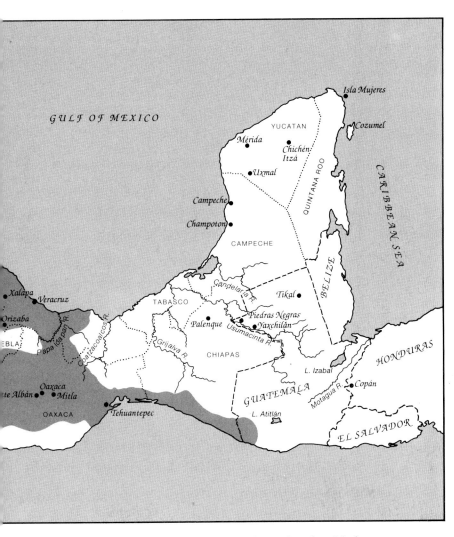

1 Map of Mesoamerica, showing the principal sites and modern Mexican states mentioned in the text, and the extent of the Aztec empire in 1519.

to destroy the old temples and idols, and to extirpate the native forms of ritual life with their myths and histories. The second phase was to implant the precepts of Christianity as the basis of the new society.

In this process of spiritual conquest certain friars such as Toribio de Benavente (Motolinía), Bernardino de Sahagún, and Diego Durán, as well as descendants of the Indian nobility such as Fernando de Alva Ixtlilxóchitl, Hernando Alvarado Tezozomoc, and Domingo Cuautlehuanitzin Chimalpahín, began to compile extensive records of the indigenous way of life.[2] This knowledge would both help the process of converting the Indians and would record a whole way of life before its memory vanished. There can be no doubt that, despite their religious convictions, the friars were deeply impressed by the sophisticated civilization they encountered. Their records reflect a probing intellectual effort and concern for accurate and comprehensive descriptions. Who were the Mexica, the Acolhua, and their neighbors, who came collectively to be called the Aztecs? Where had they come from? What was their history? What could be said of their laws, their government, and social organization? What principles ruled their beliefs and rites, and religious symbolism? And what might be recorded about their daily life and the land they lived in? Such questions lay behind the compilation of encyclopedic texts, prepared by friars who learned the native Nahuatl language and interviewed members of the old intelligentsia. These written sources form a priceless record, the largest and most detailed body of information on any of the New World peoples encountered by Europeans in the 16th century.

Toward the end of the 18th century, interest in pre-Hispanic civilization reappeared in a different context within colonial New Spain. Despite the general success over the past two centuries of the church and state in the creation of an enduring and coherent new society, the complete replacement of Indian life had never really been possible. In countless ways and in thousands of Indian communities, Spanish culture was adapted, transformed, and incorporated into traditional cultural frameworks in which the rhythms of life were governed by age-old aboriginal notions of time, space, and the relationship with nature. In the more thoroughly Hispanic towns and cities, new *Mestizo* populations of mixed racial origin, and *Criollos* of Spanish ancestry born and raised in Mexico, were increasing in numbers and influence. These people, who neither regarded themselves as Indians, nor were perceived as Spanish by the governing colonial elite, began to seek a greater voice in the affairs of colonial society. This aspiration was accompanied by a growing perception that official histories, which only began with the conquest of Mexico, were too restricted to meet their need to identify themselves with an older, indigenously "American" tradition. A search began in which the unknown pre-Hispanic past figured as something that made the New World different from the Old. The Aztecs became symbolic in a rising quest for social and cultural history – a quest that was itself an early expression of growing nationalism.

What had begun as a debate about colonial society was gradually transmuted into an ideology devoted to securing a national identity. This interest was reflected in a changing attitude toward archaeological remains. When the Aztec "Stone of Tizoc" (ills. 49,50) and the so-called "Calendar Stone" (ills. 70,71) were discovered in the late 18th century, beneath the pavement of the Zócalo plaza in central Mexico City, they were removed and displayed in the protective environment of the Cathedral atrium.[3] The importance of Aztec history was further strengthened after Mexican Independence in 1821, when the tricolor flag of the new republic displayed an evocative emblem: the Aztec image of an eagle on a cactus. According to legend this had been a prophetic sign given to the wandering Mexica tribe by their deified hero, Huitzilopochtli, to signal where they should settle.

From Independence to the present, Mexico has developed a view of its past that acknowledges the heritage of its many different peoples, among whom the Aztecs occupy a place of particular interest and fascination. Serious archaeological explorations of the ruins of Tenochtitlan (now buried under modern Mexico City) began at the turn of the century. Major excavations here have continued sporadically, as well as in other places around the Valley of Mexico and elsewhere in the former provinces of the empire. The interpretation of material remains brought to light by these excavations – buildings, sculptures, artifacts, and areas of ancient cultivation – is immeasurably aided by the abundance and detail of 16th-century texts such as those mentioned above. Conversely, excavated artifacts and monuments can reveal whole aspects of Aztec life and thought that the 16th-century writers had not perceived or only partly understood, or had deliberately withheld from the record.

Today, the search for the Aztecs goes far beyond national interests. The story of this remarkable people forms one of the most extraordinary chapters of cultural evolution in the Americas. Fearless warriors and pragmatic builders, the Aztecs ruthlessly created an empire during the 15th century, that was surpassed in size only by that of the Incas in Peru. The sacrificial aspect of their religion, with its seeming indifference to human life, appalled and repelled the Spaniards. But, as early texts and modern archaeology continue to reveal, beyond the ritual violence there were more easily appreciated achievements: the formation of a highly specialized and stratified society and an imperial administration; the expansion of a trading network as well as a tribute system; the development and maintenance of a sophisticated agricultural economy, carefully adjusted to the land; and the development of an intellectual and religious outlook that was in intimate contact with the earth, the sky, and the seasons. The yearly round of rites and ceremonies in the cities of Tenochtitlan and Tetzcoco, and their symbolic art and architecture, gave expression to an ancient awareness of the interdependence of nature and humanity.

This book is about the continuing search for an understanding of Aztec culture. Archaeological excavations, historical studies, and the interpretation of art and architecture continue to broaden our perspective, and all these sources will be used in this book to examine not only what distinguished the Aztecs from their neighbors and predecessors, but also the threads of tradition that provided continuity with the civilizations of the Mesoamerican past.

Aztec King-List

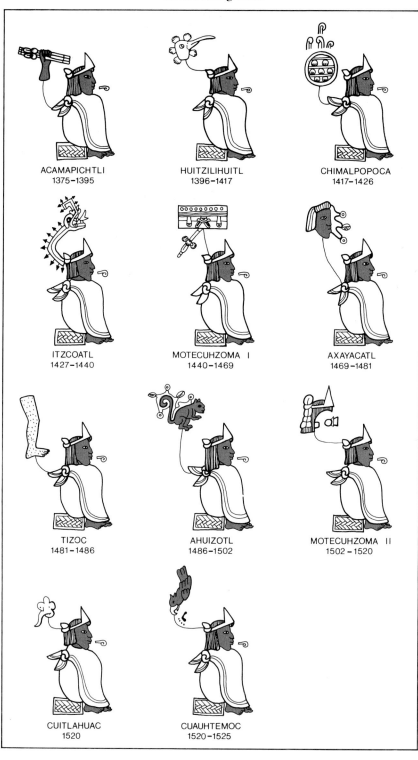

| ACAMAPICHTLI | HUITZILIHUITL | CHIMALPOPOCA |
| 1375–1395 | 1396–1417 | 1417–1426 |

| ITZCOATL | MOTECUHZOMA I | AXAYACATL |
| 1427–1440 | 1440–1469 | 1469–1481 |

| TIZOC | AHUIZOTL | MOTECUHZOMA II |
| 1481–1486 | 1486–1502 | 1502–1520 |

| CUITLAHUAC | CUAUHTEMOC |
| 1520 | 1520–1525 |

PART I

THE
CONQUEST
OF
MEXICO

1 · The Arrival of the Strangers

The expedition of Hernán Cortés

When Cortés embarked from Cuba in 1519 on his quest for the unknown kingdom, it was 27 years since Columbus had first sailed across the western ocean in search of a route to the domain of the Khan by the China Sea. Columbus' landfall on Samana Cay in the Bahamas led to three more voyages, during which he found islands and coastlines he continued to perceive as the outlying lands of Asia. It was only on his third voyage, when Columbus saw the immense volume of water flowing from the mouth of the Orinoco river in Venezuela, that he speculated that what had been found was "a very great continent, which until today has been unknown." Yet when he died in 1503 Columbus still had no clear conception of what he had achieved. By the early 1500s permanent Spanish colonies were established on the islands of Hispaniola (Haiti and the Dominican Republic) and Cuba, and other explorers were beginning to chart the eastern contour of the hemisphere. Amerigo Vespucci, Vasco Nuñez de Balboa, and others traveled along the Venezuelan, Colombian, and Caribbean coastlines.

In 1517 Hernández de Córdoba was the first to sail west to reach the Yucatan Peninsula. At Catoche, Campeche, and Chanpotón, the Spanish expedition found impressive towns with many buildings of stone, a material which was not used by the West Indian natives or on the coasts to the south. They also met armed resistance from fierce Maya formations, and at Chanpotón, where the Spaniards landed for water, a desperate battle developed in which the intruders lost some 50 men. The Spanish contingent was barely able to regain its ships with a mortally wounded commander. Undaunted by this disaster, and fired by the accounts of the towns, the prospect of gold, and new lands to conquer, Diego Velásquez, the Governor of Cuba, authorized a new expedition. This was commanded by Juan de Grijalva, who weighed anchor in early 1518. Following de Córdoba's route, the ships sailed further along the green jungle coast of Tabasco to land at the mouth of a great river, which was named after Grijalva. The Spaniards established good relations with the Indians, bartering glass beads and other prized items for gold objects and provisions. At this place they first heard the Nahuatl words *Culhua* and *Mexica*, but they did not yet know who these people could be. At a river further north on the coast, Grijalva's men were beckoned ashore by a group of men waving banners. Upon investigation the Spaniards found a delegation of finely dressed chieftains wearing cotton capes, brilliant feathers, and gold jewelry, who courteously received the strangers with an excellent feast of fowl, fruit, and tortillas. Again the Spaniards exchanged glass beads for gold and supplies but, lacking an interpreter, Grijalva was never able to ascertain who his hosts were or why he had been welcomed. Much later Hernán Cortés was to learn that these men had been representatives of the Aztec emperor Motecuhzoma, who had been receiving reports of strange sailing ships since de Córdoba's expedition. Despite the difficulties of communication it was clear to Grijalva that prizes much richer than those from the West Indies lay beyond the mountain range towards the distant interior. The expedition returned to Cuba with this remarkable news and the gold obtained in barter. The promise of such riches stimulated Diego Velásquez to call for yet another venture, and in early 1519 he named Hernán Cortés commander.

The 500 soldiers and 100 sailors who were to set sail with Cortés were of many kinds: sons with no inheritance, bored or failed planters, ex-gold miners, and men who liked soldiering, including numerous veterans of earlier voyages to South America and the Caribbean. Many had sailed on the two expeditions to the Gulf of Mexico. A number of Blacks were also included in the expedition, as testified in the later accounts of Indian witnesses. All sought a new start, adventure, and the chance to win riches fighting for Cortés. These individualistic, turbulent, and adventurous men had come to make their fortunes on the remote Caribbean frontier, yet they felt themselves bound both emotionally and legally to the Spanish Crown. They were also intensely religious, with an outlook still strongly influenced by the crusading spirit of the Middle Ages.

It was only in 1492, the year of Columbus' first voyage, that the Moorish Caliphate of Granada had surrendered to the besieging army of the Catholic kings, Ferdinand and Isabella. During the centuries-long battle to reclaim Spain from Islamic domination, Christianity had taken on a militant guise, and war automatically assumed the nature of a *jihad*. Following the recapture of Granada, the Spanish royal court discussed the prospect of extending the conquest across the Straits of Gibraltar; but, as reports filtered through from the discovery voyages, it began to seem as if there might be unclaimed realms far greater than Europe, or even Roman antiquity, across the western ocean.

The example of ancient Rome was another theme that deeply affected educated men such as Cortés, for interest in the ideas and values of the Classical world, had been diffusing from Renaissance Italy. Cortés had grown up in Medellín in Extremadura, near the ancient city of Mérida where notable Roman ruins were reminders of the greatness of that era. The impressions of these early sights were reinforced by his studies at the University of Salamanca, where Cortés would have read translations of the Roman classics during his two years preparing for a career in law. In later life he could still debate in Latin, and his letters and public speeches show that the achievements of the Romans were an ever-present example to him. Indeed, there is some evidence to suggest that Cortés attempted to reach Italy to seek his fortune; but, instead, at the age of 19, he embarked for the Caribbean colonies. Here he became a moderately successful planter on the island of Hispaniola, and eventually came to the attention of the Governor Velásquez for his able assistance in the conquest and settling of Cuba. In 1519, now in his mid-30s, he set sail for the American mainland, following the course of Grijalva.

Avoiding confrontations with the Maya towns in Yucatan, Cortés' ships proceeded to the Tabasco coast and anchored at Potonchán. A battle ensued in which Spanish horsemen, firearms, and tactics quickly won the day. Afterwards, in sign of their submission, the defeated chieftains offered food, clothing, and gold ornaments, as well as a group of young women. Among these women was one named Malintzin, called "Marina" or "Malinche" by the Spaniards. She was destined to play a pivotal role in the events to come, for she knew the Nahuatl language of Central Mexico as well as the Chontal Maya tongue spoken on the coast. Working with the Spaniard Gerónimo de Aguilar, who had learned the Maya language when shipwrecked years before in Yucatan, Malintzin became Cortés' invaluable translator and confidante. Accompanying Cortés throughout the entire campaign, she also became his consort and bore him a son, Don Martín.

At Potonchán on the Tabasco coast the Spaniards again heard the words *Culhua* and *Mexica*, which referred to a powerful people beyond the mountains to the north; but it was not until a few weeks later that the Spaniards fully grasped who these people were. The ships weighed anchor and headed up the coast, still following the route of Grijalva. A range of forested mountains appeared beyond the palm-fringed beaches, and the snow-white cone of a great volcano rose inland in the distance. The expedition reached a protected channel by the island of San Juan de Ulúa where, on the dunes of the mainland shore, camp was laid out for the men and horses in Cortés' contingent. It was here and in the nearby town of Cempoala that the Spaniards first made direct contact with subjects of the powerful Aztec empire, and came across a pair of haughty tax-gatherers from Tenochtitlan, the capital.

Motecuhzoma's embassy

Since the voyages of de Córdoba and Grijalva, Motecuhzoma had received reports of sailing vessels much larger than Indian sea-going rafts, of horses and weapons, and of men in metal armor. Now, messengers again arrived in Tenochtitlan with news of another flotilla, and of an armed camp laid out in the dunes near Cempoala. It began to seem as if the earlier voyages had prepared the way for this larger retinue. The outlandish strangers

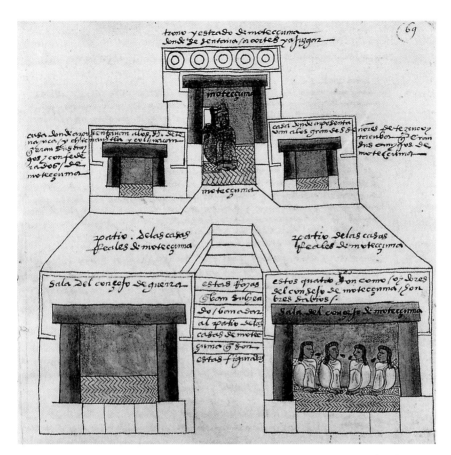

2 Motecuhzoma's palace in Tenochtitlan. Painted by an Aztec artist soon after the city's conquest, this page from the Codex Mendoza depicts the ruler seated within his throne-room (top), while a council of judges convenes in the chamber below.

had shown themselves to be troublesome, brashly mishandling the imperial tax-gatherers and fomenting discord among the Aztec tribute-paying towns of the coast. Who were these strangers? Where had they come from? What was their objective? These questions, first posed after the earlier sightings, suddenly assumed much greater importance on Motecuhzoma's agenda. As fresh news arrived reporting Cortés' expressed desire to meet Motecuhzoma in Tenochtitlan, the emperor called his council to decide the best course of action.

From the beginning, Cortés and Motecuhzoma hid their mutually hostile intentions behind diplomatic overtones. Cortés' strong religious convictions and his moral commitment to convert the Indians to Christianity were tied to his worldly ambition to acquire riches and honor. Motecuhzoma too had important religious responsibilities and he was no less a determined warrior, with a long record of conquests. Moreover, since his coronation in 1502 he had succeeded in creating a strong central administration. Yet Motecuhzoma appears to have exhibited a curious, wavering uncertainty in dealing with Cortés. Much less powerful chieftains among the Maya and at Potonchán had readily displayed an aggressive fighting spirit. So how was it that the most feared ruler in Mesoamerica had failed to take immediate and decisive action to repel the strangers, and eventually allowed the Spaniards into Tenochtitlan, precipitating a disastrous chain of events that led to the emperor's death and the fall of the Aztec empire?

These critical questions have been much discussed in innumerable accounts from early colonial times to the present.[1] Since the 16th century, many scholars have emphasized Motecuhzoma's perception of Cortés as the incarnation of a deified king, Quetzalcoatl, who was said to have prophesied in ancient times that he would return to regain his lost throne in a year "1 reed," or 1519 (the Mesoamerican time-counting system is explained in Chapter 7). According to this interpretation of the Quetzalcoatl legend, Motecuhzoma was unnerved by the prospect of the return of the god-king to reclaim his title. The legend itself describes Topiltzin Quetzalcoatl as the ruler of the powerful Toltec people, venerated predecessors of the Aztecs. Although revered and respected, the hero-king fell victim to drunkenness and, in a quarrel with a rival faction led by the sorcerer Tezcatlipoca, was tricked into committing incest with his sister. The humiliated Quetzalcoatl was forced to depart with his retinue in a year 1 reed, and made his way to the Gulf Coast, where he embarked on a seagoing raft towards the Yucatan Peninsula in the east.

As ethnohistorian Nigel Davies points out, however, in "native" versions of the myth there is no mention of any *prophesy* about the return of Quetzalcoatl in the year 1 reed, or in any other year.[2] Davies concludes that it was *after* the Spanish Conquest that the original legend was transformed with the story of a prophetic return. It therefore seems doubtful that Motecuhzoma was ever fully convinced that Cortés was the returning deity. Rather, what apparently happened was that Motecuhzoma, seeking to explain the presence of the strangers, deduced that *because Quetzalcoatl had disappeared in the east* the strange new chieftain coming from that direction *might* be the ancestral king returning to claim his throne.

More recently, anthropologist Susan Gillespie has argued convincingly that the whole story of Cortés as Quetzalcoatl was created after the Conquest by Aztec historians in an attempt to make sense of the Spaniards' arrival and victory, interpreting it as the outcome of a pattern of events established long ago, in the remote Toltec past.[3] Given that the Aztecs viewed history as a cycle of repeated events, it is highly plausible that their historians should have sought to rewrite the past in this way.

It can therefore no longer be said with any assurance that Motecuhzoma "trembled on his throne in the mountains" at the thought of meeting

Ill omens

3–5 The Spanish landing at Veracruz was illustrated decades later in Bernardino de Sahagún's *Historia de las Cosas de Nueva España*. TOP Cortés' horsemen advance in formation; Aztec messengers described them as armed men "riding on deer." ABOVE LEFT The appearance of a bird whose head was a mirror in which the stars could be seen was among the many sinister omens said to have presaged the Spanish Conquest. ABOVE RIGHT A fire at the Aztec temple of Huitzilopochtli was thought to have been started by a lightning bolt from a clear blue sky, another sign of foreboding.

Cortés as a supernatural being. Nevertheless there can be no doubt that the Spanish landing sounded a note of warning in the Aztec capital. A royal council convened to consider the strangers, and the time and place of their arrival, from various points of view.

First, the visitors were certainly unlike any other people known within or without the empire: outlandish in physical appearance, with alarming arms and armor, they showed an open, aggressive disregard for established norms of behavior. Secondly, consultation of the pictorial texts and

6,7 The Teocalli (sacred house) Stone – probably a royal throne – was modeled in the likeness of a pyramid temple. The facade is shown as a flight of stairs flanked by hieroglyphic dates and offering bowls. A sun-disk was sculpted above the "altar," representing the sun as a source of heat and life, and also the present era or "sun" in the Aztec sequence of mythical world-creations. The disk is flanked on the left by the deified hero Huitzilopochtli, attired in his hummingbird headdress, and on the right by Motecuhzoma I. Both figures carry sacrificial spines and utter the cry *atl-tlachinolli*, "water and fire," meaning deluge and conflagration – the Nahuatl word for war. This and other sun-disk monuments illustrate the Aztecs' claim to rule the world in the present era of creation. (See also ill. 35.)

calendrical records by Aztec historians and divination specialists revealed that there were also several important historical and cosmological associations surrounding the strangers' arrival. These matters gave the Spaniards a special importance in the Aztec imagination, for their presence evoked a curious parallel with the Aztecs' own history. The Aztecs had originally come from an unknown place far to the north, following a long migration to the Valley of Mexico. As strangers they had fought and eventually rose to create a powerful empire-state. Similarly, the armored strangers had come from a distant location, a place veiled in mystery; they were intruders in ordered lands; and they might well have warlike designs on the center of power. The arrival of the visitors also had powerful geographical associations. They came across the ocean, the primordial mother of waters, and they traveled from the east, traditionally held as the direction of authority among Mesoamerican peoples. Finally, the date of the Spanish landing in the year 1 reed was also significant, a date associated not only with Quetzalcoatl's banishment, but also with the influence of the plumed serpent as a cosmological sign.

Thus, several historical and cosmological themes were linked to Cortés and his armed force when they landed near Cempoala. From a European

point of view these themes would hardly seem significant. But the Aztecs placed special importance on the coincidence of events in time and space, and mythological happenings and legendary history were always compared with recent events to legitimize, justify, or otherwise explain them. From the Aztec point of view, occurrences were not unique or sequential, but were seen as episodes in an essentially cyclic concept of time and history, as has been pointed out by art historian Emily Umberger.[4] Thus, the circumstances of Cortés' arrival formed an oddly ominous pattern, warning Motecuhzoma of the gravity of the challenge he faced.

Having considered all these matters, Motecuhzoma's council recommended that it would be diplomatic to honor the visitors as royal emissaries and to acknowledge their obvious importance. The emperor decided to send an embassy with three groups of gifts that were both appropriate to the status of the strangers, and would also affirm his own supremacy. Descriptions of Motecuhzoma's gifts by Cortés, Bernal Díaz and Bernardino de Sahagún's informants differ as to the place and exact contents of the presentation. Nevertheless it is clear that two objects were especially important. The first was a disk of gold, "as large as a cartwheel," valued by the Spaniards at 20,000 ducats. This object was fashioned to represent the sun and was covered with other figures and symbols. The second was a silver disk of larger size, made to represent the moon. While the Spaniards admired these objects for their craftsmanship and intrinsic value, they had no way of knowing their significance. We shall never know exactly what the disks were like since they were eventually melted down for the value of the metal. But analysis of other artifacts and myths suggest that, as sources of light and as markers of time, the sun and moon carried profound ideas and memories about the association of rulership and the origins of things. The significance of the sun and the moon will be fully discussed in Chapter 7, but it suffices here to note that the gold and silver disks presented to Cortés spoke of the creation of the world, the place of the Aztecs in sacred history, and the divine authority of the emperor of Tenochtitlan, whose power was part of that cosmic order.

The second group of objects presented to Cortés is mentioned only in Sahagún's account. The gift consisted of four elaborate ritual costumes, of the kind worn by religious performers who impersonated the deities in the festivals of Tenochtitlan. The splendid masks, feathered headdresses, finely woven capes, and the jewelry of shell, gold, turquoise, and jade, were considered sacred items, for they were thought to be charged with sacred forces manifesting the powers and attributes of deities and heroes. It was an old and widespread Mesoamerican custom for lords and chieftains to wear, or to sponsor others to wear, the attire of deities on festival occasions, in order to maintain good relations between their communities and the heroes, gods, and the forces of nature.

Finally, Motecuhzoma sent a present of food, consisting of tortillas, maize, eggs, turkeys, and many kinds of fruit including zapotas, hog plums, guavas, tunas (nopal cactus fruit), and various kinds of pitayas (fruit of the organ cactus), as well as avocados, and possibly sweet potatoes and manioc. According to Sahagún's account, part of this was set aside as a ritual offering. As was the custom in the temples of Tenochtitlan, this special food was sprinkled and spattered with the blood of a sacrificed human being. The appalled Spaniards shook their heads at this ritual display, but turned to feast on the other food presented by the royal emissaries.

Not long after this meeting with the Aztec ambassadors, Cortés received instructions from Governor Velásquez to return to Cuba. But, knowing of the rich kingdom in the interior, he decided to disregard the governor and founded a garrison town at Veracruz. Bypassing his superior, Cortés sent a ship bearing gifts direct to Charles V of Spain. This done, he

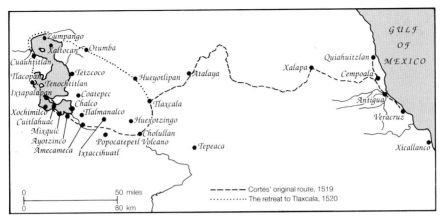

8 Cortés' route from Veracruz on the coastal plain to the Valley of Mexico, and the retreat to Tlaxcala after the Spaniards and their Indian allies were defeated in the battle of the Noche Triste.

burned all the remaining ships to forestall any thoughts of return among his men and the Velásquez supporters and, after inspiring his troops with a rousing speech, he and his tiny army set off on 16 August 1519 for Tenochtitlan.

Tenochtitlan

The despatches of Cortés and the earthy prose of Bernal Diaz del Castillo describe the crossing of the mountain ranges and the first wide stretches of the high plateau. The Spanish expedition approached the borders of Tlaxcala, an independent Indian nation that had fiercely and successfully resisted the invading armies of Motecuhzoma for many years. These veterans were now determined to stop the new Spanish invaders. Massing in overwhelming numbers, they twice attempted to envelop the Spaniards, only to be repelled and routed. In Tlaxcala the extraordinary military competence of the Spaniards against a much larger Indian army was decisively demonstrated for the first time. The defeat of the Tlaxcalan force marked a turning point in the Conquest, for it made such a profound impression on Tenochtitlan when spies reported the action that Motecuhzoma's council at last determined a course of military strategy. The Spanish success also gained powerful new allies for Cortés, who persuaded the Tlaxcalans to join his expedition on the march to Tenochtitlan. The support of these hardened warriors and the logistical base at Tlaxcala were to prove indispensable in the battles to come.

The critical element in these campaigns was the Spaniards' proficiency in battle drill as well as their arms and armor. Their disciplined maneuvers and weaponry had never been seen in Mexico, and their deadly effect on Indian formations cannot be overemphasized. The basic units of the

23

Spanish forces were infantry and cavalry to which were added separate units of arquebusiers (musketeers) and cross-bowmen, as well as the crews that manned the small cannon. The principal use of firearms was to break down the enemy charges, before these warriors could effectively launch their darts, slingstones, and arrows. Cavalry was used to break the enemy lines by lancing and following up with swords, after which the infantry moved in, wielding swords and long pikes tipped with steel blades. These weapons were more effective than the obsidian-bladed clubs carried by the Indians, for not only was more time required to lift and swing a club than to thrust and jab with a sword, but more space was needed, meaning the Indians tended to advance in loose formations. By contrast the Spanish pikemen advanced shoulder to shoulder in deep file formations, with the projecting line of pikes offering an almost impregnable barrier. By raising the pikes vertically, about-facing and lowering them again, a new threat to the rear could be repelled. Marching in tight columns, the Spanish infantry could quickly form pointed wedges to move into enemy crowds, or form squares for defense, or open out and wheel around in serried ranks to envelop or push their opponents into vulnerable positions. The troops were also protected by metal helmets and armor, although some preferred layers of leather, and many adopted the quilted cotton jackets worn by Indian warriors.

The Spaniards were always vastly outnumbered by their opponents, but their battlefield superiority was proven again and again as the fiercely spirited but more lightly armed Indian squadrons sought in vain to swamp the Spaniards after volleys of projectiles. Only when hampered by very broken terrain or confined by buildings in urban zones were the Spaniards at a disadvantage. The Spanish concept of battle (in which every man protected his neighbor and aimed to kill the enemy) was also highly effective against the Indians, who placed higher value on individual duels and heroism than close teamwork. It was an Indian warrior's priority to capture an enemy alive whenever possible, either to sacrifice the prisoner on the battlefield, or to bring him home for sacrifice on the pyramid temples. A captor was awarded the highest battlefield honors, like the Plains Indians of North America, who sought to "count coup" by touching the enemy in the heat of the battle.

Victorious in Tlaxcala, Cortés marched with his new allies to the city of Cholollan (modern Cholula). The Cholollans were allied to the Aztecs, who now sought to use them in a bold stratagem to trap and contain the Spaniards. The lesson of the Tlaxcalan battles was not lost on Motecuhzoma. Having noted the superiority of the Spanish in the open field, he was unwilling to risk an army in a major confrontation. Instead, the Cholollans were pressured to invite the Spaniards into the city as honored guests, where they might be trapped, contained, and destroyed from the rooftops and in the narrow streets. Invitations were sent out, and the Spaniards entered, while ditch traps with stakes were secretly dug and projectiles were stored upon flat roofs of the houses in the center of the city. Meanwhile, a considerable force of Aztec warriors took up hidden positions in ravines to the north of Cholollan, waiting to assault the invaders when the attack was underway. But the plot was disclosed by an informer and the tables were turned. Early one morning the Spaniards trapped the hapless Cholollan chiefs and warriors who had assembled in the central plaza. At Cortés' order his troops closed in and put many to death without quarter. Motecuhzoma heard the discouraging news with increasing consternation, and he now began to suffer a crisis of confidence that found expression in his fateful decision to welcome the Spaniards into Tenochtitlan. Nevertheless this decision may also be seen in terms of military expediency: still unwilling to risk his army in the open field against the menacing strangers, the next best thing would be to try a variant of the stratagem that almost worked at Cholollan. To allow the force of some 500 men plus 2,000–3,000 Tlaxcalans into Tenochtitlan, an island city of about 250,000–300,000 inhabitants, might be the best way of ensuring control until another action might be effectively taken.

Within a few days of their victory at Cholollan the allies were camped on the cold pass between the snow-capped peaks of Popocatepetl and Ixtaccihuatl. From this height they looked down on the spacious Valley of Mexico. A great system of interconnected lakes covered the central basin, contained on three sides by mountain ranges. The lakes are drained today and almost a third of the central valley is covered by Mexico City. But the mountains are eternal landmarks and still bear their Nahuatl names. To the east the serrated peaks of Mt Tlaloc join the snow-capped volcanoes. The southern rim is defined by another volcanic escarpment known as the Ajuscos, and another line of broken heights encloses the west horizon. The volcanic aspect of this landscape is emphasized by a long line of low cinder-cones and craters traversing the central basin from east to west. Only to the north does the valley open out into wide fields and hills, leading toward the empty steppes and ranges of the vast central plateau.

The Valley of Mexico drains to the interior, and the southern freshwater lakes of Chalco and Xochimilco once flowed through a broad channel into the slightly lower, salty water of the Lake Tetzcoco basin. Similarly, when the shallow waters of lakes Zumpango and Xaltocan rose in the rainy season, they overflowed into the wide expanse of this larger central basin. In 1519 there were many towns and cities as well as ancient ruins around the lakeshore margins. Others were scattered on the adjacent plains and higher elevations. The eastern sector of the Valley was named Acolhuacan, where the city of Tetzcoco was the capital of an independent kingdom allied to Tenochtitlan. Tetzcoco held a population of some 45,000. This second most powerful imperial city commanded tribute from numerous towns and regions extending to the east and south as far as the Gulf of Mexico. Other important urban centers were located to the west of Lake

Tetzcoco: Tenayuca with its famous pyramid, and Atzcapotzalco, the formerly powerful but much diminished capital of the old Tepanec kingdom; another town, Tlacopan, was the official ally of Tenochtitlan and Tetzcoco, in what is known as the Triple Alliance. The old towns of Zumpango and Xaltocan stood by the lakes to the north, not far from the overgrown ruins and pyramids of the city of Teotihuacan. These last monuments were much revered by the Aztec kings, as testimony of the great civilization that had flourished at Teotihuacan a thousand years before. The most developed agricultural lands were located in the south, where large sections of lakes Chalco and Xochimilco had been reclaimed for intensive farming. Here, expert horticulturalists worked the raised seedbeds known as *chinampas* that were constructed in long rectangular plots between narrow canals and lines of tall thin willow trees.

Tenochtitlan itself was built upon an island and reclaimed land towards the western side of Lake Tetzcoco. The city was connected to the mainland by three long causeways bridged in several locations, and fresh water was supplied by an aqueduct from copious springs at the hill of Chapultepec. The urban zone incorporated the city of Tlatelolco to the north. Four main roadways converged in the middle of the city, three leading in from causeways and the fourth from a landing place on the eastern side of the lake. In the center, the palaces of Aztec kings were ranged around a ritual enclosure. This sacred quadrangle contained the Great Pyramid with the dual shrines of Tlaloc and Huitzilopochtli on its summit, as well as many other temples and administrative buildings, including the *tzompantli* skull rack, where thousands of trophy-heads of sacrificial victims were strung up on public view. A regular grid of canals and walkways was laid out in all directions, giving order to the residential and manufacturing zones of the city. The principal geographic and cultural features of Tenochtitlan were noted on a map prepared at the order of Cortés soon after the Conquest, and published in 1525 in the volume of his *Letters to Charles V*.

The expedition descended from the mountain pass and moved in a long column across the plain and through the towns on the shore of Lake Chalco. Cortés and his men were visibly impressed by the ordered landscape with its gridplan towns and temple pyramids, and the regular pattern of raised fields bordered by lines of willows. Crowds of people drew close to the road in increasing numbers, reminding the Spaniards that they were only a few miles from the fearsome Aztec capital. The Spaniards camped that night at Ixtapalapan, at the head of the southern causeway. Before dawn the troops prepared for the final march. The sun rose over the dark blue ridge of Mt Tlaloc, sending a flood of light across the water of Lake Tetzcoco, and throwing the long straight causeway into bold relief. Thousands of onlookers were already swarming in fleets of dugout canoes. The sunlight caught the polished armor of the Spaniards as they marched watchfully to the rhythm of even drumbeats and high wailing fifes. Horsemen scouted the vanguard, moving back and forth;

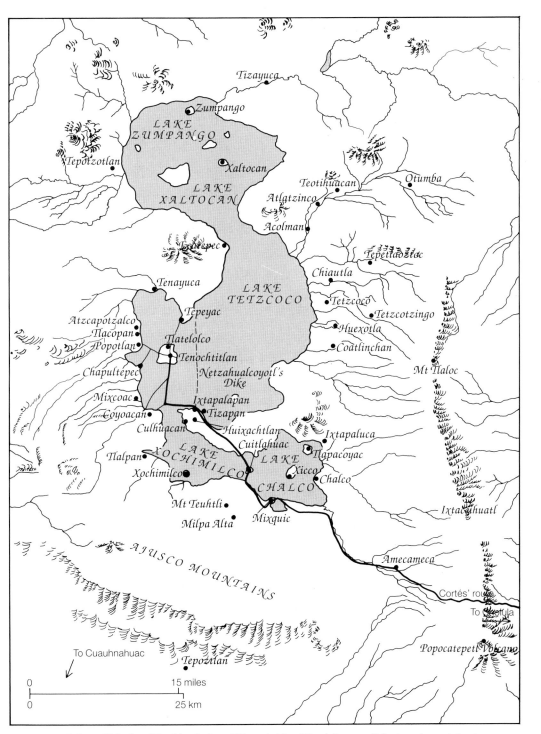

9 The Valley of Mexico. The island city of Tenochtitlan-Tlatelolco was linked to the mainland by causeways, and protected from the brackish water of Lake Tetzcoco by Netzahualcoyotl's dike. Lakes Chalco and Xochimilco to the south were fed by great springs and were the site of major *chinampa* plantations.

The Valley of Mexico and Tenochtitlan

10–12 ABOVE Miguel Covarrubias' reconstruction of Tenochtitlan and the Valley of Mexico. The ceremonial precinct of Tenochtitlan is at the center, surrounded by the royal palaces. OPPOSITE ABOVE Plan of Tenochtitlan, first published in 1524. Following contemporary cartographic conventions, the ritual precinct dominates the center of the map, with the buildings and natural features surrounding it diminishing in size and importance. OPPOSITE BELOW A schematic plan of Tenochtitlan-Tlatelolco, showing the location of the principal features, including the internal canal system and main roads to the causeways. By 1519 the two cities had become a single urban zone, inhabited by some 300,000 people. Today the area is covered by downtown Mexico City.

next came a man with the banner of Spain, followed by pikemen, cross-bowmen, and arquebusiers, and then Cortés and his captains. The white heron emblem of Tlaxcala came next, leading some 3,000 whistling and whooping warriors. Four miles ahead, gleaming pyramids rose from the thin haze and smoke of early cooking fires on the island city. At the entrance to Tenochtitlan, Motecuhzoma came out to meet Cortés on a palanquin borne by four nobles. His iridescent green plumes of the quetzal bird, turquoise diadem, and golden jewelry signaled his royal status. Descending, Motecuhzoma approached the Spaniard supported on the arms of two chiefs. This was a ceremonial manner of walking to express his highest respect. Motecuhzoma reached out and bestowed on Cortés a necklace of golden crabs. He received in return a prized necklace of Venetian glass beads, strung on a golden filament and scented with musk. With an elegant speech he welcomed Cortés into the city:

> O our lord, thou hast suffered fatigue; thou hast spent thyself. Thou hast arrived on earth; thou hast come to the noble city of Mexico. Thou hast come to occupy thy noble mat and seat, which for a little time I have guarded and watched for thee. For thy governors of times past have gone – the rulers Itzcoatl, Motecuhzoma the Elder, Axayacatl, Tizoc, Ahuitzotl – who, not very long ago, came to guard thy mat and seat for thee and to govern the city of Mexico. Under their protection

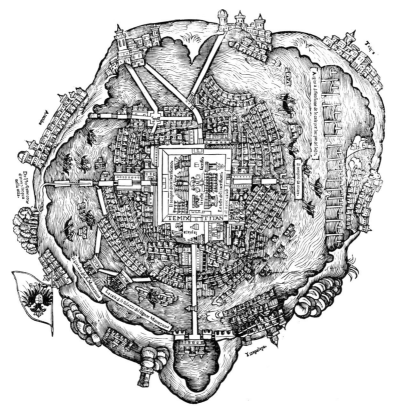

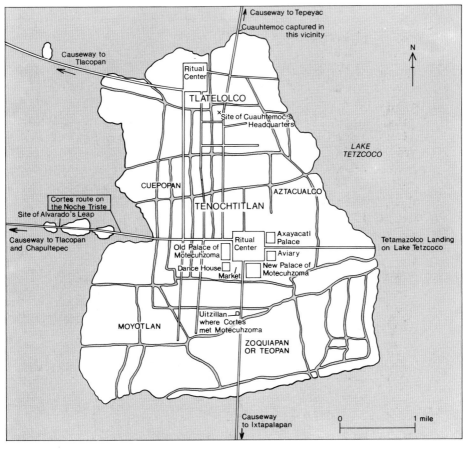

Causeway to Tepeyac
Cuauhtemoc captured in
this vicinity

Causeway to
Tlacopan

N

Ritual
Center

TLATELOLCO

× Site of Cuauhtemoc's
Headquarters

LAKE
TETZCOCO

CUEPOPAN

AZTACUALCO

TENOCHTITLAN

Cortes route on
the Noche Triste
Site of Alvarado's Leap

Causeway to Tlacopan
and Chapultepec

Tetamazolco Landing
on Lake Tetzcoco

Axayacatl
Palace

Ritual
Center

Old Palace of
Motecuhzoma

Aviary

Dance House

New Palace of
Motecuhzoma

Market

Uitzillan
where Cortes
met Motecuhzoma

MOYOTLAN

ZOQUIAPAN
OR TEOPAN

Causeway
to Ixtapalapan

0   1 mile

The ritual precinct

13–15 BOTTOM Ignacio Marquina's reconstruction of the Great Pyramid and adjacent buildings as they might have appeared to Cortés and his men in November 1519. RIGHT Marquina's plan of the ritual precinct. LEFT Schematic representation of the sacred precinct from the Codex Matritense. The twin-towered pyramid of Tlaloc and Huitzilopochtli is shown in the middle. Other prominent monuments include the circular gladiatorial stone, the skull rack, the I-shaped ballcourt, the Yopico temple (lower right), and two other temples (lower left).

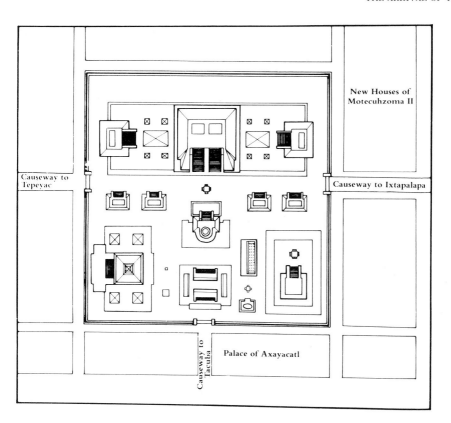

New Houses of
Motecuhzoma II

Causeway to
Tepeyac

Causeway to Ixtapalapa

Causeway to
Tacuba

Palace of Axayacatl

16 Motecuhzoma II and Cortés hold discussions in the palace, with Malintzin interpreting. The bound deer, quail, and maize at their feet represent supplies given to Cortés and his Indian allies by their Aztec hosts; from the Lienzo de Tlaxcala.

the common folk came here. Could they, perchance, now find their descendants, those left behind? O, that one of them might be a witness to marvel that to me now hath befallen what I see, who am the only descendant of our lords. For I dream not, nor start from my sleep, nor see this as in a trance. I do not dream that I see thee and look into thy face. Lo, I have been troubled for a long time. I have gazed into the unknown whence thou hast come – the place of mystery. For the rulers of old have gone, saying that thou wouldst come to instruct thy city, that thou wouldst descend to thy mat and seat; that thou wouldst return. And now it is fulfilled: thou hast returned; thou hast suffered fatigue; thou hast spent thyself. Arrive now in thy land. Rest, lord; visit thy palace that thou mayest rest thy body. Let our lords arrive in the land.[5]

After Cortés' return address the allied army was quartered in the old palace of Axayacatl, to the east of the ritual enclosure in the middle of the city. In the days that followed the Spaniards were shown the sights of the imperial capital. Bernal Diaz, who accompanied Cortés on one of these memorable outings, described the visit to the Tlatelolco pyramid and the adjacent market. Cortés and his party were led up the pyramid stairs to be received by Motecuhzoma on the upper platform. Taking Cortés by the hand, the emperor walked to the edge and invited him to view the city.

The Great Pyramid of Tenochtitlan could be seen across the intervening residential zones two miles to the south. Rising in tiers with twin temples on its summit, its white lime-plastered surfaces and brightly painted temple houses in blue and red stood out against the dark background of the mountains in the distance. Elsewhere the urban skyline was dominated by other pyramids rising above lesser ritual centers in the four wards of the city. Aztec architecture, with its open-volume forms, was a far cry from the vaulted cathedrals and pillared halls of mosques familiar to the Spaniards. The ritual precincts of Tenochtitlan and Tlatelolco were designed in similar fashion, bounded by a raised quadrangular platform forming a hollow square, within which the regular geometrical shapes of ceremonial buildings were symmetrically arranged. These enclosures of repeated platforms, stairways, and house-like temples established a visual hierarchy oriented to the four directions along a dominant east-west axis, with the pyramids and plazas echoing the conical volcanic shapes and the broad reach of the lake and plain.

The royal palaces and the houses of notables were close to the ritual precincts, while the thatched huts and wattle compounds of the lower social orders reached out towards the periphery. A few sections of

17 The excavated ruins of the Tlatelolco pyramid. The series of stairways extending towards the front correspond to successive enlargements of the pyramid. The market of Tlatelolco was located to the rear of the pyramid.

Tenochtitlan and outlying islands were more agrarian in nature, with ordered rows of cultivated *chinampa* plots extending into the lake. Such a district is shown on a fragment of an early colonial plan, the *Plano en Papel de Maguey* (ill. 39). A dense grid of walkways and narrow canals provided routes for foot traffic and canoes, for there were no wheeled vehicles or beasts of burden in ancient Mexico. Everything was transported by water or by long lines of human porters. The greatest marketplace in Mexico lay below and to the south of the Tlatelolco pyramid (Chapter 10). From their vantage point Cortés and Motecuhzoma could hear the rising hubbub of voices and see the colorful crowds. Thousands of people were attracted on that day in larger numbers than usual because of the strangers' presence.

Tenochtitlan was the product of imperial strategy, based economically on trade and agriculture as well as a regular tribute of incoming goods and labor. The subject towns that were required to send men and products at established times numbered in the hundreds, from lands on the coast and highlands which the Spaniards had hardly yet envisioned. The imperial tribute system was enforced by the terror of retribution from a fierce army, whose authority was proclaimed in the capital by skull-racks of sacrificed victims. Yet Tenochtitlan was not simply the product of a state-organized agriculture, traders and markets, and a ruthless series of conquests. What the Spanish soldiers did not see and could not have understood were the deeper historical and symbolic relationships between the city and its inhabitants. The city's plan, its buildings and monuments, and its place in the natural setting, were visible expressions of religious and aesthetic forces that flowed through the life of the people. In great measure the Aztec state drew its power from the yearly procession of seasonal rites and their panoply of signs and symbols. No aspect of Aztec life was more carefully orchestrated than these religious activities. In part such ceremonies celebrated individual achievements and specific historical events, but more importantly they brought the community into direct contact with the elemental life of the land – the mountains, clouds, rain and thunder, the wind, the lakes, and the sun. In this communal religious effort, Motecuhzoma himself was chief.

From their vantage point on the pyramid of Tlatelolco, the Spaniards saw a city that would seem to be invulnerable. Yet on the long march to the capital they had already begun to understand its inner tensions and instabilities – in Tlaxcala, in the streets of Cholollan, and even now while standing next to the emperor Motecuhzoma. In his person all power and decisions were concentrated, and it would be in their dealings with him that the future would be decided.

2 · The Fall of the Aztec Empire

The events that followed the Spanish entry into Tenochtitlan are recounted in the colonial narratives and by Sahagún's Indian informants. It is not our purpose to repeat their descriptions, yet certain episodes are especially significant for what they tell us about Aztec politics and strategies, the weaknesses and strengths of their empire, the role of religion in the conduct of war, and the duties of kings towards their people. These themes were interwoven in the epic of the final catastrophe.

The death of Motecuhzoma

The Spaniards and Tlaxcalans had been in Tenochtitlan for some two weeks when Cortés and his captains began to think of how to advance their purpose. They were guests of the Aztec state, but they were well aware that the Chololian trap might be tried again. They were hostages in the center of a city from which there would be no easy escape across the causeways and bridges. However, they might both ensure their safety and proceed with their plan of conquest if they could capture Motecuhzoma. Under the pretext that an Indian attack on the garrison at Veracruz had been secretly ordered by the emperor, Cortés and his most steadfast captains asked for an imperial audience. Once admitted to the royal apartments they swiftly seized Motecuhzoma. From the Aztec point of view this move was unimaginable, for the authority of Motecuhzoma was paramount and he was to some extent a sacred person. Such a danger within the palace was therefore utterly overlooked. Taken by surprise Motecuhzoma had no choice but to submit or possibly lose his life. This calculating and ruthless monarch, who was counted among the most successful in Aztec history, had failed to assess the unswerving purpose of Cortés. In the shock of surprise, he allowed himself to be conducted across the plaza to Axayacatl's palace where the Spaniards were quartered. To cover the humiliation of his capture he gave out that he was going willingly as a guest of Cortés. But Motecuhzoma had lost the initiative, for those whom he thought to be hostages in Tenochtitlan now held *him* hostage.

Even so, Motecuhzoma continued to conduct the affairs of state with his advisers and commanders from the guarded apartments. Outside, the population of the city remained submissive beneath a growing sense of disquiet. In the months that followed Motecuhzoma developed a policy of appeasement while keeping up the civilities and expressions of affection with the Spanish troops. Members of Cortés' party were sent to the provinces to visit the gold mines and other sources of imperial tribute. By early 1520 Motecuhzoma had formally declared his vassalage to Charles V of Spain, and gave a hoard of treasure stored within the palace to the soldiers of Cortés. Another extraordinary concession was then demanded by Cortés, who asked for a place of Christian worship on the Great Pyramid. A crucifix was installed there with an image of the Virgin, and the Spanish leaders ascended the stairs to kneel for mass at the summit. This act of worship, conducted in full view of the city, was seen as a symbolic appropriation. The dramatic sight precipitated suppressed anger among the Indians, and a faction of Motecuhzoma's chieftains began to take concrete steps to rid Tenochtitlan of the visitors. The time of appeasement was over and demands for action were made. Spurred by these restive and warlike men, Motecuhzoma informed Cortés that the mood of the city was such that he could no longer guarantee safety. He suggested that the Spaniards and their allies should depart or face an armed uprising.

At this critical point Cortés was unexpectedly called away to the base at Veracruz, taking a contingent of troops and leaving Pedro de Alvarado in charge of affairs in the capital. A new Spanish force had landed on the coast under Pánfilo Narvaez, who was charged by the governor of Cuba to arrest Cortés and take control of the expedition. Governor Velásquez had long since learned (with great pique) that Cortés had broken from his control and was writing directly to Charles V. But Cortés crossed the mountains, surprised Narvaez, and captured him in a skirmish. He then persuaded Narvaez' troops to join his own forces in Tenochtitlan. Upon returning to the city they found the streets strangely deserted and silent. Alvarado had committed a grave blunder by attacking and killing a contingent of Aztec lords. This was done, he said, to destroy a threatening conspiracy. The city now waited in shock and silence as their leaders conferred. Motecuhzoma, by failing to put his life on the line, had broken his warrior's code; his appeasement policy had proved disastrous; and now Cortés returned with reinforcements to place the city in peril.

Long smothered resentment now burst forth in a furious cry for vengeance as squadrons of Aztec warriors assaulted the Spaniards and Tlaxcalans in their palace stronghold. A 16th-century pictorial document called the Lienzo de Tlaxcala depicts this episode, when the Aztecs propelled stones and darts into the patio and the Spanish retaliated using cannons to clear the gate of charging enemy formations (ill. 18). The first attack was no sooner repelled than another was mounted. Motecuhzoma was persuaded by the Spaniards to address his people from the rooftop parapet. The warriors dispersed, submitting to the imperial command even in these extreme circumstances. But it was Motecuhzoma's last effective act, for all could see that he no longer embodied the Aztec ideal of kingship.

Motecuhzoma's brother, Prince Cuitlahuac, was elected as the new leader and the attack was renewed with conviction. The humiliated Motecuhzoma was again persuaded to calm the besieging warriors. His words were received in incredulous silence; then amid whistles, taunts, and jeers a hail of stones and arrows was flung. Motecuhzoma fell with concussion and was taken to his rooms where he lingered and died – the result of the stoning said the Spaniards; the result of a secret strangling according to later Indian accounts. (Only once before in Aztec history had a king so failed his office, when Tizoc in 1482 proved unsuccessful in battle. His unlucky rule, marked by rebellions, ended when he was removed by poison.)

Storming the Great Pyramid

The Great Pyramid rose above the ritual enclosure and overlooked Axayacatl's palace, where the Spanish were housed. From this high platform the Aztec warriors continually launched missiles towards the roof and courtyard below. Cortés was determined to capture the pyramid and he personally led the attack, supported by fire from muskets and crossbows. Missiles, beams, and burning logs were hurled down the stairway by the defenders, who massed at the landings to contest the passage of the determined Spanish force. The assailants pressed on, pushing the Aztec soldiers back to the upper platform. At the top the opponents faced each other in full view of the city. No quarter was asked or given as the Spaniards drove in their attack. Struggling men fell or were pitched over the edges of the pyramid. Superior weapons and battle discipline soon gained the upper hand and as the last group of Aztec warriors defended themselves, the Spaniards rushed to the chambers of the pyramid temples. The Christian shrine had disappeared. Seizing the idols, the troops cast them down the stairways and set fire to the shrines before the eyes of the horrified city. A column of smoke rose behind the victorious troops as they descended the steps of the pyramid. This was indeed a dreadful sight to the Aztec population, for in their practice of war, to capture and burn an enemy temple was the ultimate sign of victory. The casting down of the idols was also deeply shocking for, as will be shown in Chapter 8, the pyramid was directly associated with a mythical battleground on which the defending hero Huitzilopochtli had toppled his enemy Coyolxauhqui and defeated her assaulting warriors.

Despite his success, Cortés knew that his position was untenable and resolved to escape from the city in the dark of the night. The Spanish knew that four of the eight bridges in the causeway were missing, and to secure passage over the remaining gaps a portable bridge was constructed. Hidden by the darkness, and taking every care not to make any noise, the allied forces opened the gates of the palace and made their way towards the Tlacopan causeway. War was not traditionally waged at night by the

18 This scene from the Lienzo de Tlaxcala portrays the Spaniards and their allies besieged in the palace by Aztec warriors. The defenders group in the courtyard and a cannon is fired against an Aztec formation charging the principal entrance.

Aztecs, and no sentries had been posted. The alarm was finally given by a group of women at a watering place. Hurrying on, the army was strung out along the causeway when the first gap was reached. The portable bridge was fitted and the crossing began, but the vanguard soon reached the second gap before everyone had crossed the first. The portable bridge had jammed and panic ensued as thousands of Aztec warriors began to appear in canoes along the sides of the narrow causeway. In the darkness, the Spaniards and Tlaxcalans pushed forward amid an unceasing hail of stones, darts, and arrows. The gap began to fill with baggage and bodies as the troops pressed on pell mell. Many fell victim to their greed as they were borne under the water by the weight of booty taken from the palace. Dawn approached, and in the grey twilight the wild melee and carnage continued along the length of the causeway. Those Spanish captains who had reached the relative safety of the shore now spurred back into the disaster to the aid of their comrades. Trapped on the far side of the gap, Alvarado saved himself by placing his lance into the debris below and vaulting across. At last the main body of the army made the crossing, and

19 The Spaniards attack the Great Pyramid, supported by cavalry and Tlaxcalan warriors in the plaza below. From the Lienzo de Tlaxcala.

regrouped to continue their escape as the Aztecs turned their attention to booty and captives.

Why the Spaniards were allowed to escape from this battle (often referred to as the Noche Triste) can only be attributed to the fact that the Indians had no concept of fighting "to the bitter end." The Aztec's ritual duty to capture booty and sacrificial victims, and the achievement of high status were more important objectives. The main purpose of war was to secure tribute, and it made no sense to completely wipe out the enemy.

The allied expedition thus made its way to the base in Tlaxcalan territory after defeating yet another Aztec army on the open plains near Otumba. That the Spaniards were able to find sanctuary in Tlaxcala speaks of the deep and rancorous divisions among Indian nations who could have made common cause against the foreign invaders. But deep-seated feelings of enmity, the result of decades of military threat and economic and political oppression from Tenochtitlan, had already gained invaluable Tlaxcalan assistance for Cortés, and would lead to other alliances. As the army recuperated in the coming months, Cortés made

20 The disaster of the Noche Triste, from the Lienzo de Tlaxcala. At a gap in the causeway the Spanish and Tlaxcalan forces, exposed down the length of the causeway, were assaulted from the lake by thousands of men in canoes.

diplomatic overtures to the nearby town of Tepeaca. The Cholollans also saw the chance to secure their own independence from Aztec domination and decided to join the allied force. By April 1521 the allied army departed again for the Valley of Mexico. This time their objective was to lay siege and to capture Tenochtitlan.

The siege and surrender of Tenochtitlan

A critical part of Cortés' strategy was to gain a landing place from which a fleet of armed brigantines – constructed on the lake – could blockade the island city. Nowhere was more suitable than the city of Tetzcoco on the eastern side of the lake. This old partner of Tenochtitlan had in fact long resented the high-handedness of its neighbor and the arrogance of Motecuhzoma, who had precipitated the decline in power and prestige of the Tetzcocan court. With Motecuhzoma gone, the movement towards centralization and authoritarian control had lost its most forceful figure. The bonds of the old alliance, already strained, were now severely questioned by the Tetzcocan chieftains. As the Spaniards and their allies approached, a pro-Tenochtitlan ruler fled by canoe and a new ruler was appointed by the dissident faction. This man shortly died of disease, and Prince Ixtlilxochitl was elected with the approval of Cortés. This ebullient youth had won high honors as a warrior. Hating Motecuhzoma, he lent his full support to Cortés and was to prove an invaluable ally in the coming campaign.

The empire of the Aztecs was beginning to unravel with this Tetzcocan defection. Collaboration among the city-states was at best uneasy in a land where the political independence of each community was jealously maintained. Before the rise of Tenochtitlan, Tetzcoco, and Tlacopan as paramount powers during the 15th century, incessant war was the normal state of affairs between the many rival cities. These local wars had seldom resulted in total defeat or victory, because their primary purpose was to obtain tribute. As the authoritarian structure personified by Motecuhzoma began to collapse, the old underlying tendency towards fragmentation reappeared.

Step by step Tenochtitlan was isolated. Cortés led an expedition south to Chalco and neighboring *chinampa* towns, while another column circled north to Zumpango and Xaltocan, and on around the western side of the lake to reach Tlacopan. Later, Cortés marched down into the rich Tlahuica territories on the road to Cuauhnahuac (modern Cuernavaca). Meanwhile the fleet of armed brigantines built and based in Tetzcoco kept up a blockade along the lakeside landing places of Tenochtitlan. The isolation of the city is schematically shown on a page from the Lienzo de Tlaxcala. By early summer 1521 the Spaniards and their allies, divided into three forces, were in position at the head of the causeways – Gonzalo de Sandoval stationed to the north, Pedro de Alvarado to the west, and Cortés and Cristóbal de Olid to the south. The three-pronged attack met fierce resistance, and the Aztecs caused considerable damage as the fighting see-sawed back and forth. The besieging army of about 900 Spaniards plus several thousand Indian allies was minute compared with the huge population of the city, and the gains made on one day were often lost on the next as the defenders came back by circuitous routes and regained the rooftops. Several pages from the Lienzo de Tlaxcala portray the scenes of fighting. The Spaniards began systematic demolition: as bridges were captured and advances were made, all buildings were razed, clearing the ground to give the troops wider space to maneuver.

These slow but effective tactics gave the attackers the upper hand. Slowly the siege was tightened, while the city's population was gradually decimated by starvation, disease, and lack of fresh water, and by frightful massacres perpetrated by the Tlaxcalans. The ferocity of the Indian allies against their former oppressors could not be restrained by the Spaniards, who were shocked by the thousands of women and children who perished in the wholesale slaughter. The advance continued day by day amid piles of bodies and the rubble of buildings. The Great Pyramid and the royal palaces were captured as the Aztecs were hemmed into the northern district of Tlatelolco. Cortés sent messages to Prince Cuauhtemoc, the new Aztec commander, inviting him to surrender. But these communications were steadfastly refused. Determination to resist had changed to a will to perish. After 93 days of siege, on 13 August 1521, Cuauhtemoc was captured with his wife and chieftains as he tried to escape by canoe, seeking to continue the war from some other sanctuary. Cuauhtemoc was taken to a rooftop where Cortés received his brave surrender with honor and respect. The scene is depicted in the Lienzo with the Nahuatl inscription: "This is where came the end of the Mexica [Aztecs]."

Many factors played a part in the fall of Tenochtitlan: the coincidences surrounding the Spaniards' arrival; the brilliance of Cortés as a commander-in-chief and the superior Spanish arms and tactics; Motecuhzoma's unsuccessful strategy of entrapment and appeasement; and the Aztec way of waging war, tied to religious practice. Also significant was the inherent instability of an empire where coercion and fear had exacted tribute from cities that otherwise tended to maintain a strong sense of independence. Despite decades of effort by the Aztecs to build alliances, kinship connections, religious obligations and systems of patronage throughout their dominions, an infrastructure of imperial government that might have successfully resisted the invaders had not yet been achieved. Finally, there was the inflexibility of a strongly centralized chain of command that depended on final decisions by the emperor himself.

Cuauhtemoc's surrender marked more than the demise of Tenochtitlan. It also signaled the end of all the great Indian nations and civilizations that had flourished in Mesoamerica for almost two millennia. The empire built by the Aztecs represented the outcome of a long process of adaptation that had begun in the 13th century when barbarian newcomers arrived in an old environment, grafting themselves upon the land and the social order already established by earlier populations. The rise of the people we now call the Aztecs began as several different groups of migrants – including Acolhua, Tepanecs, Chichimecs, and Mexica – arrived and settled in separate districts of the Valley of Mexico. In the following chapters we shall see how these diverse peoples began to find, within a certain shared experience, subtly divergent and distinct patterns of existence.

PART II

IMMIGRANTS, SETTLERS, AND THE FIRST STATE

3 · Urban Traditions and Tribal Peoples

The Aztec empire encountered by the Spaniards in the 16th century was but the most recent phase of 3,000 years of settlement in the region. It is impossible to separate Aztec history from that of Mesoamerica as a whole, for the Aztecs inherited a wide range of institutions, beliefs, and practices from their Mesoamerican forebears. In this respect, we can trace the cultural patterns of Aztec life well beyond the relatively recent history of their state and earlier tribal migrations, to the Toltecs (*c.* AD 900–1170), back through the great civilization of Teotihuacan (*c.* 200 BC–AD 750) to the earliest complex societies which first developed in Mesoamerica some time before 1500 BC.* But within the compass of this book we will focus on the people to whom the Aztecs felt a special affinity: the Toltecs.

The Toltec precedent

The violent fall of the Toltec capital, Tula, around the year 1170, set in motion a dispersal and migration of people in the highlands. Some refugees from Tula itself went to settle among old villages and towns of the southern Valley of Mexico. Others, of tribal origin, emerged from the northern ranges to begin their long and gradual trek to reach the central plateau. Our understanding of the Toltec world is still only beginning, yet it can be seen from the harsh, military character of its archaeological remains that Toltec society unquestionably had widespread political and cultural influence in its own brief time.[1] The Toltec empire collapsed 250 years before the rise of the Aztec state, yet Tula was still remembered as a center of power and civilization, whose cultural legacy held much prestige among the urban populations: to be a "Toltec" was synonymous with being "civilized."

Located in the broad, semi-arid plateau some 40 miles north of the Valley of Mexico, Tula commanded an extensive domain whose scattered archaeological remains are yet to be fully explored.[2] Roughly speaking, the northern reaches appear to have extended in an east–west line from the border of the Veracruz Huaxtecs (a people related to the Maya), across the mountains and upland plains of Querétaro and Guanajuato states, and into adjacent parts of Jalisco and Michoacan. The heartland of the Toltec empire was more restricted, embracing the region around Tula itself, parts of the nearby Tulancingo and Toluca basins, and probably the northern

---

*Mesoamerican history is divided into four periods: Archaic (*c.*7000 BC–2000 BC), Preclassic or Formative (*c.*2000 BC–AD 250), Classic (*c.*AD 250–AD 900), and Postclassic (AD 900–1521).

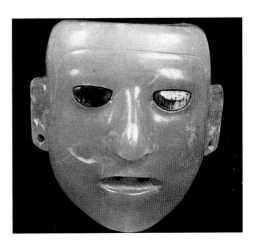

21–23 The Aztec custom of using stone masks in rituals derives from a tradition established over 1000 years before, during the ascendancy of Teotihuacan. RIGHT Aztec green alabaster mask recovered from the foundations of the Great Pyramid at Tenochtitlan. CENTER Another stone mask found at the Pyramid, inset with shell and obsidian, originally made in Teotihuacan. BELOW The Ritual Way and Pyramid of the Sun at Teotihuacan.

Teotihuacan

Valley of Mexico. There may well have been independent enclaves within this sprawling territory, such as the domain of Teotenango in the southern Toluca valley, just as Tlaxcala was later to remain independent within the Aztec dominions.

The name Tula, or Tollán, signifies "place of reeds," figuratively meaning a densely inhabited place where people were "as thick as reeds" around the highland lakebeds. In this sense the name Tollán had been applied to other cities, including perhaps Teotihuacan centuries before. That Tula was powerful and prosperous is attested by the archaeological ruins of its ceremonial center and outlying residential districts. The ethnohistoric texts of Sahagún describe Tula as a wealthy place where the ruler Quetzalcoatl had his greenstone house, his gold and silver house, his coral house, his shell house, his house of beams, his turquoise house, and his house of precious feathers, alluding certainly to buildings where tribute and trade-goods were stored.[3] Other passages give accounts of marvelously skilled artisans, and of squashes, ears of maize, and amaranth plants of amazing dimensions, as well as fields where cotton was grown in colors of red, yellow, violet, green, white, grey, and brown. Of special interest to Aztec historians was the story, recounted in Chapter 1, of Quetzalcoatl's legendary struggles with the wizard Tezcatlipoca.

The southern reach of Tula's influence presents complex archaeological and historical problems concerning the connections between the Toltecs and the Maya peoples to the south. Traditionally it has been held that warriors from central Mexico – collectively called "Toltecs" – led the conquest of Yucatan and the formation of Toltec–Maya states. Chichén Itzá was the most powerful of these Yucatan capitals between the 11th and 13th centuries. It was long assumed by archaeologists that the strong architectural and sculptural similarities shown by Tula and Chichén Itzá indicated that Tula was the primary generative center and Chichén Itzá the recipient; and these notions seemed to be supported by ethnohistoric texts. But as art historian George Kubler observed, the Yucatecan site of Chichén Itzá is the more elaborate city, where certain types of buildings and sculptures had a long history of development in late Classic Maya centers. Today, archaeological investigations are revealing that the movement of peoples or cultural influences between the Maya lowlands, Yucatan, and central highland Mexico was from south to north as well as from north to south. The relationship between these regions is part of a broader, complex picture whose roots lie deep in the dissolution of Classic Mesoamerican cities such as Teotihuacan in the Valley of Mexico, and Tikal, Palenque, and others in the lowland Maya region.[4]

As the social order represented by ancient centers collapsed in the 8th and 9th centuries, new seats of power such as Cacaxtla and Xochicalco were established in the highlands under the patronage of rulers anxious to forge new political organizations and to affirm their military might and territorial claims. The social, economic, and political changes taking place at this time were reflected by changing patterns of beliefs and practices. This is clear from examination of contemporary art and architecture, which borrowed from and adapted pre-existing Classic traditions. Tula, in the 11th century, was no exception in this incorporation of ancient forms, but new themes and emphases began to appear as well.

Architecture and sculpture at Tula continued to exhibit distant affiliations with late Classic Maya and Teotihuacan styles. Thus, a series of crudely carved stela-like stone monuments depicts members of the Toltec aristocracy, with symbols of rank and authority that ultimately derive from Maya sources; and ballcourts around the ceremonial center reflect similar origins. The architectural legacy of Teotihuacan appears in pyramid-platforms, arranged in panel-and-slope (*talud-tablero*) profiles with repeated animal friezes, and in the use of colossal architectonic sculptures. But at Tula – as at Chichén Itzá – it is difficult to find evidence of interest in those agricultural, mythical, and cosmological themes that characterized the symbolism of Classic-period sites, especially Teotihuacan. Instead, Toltec imagery displayed a narrow military focus, emphasizing scenes of conquest and sacrifice, processions of warriors, and emblems of rank and authority. Age-old signs of the four directions, once primarily associated with the earth and agricultural fertility, now signaled conquered land in scenes of sacrificial rites; solar disks, ancient symbols of the heat of the sun and its regenerative force, now primarily expressed the ascendancy of victorious commanders; and plumed serpents, traditional sky-symbols identified with the seasonal appearance of rainstorms, came to be state emblems of rulership and military formations. To be sure, such cosmic signs and symbols had always carried a degree of temporal as well as religious meaning; but their use in almost exclusively military contexts at Tula and Chichén Itzá affirmed the new ethos of warrior nations whose interest lay in seeking wealth and nobility through conquest.

It is significant to note that the long life of the Classic cities (AD 250–900) contrasts with the 150–175 year period of Toltec ascendancy. The violent destruction of Tula around AD 1170 is well attested by adobe bricks from residential zones which show signs of baking in a conflagration; there are also abundant deposits of ash and carbon; and in addition skeletal remains of those killed in combat have been unearthed. Furthermore, the colossal atlantean columns atop the commanding pyramid were toppled and buried in a trench dug into the building, a way of expressing the death of a ruling order which had much older precedent in the mutilation and burial of Olmec monuments at Gulf Coast sites during the first millennium BC. According to some archaeologists, the destruction of Tula may be linked to a drought that affected the northern marches and unleashed a major population movement with ensuing disorders and conflicts.

At present too little is known of the laws, government, political structure, tribute-economy, and ritual life at Tula to understand fully the web of its

Tula and Chichén Itzá

24–26 The Aztecs drew on ancient artistic themes to associate themselves with the great traditions of Mesoamerican antiquity. Recumbent figures of ritual attendants (chacmools) from Chichén Itzá (TOP), the Toltec capital of Tula (CENTER), and an Aztec sculpture from Tenochtitlan (BELOW).

Opposite:
27–30 The art and architecture of Tula and Chichén Itzá are dominated by images of warfare. TOP The so-called Pyramid of the Morning Star at Tula was in fact the seat of supreme authority at the city. BELOW LEFT Made in drum-like segments fitted together, the colossal warrior sculptures of Tula stood guard in the Pyramid's council-chamber. CENTER An eagle devouring a blood-offering from a frieze on the Pyramid. Eagles, coyotes, and jaguars were emblems of Toltec military orders and were adopted by the Aztecsat Tenochtitlan. BELOW RIGHT Figures from sculptural columns at Tula (left) and Chichén Itzá (right).

social order and the reasons for its relatively short existence. One possible explanation of the collapse lies in the almost exclusively military character of public sculptural imagery. The emblems of the warrior societies, sacrificial themes, detailed weaponry, and processions of allegiance and submission suggest political methods hardly developed beyond the threat of force over tribute-paying peoples. The reductive art visible at Toltec towns and cities bespeak ill-knit polities that could not withstand the pressures of a sustained natural disaster. Was the apparent lack of a deep-seated, flexible state religion with links to the basic cults of the farming peoples a major reason for Toltec collapse in time of drought and social stress? We do not know. But the need to develop adequate mechanisms for integrating far flung social groups was likewise to prove a central problem for Tula's eventual successors, the Aztecs, whose ancestors at this stage were still only nomads in the open lands far north of the Valley of Mexico.

In the 13th century, the site that eventually became Tenochtitlan was a cluster of small islands in the Lake Tetzcoco marshes, with willow groves, waving reedbeds, and nopal cacti growing among upturned rocks. Eagles, herons, ducks, cranes, and many other waterfowl shared this wetland setting with its teeming aquatic life. The eastern side of the valley was virtually uninhabited, as it had been for centuries, since the collapse of Teotihuacan. Here forests covered the heights of Mt Tlaloc and extended to the foothills, and down into the piedmont plain close to the line of the water. To the north, the small towns of Xaltocan and Zumpango stood amid the marshes of the shallow lakes. The western shore was by contrast more populated. The principal center was Atzcapotzalco, a town initially established in the time of Teotihuacan. Subsequently, perhaps during Tula's hegemony, this district was occupied by Tepanec people originally from the Toluca Valley, who were destined to make Atzcapotzalco a major political center. Southern communities around lakes Chalco and Xochimilco may have retained their independence from Tula, but they became recipients of major refugee groups at the time of the Toltec dispersal. This southern district was economically stable, for it had copious summer rains, freshwater springs, and a long tradition of *chinampa* agriculture and hillside farming terraces. The arrival of leading Toltec families meant that towns such as Culhuacan, Xico, and Chapultepec came to be identified with Toltec culture.

Archaeological excavations have yet to explore thoroughly this period in the life of the *chinampa* towns; yet the lack of major ruins, plus the accounts of pictorial codices and colonial written histories, indicate that the slow pace of provincial life was not substantially altered by the activities of Tula. The rhythm of these communities was predominantly set by the eternal round of the agricultural cycle, enlivened by the drama of ritual festivities and the seasonal excitement of endemic raids and small-scale hostilities.

The migrants: Chichimecs, Acolhua, Tepanecs, and Mexica

Among many migrant groups that began to arrive in the Valley of Mexico in the 13th century, four were destined to play a critical role in the rise of the Aztec empire. The traditional histories of these groups reflect "official" versions prepared long after the actual events. These accounts were again recorded in the early Spanish colonial histories of native communities, many of which were written by descendants of the Indian nobility. The "official" versions of the migration stories show how the Aztecs and their neighbors manipulated history by interweaving legends with actual happenings, sometimes narrating supposedly unique events in terms directly borrowed from much earlier peoples and places. In great measure these efforts reflect the longing of the incoming peoples for an acceptable ancestry.

The first major group were the *Chichimecs* (this name also applied generically to all the immigrant groups), said to have been led by the chieftain Xolotl, whom we may view as a semi-legendary personification of various tribal leaders whose names appear in different histories. The *Tepanecs* were a second group, probably tracing their origins to the Valley of Toluca and the Matlazinca and Mazahua ethnic stock of that region. The Tepanecs intermarried with the existing peoples of the Valley of Mexico and eventually settled at Atzcapotzalco on the western side of the basin. The *Acolhua* were a third migrant contingent, who moved into the eastern side of the basin in what was then unoccupied land. By the time the fourth and last major group arrived towards the middle of the 13th century, few lands remained unclaimed. This group, itself a mixture of various others, also intermarried before settling on the islands that became Tenochtitlan and proclaiming themselves the *Mexica*. The involvement of these incoming peoples with the older urban communities set the stage for dynamic changes in the 15th century.

The arrival of the Chichimecs and Acolhua is chronicled in the 16th-century colonial pictorial manuscripts such as the Codex Xolotl, Mapa Quinatzin, and Codex Aubin, and in the written history of the 17th-century historian Fernando de Alva Ixtlilxóchitl. The codices and the written text are very closely related, for they drew on earlier pictorial manuscripts and oral histories. These sources portray a simple, dramatic version of what was actually a complex process of adjustment to the urbanized culture of the settled valley peoples. The initial page of the Codex Xolotl shows the Chichimecs approaching the Valley, scouting for land to settle.[5] They dressed in hides, carried light bows and arrows, and other implements for survival in the desert. Xolotl, the chieftain, is depicted establishing a base at the site of Tenayuca in the northwest of the Valley, where a large dual pyramid would later be built. The remains of this structure may still be seen in a suburb of modern Mexico City. The Codex continues with an account of colonization on the eastern side of the Valley. Xolotl's son Nopaltzin set out from Tenayuca on a reconnaissance of the eastern side. He viewed the unclaimed landscape from the foothills of Mt Tlaloc, and even climbed the summit to survey the entire region. The hill of Tetzcotzingo, which was later to become an important ritual place, is another significant landmark. Following Nopaltzin's favorable report, incoming nomadic bands of Acolhua – linked to the Chichimecs – were directed to this district. The Mapa Quinatzin and Codex Aubin depict them as they settled in rockshelters and other places along the foothills and the piedmont. These settlements eventually became important towns such as Oxtoticpac, Tzinacanoztoc, Coatlinchan, and Huexotla. Tetzcoco, later the Acolhua capital, may already have existed as a primitive settlement prior to these arrivals. Nopaltzin's son Tlohtzin was eventually made ruler of this eastern district and established his seat at the hill of Tetzcotzingo. It was not until the 1420s that Tlohtzin's son Quinatzin moved the center of government to Tetzcoco.

However rudimentary their economy, the early settlers must not be imagined in terms of simple bands of hunting and gathering nomads. Even allowing for the exaggerations of this epic, the actions of the chieftains Xolotl and Nopaltzin suggest the existence of a social order of at least a tribal level. Xolotl played a part of considerable authority in "assigning" different groups to specific areas of settlement. He also extended his influence to the north, and formed alliances by arranging marriages between leading Chichimec families and those of the lords of neighboring towns. It is likely that the urban peoples quickly appraised the military skills of the newcomers, and were eager to enlist their support in the small-scale wars and raids endemic in the Valley. At the same time, economic power was increasingly vested in the Chichimec and Acolhua leaders – a significant step away from the economic egalitarianism of bands or even tribal societies. Among the first manifestations of this tendency was the construction of special hunting enclosures in the foothills of Mt Tlaloc. The Codex Xolotl depicts these enclosures with Xolotl and Nopaltzin, showing how the preserves were supplied with rabbits and other game obtained as tribute from communities to the north and east. Knowledge of agriculture and the acquisition of farming lands was another step to economic privilege. The Chichimecs and Acolhua probably had basic knowledge of farming when they arrived in the Valley, but this was far from the specialized indigenous practice of *chinampa* and terrace-farming. The Codex Xolotl depicts the agricultural zones of the southern district, where Chalco, Atenco, and other towns are shown with canals and canoes representing *chinampa* farming. When Nopaltzin married a lady from Chalco, his son Tlohtzin was largely brought up in that town, where he learned about intensive cultivation. Upon inheriting the authority vested in his father, Tlohtzin proclaimed his intention of converting the still semi-civilized Chichimecs and Acolhua into a settled farming people:

31 This page from the Mapa Quinatzin illustrates the Chichimec migrants arriving in Acolhuacan.

Once sworn in, and having received the empire, Tlohtzin placed special care on the cultivation of the land. And since he had lived for the most part in the province of Chalco since the time of his grandfather Xolotl, and what with the communication that he had there with the Toltecs and Chalcoans (his mother was a lady native to these peoples), he saw how it was that corn and the other seeds and vegetables were necessary for human sustenance. And he had especially learned from Texpoyo Achicauhtli, who had his house and family on the hill of Xico; he had been his guide and teacher, and among the things that he had taught him was the way to cultivate the land. And, as a person habituated to this, he now gave order that everywhere the land should be cultivated and worked. And even though many Chichimecs thought that this was a convenient thing and they put it into effect, others who were still in the backwardness of their ancestors left for the hills of Metztitlan and Tototepec ... and from that time on the land began to be cultivated everywhere, and the corn was sown and harvested, and other seeds and vegetables, and cotton in the warm country for their clothing.[6]

Although archaeological evidence is lacking for this period, written and pictorial sources portray the essential aspects of the process of acculturation. By the time Tlohtzin's son Quinatzin assumed power, three large special enclosures had been constructed near Tetzcoco under the control of ruling families. The Codex Xolotl shows that two of them were for agriculture, as indicated by a pointing digging implement, the *coa*; the third enclosure curiously combined agricultural and hunting functions, for the *coa* was also shown with a rabbit and a hare. In addition to these special lands, the Codex shows other lands with signs of particular ownership: one, with a small temple, may be *teopantlalli*, "land belonging to the temple;" another, with a small building, may be *tecpantlalli*, "palace land;" and yet another may be *calpultlalli*, "communal land of a town or district." As the immigrant peoples adopted agriculture, they incorporated ways of organizing the soil that reflected the stratified society of the older towns, and their rulers began to assume new roles and status in promoting agricultural prosperity.

The claiming of a large and unsettled territory with varied natural resources; the pattern of alliances and intermarriage with the townspeople; the adoption of agriculture (and doubtless its cults); the tendency to consolidate authority and economic power in the hands of a governing elite; and the tendency of that elite to adopt the language and culture of the city populations, all formed part of a conscious movement during the 13th and 14th centuries that established the base of a new social order from which the future state of Acolhuacan (Tetzcoco) began to evolve.

The Mexica

Of all the migrant groups, the early history of the Mexica is the most well known. The legends of their origins, travels, and adventures, and their various settlements and battles before founding Tenochtitlan are recounted in the schoolbooks of Mexico today. The orthodox version of their migration was composed from various original written and pictorial sources. In these accounts episodes are not always sequential, and facts are often expressed in metaphoric terms, sometimes describing magical or fabulous events that cannot be pinned down historically with confidence. Many questions remain open concerning the tribe's place and time of departure, the subsequent route of travel, and the significance of certain events and places described in the textual sources. Indeed, scholars such as Susan Gillespie, Rudolph Van Zantwijk, and Nigel Davies regard the Mexica migration as a composite of stories assembled by a small tribe after arriving and intermarrying in the Valley of Mexico, since many motifs appear to have had a long earlier history among the urban peoples.[7] Yet there can be no doubt that the legend was thought of as historical fact by the inhabitants of Tenochtitlan, just as the epic of Troy, the legendary travels of Aeneas, and the story of the founding of Rome were

32 The Aztec migration begins from the legendary island of Aztlan (left), led by a priest carrying an effigy of the deified hero Huitzilopochtli (right). From the Codex Boturini.

true historic events to the Roman population. The following outline will show how this legendary history took root in the Mexica collective imagination, coloring their ideas, rites, and eventually affecting the fabric of their empire.

Probably during the early 12th century a tribe departed from its ancestral homeland, described as an island within a lagoon somewhere to the north. The name of this place was *Aztlan*, meaning the "place of cranes," from which the archaic name *Aztec* was taken. It was not until later during the migration that these peoples assumed the name *Mexica* by which they were known by the Spaniards. The original term "Aztec" reappeared again in scholarly studies of the 18th and 19th centuries, and is now accepted as a generic name for the peoples of the Valley of Mexico at the time of the Spanish Conquest.

According to oral histories recorded by Fray Diego Durán late in the 16th century, the tribe had originally emerged from caves or springs in the time of genesis.[8] This is a localized version of a virtually universal motif in Mesoamerican mythology, alluding to the birth of people from the female earth, the primordial mother of things. The legend describes Aztlan as an island surrounded by reeds in the middle of a lagoon. The geographic location of this place has been much debated among modern scholars, as it was among the Mexica themselves by the middle of the 15th century. Some researchers have thought that Aztlan corresponds with one of several highland lakes in Michoacan or Guanajuato states. Others have suggested the lagoon named Mexcaltitlan on the more distant Pacific coast of Nayarit, where an island-town still preserves its aboriginal four-quarter layout. Yet more hold that Aztlan was the Isla de los Idolos in Tamiahua lagoon, on the Gulf of Mexico in northern Veracruz.

The quest to find the original Aztlan was actually begun by the emperor Motecuhzoma I, probably during the 1440s. By that time the location of the original homeland had become a mythic memory, but as the Mexica empire expanded and its rulers became actively engaged in building a sense of national identity, the notion of finding their place of origin assumed special significance. Motecuhzoma I despatched an expedition, curiously consisting of some 60 priests and shamanistic mediums. They traveled north, beyond the site of Tula. Diego Durán describes this odd adventure, saying that they journeyed to a place reputed to be the birthplace of their ancestral deity, Huitzilopochtli. There the delegation was met by a supernatural being who contrived by magical means to transform them all into birds and other winged beasts. In this guise they flew to Aztlan where they resumed their human form, and were greeted in Nahuatl by kinsmen paddling canoes. The migration legend continues with a "perilous journey" story of how, having arrived in Aztlan, the royal messengers were taken to an aged man, said to be related to Huitzilopochtli. After a series of questions, this guide took them on another journey full of dangerous trials. During the travels he revealed his magical powers, and scolded the Mexica for their soft and luxurious life in Tenochtitlan. At last they were brought into the presence of Huitzilopochtli's ancient mother, to whom they offered rich presents and recounted the history of the successful and powerful state. But she replied with a dire prophesy to the effect that they would be conquered one day just as they had conquered others. With this oracular pronouncement the visitors returned to report to Motecuhzoma. The magical quest was not really an effort to reach a geographical place, but the search for a consultation with a prophetic divinity also identified with Mexica tribal origins. Aztlan thus emerges as more of a concept than an actual location.

The original Aztecs may have had some knowledge of agriculture, for it was not until after leaving their homeland that they were joined by a second group of nomad hunter-gatherers who called themselves "Mexica." According to legend it was Huitzilopochtli – probably at this time a living leader, later to be deified – who ordered the tribe to change its name and to carry the equipment of nomad peoples: bows, arrows, and nets. The tribe wandered on across the tablelands and mountain ranges, settling in favorable places for as long as 20 years before moving on to a newer location for another two or three years. They ate meat, yet also retained basic farming skills and raised beans, amaranth, chia, chiles, squash, and tomatoes, as well as maize, the basic staple. It is said that they even built temples and ballcourts at their longer stopping-places, yet they always did move on urged, it was said, by a vision of destiny conveyed posthumously by Huitzilopochtli through his priestly mediums.

> We shall proceed to establish ourselves and settle down, and we shall conquer all peoples of the universe; and I tell you in all truth that I will make you lords and kings of all that is in the world; and when you become rulers, you shall have countless and infinite numbers of vassals, who will pay tribute to you and shall give you innumerable and most fine precious stones, gold, quetzal feathers, emeralds, coral, amethysts,

and you shall dress most finely in these; you shall also have many kinds of feathers, the blue cotinga, the red flamingo, the *tzinitzian* and all the beautiful feathers, and multicolored cacao and cotton; and all this you shall see, since this is in truth my task, and for this have I been sent here.[9]

Such curiously "imperial" prophesies from the deified leader may well have been added to the official Mexica history by chroniclers from Tenochtitlan during the 15th century. Nevertheless, despite such later manipulations, the original tribe emerges as a people with an economy more varied than that of the Chichimec and Acolhua nomads of Xolotl and Nopaltzin. The Mexica also knew of the Mesoamerican ritual calendar, for they marked the passage of every 52 years (a "century" in this system of time-counting) with elaborate ceremonies of renewal and sacrificial offerings (see Chapters 7 and 8).

The migration legend describes a route of travel leading to two important places: *Culhuacan*, "Curved Mountain," and *Chicomoztoc*, "Seven Caves." The exact location of these sites remains unclear, although there is agreement among some scholars that they lie somewhere between 60 and 180 miles to the northeast of the Valley of Mexico. (The mountain Culhuacan is not to be confused with the town Culhuacan in the Valley of Mexico.) Mt Culhuacan may well be a height near the present town of San Isidro Culhuacan, and the site of Chicomoztoc may be not far to the east. Indeed, the scholar Paul Kirchhoff argued effectively that the seven caves (Chicomoztoc) were actually a feature of the curved mountain Culhuacan.[10] Chicomoztoc-Culhuacan was also known by ten other names, one of which was Amaneme or Amequemecan, mentioned as the place where Xolotl's Chichimec groups had departed on their journey to the Valley of Mexico.

The manuscript Historia Tolteca-Chichimeca records that earlier migratory groups had abided here, before continuing to settle in Puebla-Tlaxcala. A famous page from the manuscript (ill. 33) depicts Culhuacan-Chicomoztoc as a mountain with womb-like caves, representing the ancient notion of the mountain as a procreative entity. The manuscript portrays a Chichimec priest enacting a creation myth, symbolically bringing forth the tribes from the earth as a sign of their passage from hunting and gathering in the search for a new place of agriculture. The importance of this consecrated site was as a place of religious renewal, where a course of action might be sanctioned, or a people "reborn" with a connection to the primordial forces of life, or where new leaders might be installed in office through a rite of passage. The wandering Mexica portrayed themselves as stopping at this ancient shrine and if indeed they did so, they surely undertook similar rites of regeneration and collective rededication of purpose.

The narrative continues by describing a series of tribal quarrels. A

33 LEFT The Historia Tolteca-Chichimeca depicts the curved peak of Culhuacan and the seven caves of Chicomoztoc as the womb of the mountain. Seven tribes are shown within, and a priest strikes the entrance with his magical staff.

34 RIGHT The earth goddess Coatlicue (Serpent Skirt). Serpents were seen as a symbol of regeneration, while the proximity of her breasts to her necklace of hands and hearts associates the idea of nurture with the need for reciprocal sacrifice. Twin serpents rise symmetrically from her severed neck, representing streams of blood; ritual impersonators of this earth-deity were decapitated as a blood-offering.

faction split from the main body, followed by another more serious division when Huitzilopochtli's "sister" Malinalxochitl was abandoned with her group. These people are said to have made their way separately to found the town of Malinalco, deep in forested mountains some 45 miles southwest of the Valley of Mexico. Another more serious internal challenge to Huitzilopochtli's main group came at a celebrated place named Coatepetl, "Serpent-Mountain," now thought to be somewhere near the site of Tula. The dramatic events at Coatepetl are described in metaphoric terms. The summit was crowned by an earth-shrine, the home of a guardian priestess, Coatlicue. Her title, meaning "Serpent Skirt," was a ritual name for the sacred earth itself, and she is described as an aged woman, meaning that the cult was very old. She is also described as the "mother" of a powerful woman named Coyolxauhqui and of a host of others known as the Centzon Huiztnaua, the "Four Hundred Huiztnaua." The myth says that one day the priestess Coatlicue was sweeping the shrine at the mountaintop when she was magically impregnated by a ball of feathers that fell from the sky. This was the supernatural conception of Huitzilopochtli. We must remember that although Huitzilopochtli had already appeared in the

migration story as an ancestral leader, the point of this episode is not to observe chronological accuracy, but to describe events in poetic and metaphoric terms. Thus, Huitzilopochtli is to be "reborn" as a way of indicating a renewal of his tribal authority. Upon learning of Coatlicue's impregnation, the outraged Coyolxauhqui and the Four Hundred gathered on the plain below in order to storm the hill and kill their dishonored mother. However, one of them ran ahead to inform Huitzilopochtli, still within the womb, of the impending attack. As the enemy reached the shrine, Huitzilopochtli was suddenly born as a fully armed and invincible warrior. Wielding a *xiuhcoatl*, "Fire Serpent" (a heat ray of the sun), he quickly dispatched Coyolxauhqui, whose dismembered body rolled down the slope, and then scattered the Four Hundred in all directions. At imperial Tenochtitlan centuries later, the Great Pyramid with Huitzilopochtli's shrine would be named Coatepetl, in commemoration of this mythic battle on the mountaintop, and at the pyramid's foot lay a huge dismembered sculpture of Coyolxauhqui. Even this episode has been traced by scholars to stories that had a long prior history in the central highlands, and Huitzilopochtli himself may originally have been a Toltec deity whom the primitive Mexica adopted.

The Mexica left Coatepetl and made their way to Tula, where they camped among the ruins before continuing to the Valley of Mexico. When they arrived they made their way along the western lakeside, stopping briefly at Tenayuca before passing on by Atzcapotzalco to arrive at Chapultepec, where they settled *c.*1300 near the springs at the base of the hill. The following period of about 25 years (or 45 by some accounts) was critical for the newcomers. Unlike the Chichimec-Acolhua, who had settled on tracts of unclaimed land, and unlike the much earlier Tepanecs who had intermarried and became integrated in the old town of Atzcapotzalco, the Mexica faced a hostile and contemptuous reception. The first threat came from a distant relative named Copil, who was the "son" (a descendant) of Huitzilopochtli's dissident "sister" Malinalxochitl. Now based at Malinalco, the leader Copil began to intrigue among the older towns to throw out the newcomers. In the battle that followed the Mexica were driven from Chapultepec, although Copil himself was killed. According to legend his heart was cut out and thrown across the water to land on the island where Tenochtitlan would later be founded.

At this point the migration myth enters the realm of actual history. Returning to Chapultepec, the Mexica soon faced another threat, this time from a coalition led by the Tepanecs of Atzcapotzalco and supported by neighboring Culhuacan. The coalition aimed to regain control of the copious springs at Chapultepec, a coveted resource located between the territories of the two communities. The Mexica were seen to be dangerous squatters and were decisively defeated in the woods in the area of modern Chapultepec Park in Mexico City. The refugees dispersed around the countryside and nearby marshes of the lagoon, while the

Mexica leader was taken to Culhuacan for sacrifice. Eventually the main group of refugees, without clothing or possessions, made their way to Culhuacan to beg protection of its rulers. The council of Culhuacan decided to grant the supplicants some land at Tizaapan, the lava-flow near today's University City. Displaying courage and endurance, and drawing on their long experience of hunting and gathering, the Mexica proceeded to adapt themselves to this unlikely environment. Small agricultural plots were built among the crags and boulders, and gradually the people were allowed to trade in nearby Culhuacan.

As a degree of acceptance grew, courtship and intermarriages also began. Soon the Mexica were styling themselves "Culhua-Mexica;" and by virtue of newly established bonds of kinship, they began to regard themselves in some measure as a part of "Toltec" civilization, for Culhuacan was the town where Toltec refugees had settled after the fall of Tula. The Mexica position within Culhuacan was strengthened when they were enlisted as allies in a small-scale war against neighboring Xochimilco. In the ensuing battle along the lakeshore the Mexica warriors saved the day. As proof of their triumph they presented the Culhua ruler with a pile of ears from Xochimilco warriors captured or killed in the battle. Aspiring now to higher status the Mexica boasted of their achievements in the marketplace. This insolence failed to impress the old Culhua nobles, since they still viewed their neighbors as barbarous inferiors while remaining uneasy of their warlike nature. A debate ensued in the city council concerning the future of the Mexica as residents in the Culhua domain.

As discontent arose, the Mexica themselves precipitated their own violent departure. Obeying the promptings of Huitzilopochtli's priests, they had approached Achitometl, one of the Culhua magnates, asking for his beautiful daughter as their "sovereign" and "wife of Huitzilopochtli." Not understanding the implications of this request, Achitometl acceded to the honor; his daughter went to Tizaapan, where she was splendidly arrayed and sacrificed. Following an old custom, the body was flayed and a priest donned her skin in an ancient agricultural rite symbolizing the renewal of life. The unsuspecting chieftain Achitometl, invited to participate in the concluding festivities, suddenly recognized the skin of his daughter on the body of the priest. The outraged Culhua took arms and were joined by others and, in the wild melee of javelins and arrows, the Mexica were once again driven into the reeds and brackish swamps of Lake Tetzcoco. The next day they made their way in canoes and makeshift rafts across the water to the uninhabited islands.

Although this episode reads as a single event in the migration, it is actually a stylized way of expressing the tribe's intention to become a settled agricultural people by ceremonial marriage with a female who was the symbolic personification of an "earth mother" deity. A similar motif is contained in the earlier stories of Xolotl's Chichimec warriors marrying noble ladies who brought knowledge of cultivation from the old *chinampa* towns. As Susan Gillespie has remarked, the women in these "historical" stories represent agricultural fertility – and in the case of Achitometl's daughter, an agricultural deity.[11] In later times these female earth-divinities were known by various names, including *Toci*, "our grandmother," *Teteo innan*, "mother of deities," *Tonan tlaltecuhtli*, "our mother earth-lord" (lady), and *Coatlicue*, "Serpent Skirt." The Mexica account grows still more stylized in the episode that follows.

When the refugees arrived in the reedbeds, one of Huitzilopochtli's priests is said to have had a vision in which the ancestral deity appeared, reminding him that Copil's heart had been thrown to land nearby, and that this sacred spot would be marked by a large nopal cactus upon which an eagle would perch. This would be Huitzilopochtli's sacred sign for where the tribe was to found their city. As the Mexica spread out the following morning they saw an eagle on the cactus, where they quickly erected a rude platform with a reed hut temple as the shrine of their tribal divinity. This humble structure was the precursor of the Great Pyramid of Tenochtitlan that was eventually built on the foundation place. Other sacred signs were said to have been witnessed, such as springs of blue and red water: once again these motifs were prefigured in foundation myths of earlier peoples. The Mexica thus claimed the island as their permanent home. The name Tenochtitlan refers to *tetl*, "rock," *nochtli*, "cactus," and *tlan*, the locative suffix. These events took place in the year 2 House

35 The rear of the Teocalli Stone, depicting an eagle on a cactus. According to legend, this was the magical sign which was to indicate where the Aztecs should found their city. (See also ills. 6 and 7.)

36 The opening page of the Codex Mendoza illustrates the legendary founding of Tenochtitlan, with the eagle on the cactus at the center. The crossed bands signify the waters of Lake Tetzcoco; early Aztec tribal chieftains are portrayed with their name-hieroglyphs.

(1325 by some reckonings, 1345 by others). Following prescribed custom the new settlement was laid out in four districts as the community began to reorganize.

The founding of Tenochtitlan, and within a few years the neighboring community Tlatelolco, brought the long period of migration to a close. The Mexica were now established in their place of permanent residence. Unlike the Tepanecs long before they had not become assimilated in an older city. Unlike the Chichimec-Acolhua, they had not found a large tract of unclaimed land upon which to settle. Their reception in the Valley had been marked by two major battles and displacements. Through adverse fortune they had come to rest on the islands of a lagoon, where agricultural prospects were meager, building materials were lacking, and they were surrounded by indifferent or aggressive neighbors. Remarkably, they had the determination to begin anew. These hard circumstances were to have a profound effect on Mexica attitudes and actions.

There were positive features of the island site. Birds, fish, and many other edible forms of aquatic life were abundant. Communication and transport by canoe to other lakeshore cities could be achieved with minimal effort – an advantage in this land where there were no wheeled vehicles or beasts of burden. And the islands were strategically placed between the three most important peoples – the Culhua to the south, the Tepanecs to the west, and the Acolhua on the eastern side of the basin. Tentatively at first, and then with increasing assurance, the Mexica strengthened their position. A council was held among the elders, who debated the possibility of offering the tribe as subjects to one of their powerful neighbors in exchange for wood, stone, and other supplies from which to build a permanent city. But this notion was dropped in view of their neighbors' scorn and their own concern to avoid further ill-treatment. As it turned out, it was the Mexica women who initially strengthened the economy by carrying fresh fish, frogs, birds, and various greens gathered from the lake, to sell at the weekly markets around the lakeshore towns. Markets were also established at Tenochtitlan and Tlatelolco, as described by the 16th-century Spanish historian Fray Diego Durán:

> They began to fill their city with people from neighboring towns and to take them in marriage. In this way they won over the people of Tetzcoco and others. They treated travelers and strangers well, they invited merchants to come to the markets of Mexico with their goods for such commerce always enriches a city (and this same Aztec nation today has this quality; for to towns where a man is well received and flattered and given to eat and drink he will go willingly, especially if he sees inviting faces, which is what most appeals to him).[12]

These modest beginnings laid the foundation for what eventually became a far-reaching trading network with the most famous market at Tlatelolco, described by Cortés and Bernal Diaz in the year 1519 (see Chapter 10).

Efforts were also made to construct a *chinampa* system. This was a long-term, laborious task, and was only of true agricultural value on the freshwater (western) side of the islands. The problem of acquiring agricultural land became all too apparent, and was to remain a critical concern for the island communities. Even at the time of the Spanish Conquest the *chinampas* of Tenochtitlan and Tlatelolco were far from meeting the needs of the populous cities. Military conquest was to be the final means of solving the need for productive land, but it was not until later that such action began.

Changes in social organization began to take place as the communities settled. At the time of the city's foundation the Mexica were led by the chieftain Tenoch. He is depicted with others on the opening page of the famous Codex Mendoza (ill. 36), with his name-glyph *tetl* (rock) and *nochtli* (cactus). The emblem of Tenochtitlan, derived from this chieftain's name, is painted in the center of the page with the eagle perched above. The status of Tenoch as *tlatoani* (pl. *tlatoque*), "speaker" or "commander," is indicated by the speech-scroll in front of his mouth.

Tenoch was a chieftain elected to office by a council of elders, and he governed in continual consultation with this group. It is probable that his authority was also derived from descent from a leading family or clan. Among tribal people who honor kinship above all other bonds of loyalty, the strength of a ruler is closely connected with blood-relationships. But the Mexica faced new problems as a settled community, and the need to achieve higher status and stability through different leadership became apparent. Therefore, when Tenoch died some 25 years after the founding of Tenochtitlan, a Mexica delegation was sent to their former enemies, the Culhua. During the brief time when the Mexica had been allowed by the lords of Culhuacan to reside in the lava-beds of Tizaapan, a degree of intermarriage had taken place between the two communities. Now the Mexica hoped that despite tensions incurred when they were expelled, the blood-ties that still bound some of their people with the Culhua would affirm closer ties with a dominant town of the Valley. (The Culhua aristocracy, it will be remembered, held the most prestigious lineage since they claimed direct Toltec descent.) A Mexica delegation approached the Culhua lords with a petition to ask for Acamapichtli to become *tlatoani* as a noble descended from Mexica and Culhua families. The choice of Acamapichtli was astute, for his family also had connections with leading Acolhua families in Coatlinchan. Soon thereafter Acamapichtli was ritually installed as ruler of Tenochtitlan, and in that same year (1375) the people of Tlatelolco installed a son of the Tepanec ruler of Atzcapotzalco.

By this time the old tribal clans, or *calpultin*, were increasing in size and number, and were becoming closely identified with specific locations. When Tenochtitlan was founded, according to ancient custom each *calpultin* was assigned its own place, with its temple and local cult, within the four-quarter plot of the city. These *calpultin* territories were owned communally; and as agricultural *chinampas* were developed, individual families were assigned hereditary farming rights to particular tracts. The users paid a form of tax or tribute for their farming privileges, and the land could be reassigned if it was neglected or if the user died without heirs. These farmers – the *macehuales* – were the free commonfolk of the nation.

As the Mexica leaders began to intermarry with the nobility of neighboring towns, the community became increasingly stratified in terms of socio-economic classes, just as among the neighboring Acolhua-Chichimecs. The *tlatoani* speaker (leader) and the *pipiltin* (nobles) possessed lands, or the income from lands, owned outright or eventually captured in war. This gave them a basis of economic power independent from the *calpultin*. In the early years of Tenochtitlan private control of land was hardly established; but as the practice of war began to increase, land was to become a principal reward for the rising warrior class, as well as a dominant factor in the changing economy.

4 · The Birth of an Empire

The Tepanec expansion

In the years after Acamapichtli came to Tenochtitlan, the city became increasingly tied to the Tepanec city-state. At the Tepanec capital of Atzcapotzalco an extraordinary man became ruler in 1371. This was Tezozomoc, whose ruthless genius for political intrigue and skill as a warrior-commander lay behind the creation of the first state-like society in the Valley of Mexico since the fall of Teotihuacan some 600 years before. Tezozomoc was destined to rule for 50 years. When he died in 1426, the towns paying tribute to Atzcapotzalco included many beyond the Valley to the north, south, and west. The story of Tezozomoc's shifting alliances, dynastic relationships, military campaigns, and ceaseless intrigues was chronicled by Diego Durán, Fernando de Alva Ixtlilxóchitl, Alvarado Tezozomoc, and Domingo Chimalpahín, each writing from his own perspective in the early Spanish period. Their narratives, based on oral histories and pictorial manuscripts, show Tezozomoc as a shrewd military strategist who also made effective use of flattery, bribery, assassination, and treachery in a career worthy of a Machiavelli. Here, no less than in Renaissance Italy, the pragmatic aims of politics were never confused with idealism, much less with morality. But also like the tyrants of the Italian states, this ruler's accomplishments and fortunes were interwoven with the changing life of a civilization. From the perspective of the Mexica and the Acolhua, the expansion of the Tepanec empire constituted a critical stage in an experience that was to propel them from subservient status into states in their own right, with concomitant developments in the systems of law, administration, economy, religion, and military organization.

The political events described by the early Spanish colonial historians provide a framework from which to outline this cultural transformation. During Acamapichtli's rule the Mexica were obliged to pay tribute to Tezozomoc in Atzcapotzalco. One form of tribute was to send levies for his army. The Mexica thus took part in a series of campaigns under Tepanec command. Eventually they were allowed by the Tepanecs to wage war on their own. In this way the Mexica took several *chinampa* settlements in the Xochimilco area to the south of the Valley. Other expeditions were carried out in conjunction with the Tepanecs as far south as Cuernavaca, west into the Toluca valley, and also in the old Toltec lands to the northwest. A war was also begun with Chalco that was to persist intermittently for two generations. This state of affairs continued when Acamapichtli's son, Huitzilihuitl, became *tlatoani* of Tenochtitlan in 1396. Following ancient custom this ruler was elected by the council of elders, for authority was never automatically passed from father to son. Huitzilihuitl married one of Tezozomoc's granddaughters and thereby ensured a special place for the Mexica among the Tepanec vassals. Continuing to participate in Tepanec conquests, they fought in a major campaign against Xaltocan, for which they were awarded significant tracts of land. Another expeditionary force was sent to Cuauhtinchan in the Valley of Puebla, and yet another war pitted them against the Acolhua of Tetzcoco.

Tezozomoc's ambition to conquer Tetzcoco was partly provoked by the injudicious claims of the new Tetzcocan ruler, Ixtlilxochitl, a descendant of the Chichimec chieftains Xolotl and Nopaltzin. This Ixtlilxochitl had married a princess of Tenochtitlan, a daughter of the future Mexica *tlatoani* Chimalpopoca. He rashly proclaimed himself "Lord of the Chichimecs," and urged the Mexica to join him against the despot Tezozomoc. But when Chimalpopoca became *tlatoani* of Tenochtitlan in 1417, he remained allied to Atzcapotzalco. Political maneuvers and sharp military actions then took place, in which Ixtlilxochitl almost succeeded in besieging Atzcapotzalco; but the Mexica-Tepanec alliance stood firm and by 1418 Ixtlilxochitl's forces were compelled to retreat and then to abandon Tetzcoco itself. The hapless Ixtlilxochitl was trapped in a ravine in the foothills of Mt Tlaloc and killed. The murder was observed from a tree by his young son, Netzahualcoyotl, who was destined to become one of the most famous men in all of ancient Mexico. In the following debacle Tetzcoco was captured and awarded to the Mexica as a tributary city, while Netzahualcoyotl fled to the mountains. By 1426 the Mexica had thus risen from tributary status to *de facto* allies of Atzcapotzalco, for they were now tribute-gatherers in their own right and serious contenders for power.

A decisive turning point in the relationship between the two allies was reached that same year, when the aged Tezozomoc died and his son, Maxtla, assumed authority after murdering a rival brother. This touched off a series of intrigues and struggles between the two peoples that eventually led to the assassination of the Mexica *tlatoani* Chimalpopoca. With his death a new ruler, Itzcoatl, was elected in Tenochtitlan. This able warrior was supported by Motecuhzoma Ihuilcamina, a seasoned commander who himself would be *tlatoani* one day, and by the latter's younger brother Tlacaelel, who was not only an extraordinarily audacious warrior but a wily strategist whose statecraft would equal that of Tezozomoc. These three hard-thinking men of action saw the opportunity to throw off their remaining vassalage to Tepanec Atzcapotzalco. Speeches were made and tension grew as more cautious representatives of the Mexica population voiced their apprehensions about the fearsome Tepanecs. Tenochtitlan was blockaded by Tepanec guards at the approaches to the city, and Maxtla placed Atzcapotzalco on a warlike footing. Lacking the diplomatic skills and intelligence of his father, and further hampered by a violent temper, Maxtla's bitter resentment was directed against the Mexica. In angry outbursts he insisted they renew paying tribute as a sign of their submission.

An atmosphere of crisis developed, and signs of wavering were seen in Tenochtitlan as the commoners sought compromise, some suggesting that the image of Huitzilopochtli be sent captive to Atzcapotzalco as a symbol of subordination. Deputations crossed the lagoon between the island and the mainland. One of these delegations was led by Tlacaelel, who succeeded in delivering to Maxtla a ritual declaration of war. Returning after this dangerous mission he encouraged the hesitant Mexica people. A heated discussion ensued. According to the official Mexica account, the warriors struck a bargain with the commoners: "If we are unsuccessful in our undertaking, we will place ourselves in your hands that our bodies may sustain you, and you may thus take your vengeance and devour us in dirty and broken pots." The people then replied: "And thus we pledge ourselves, if you should succeed in your undertaking, to serve you and pay tribute, and be your laborers and build your houses, and to serve you as our true lords."[1]

At this point a surprising new player entered the scene: Netzahualcoyotl, son of the murdered ruler of Tetzcoco, Ixtlilxochitl. It will be recalled that as a youth Netzahualcoyotl had witnessed his father's demise during the 1418 war with Tezozomoc. The young prince had fled southeast across the mountains to Huexotzingo, and had returned in 1422 to live with relatives in Tenochtitlan. While in the city he came of age as a warrior and is said even to have presented war captives to Tezozomoc himself. For a brief period after Maxtla's accession in Atzcapotzalco, Netzahualcoyotl returned to his ancestral seat in Tetzcoco. A delegation from Atzcapotzalco was sent, posing as an embassy but in fact charged by Maxtla to murder him. Their plot was discovered by Netzahualcoyotl's attendants, and for the second time the prince fled his homeland across the mountains to stay among his friends in Huexotzingo. Word soon came to him of Maxtla's new difficulties with the Mexica *tlatoani* Itzcoatl (Netzahualcoyotl's uncle), and when a delegation from Tenochtitlan arrived seeking alliance with Huexotzingo, Netzahualcoyotl promptly seized the opportunity to present his own petitions.

Itzcoatl's request for support was successful, and Netzahualcoyotl returned to Tetzcoco at the head of an allied force to dislodge Maxtla's Tepanec garrison. A base of operations was established here for war against Atzcapotzalco. Netzahualcoyotl and his Huexotzingan allies then crossed the lake in a fleet of canoes to land and move south to besiege Atzcapotzalco. Simultaneously the Mexica, joined by allies from the

37 A page from the early 17th-century Codex Ixtlilxóchitl depicting the heroic founder-father of the Tetzcocan empire, Netzahualcoyotl.

rebellious Tepanec town of Tlacopan (or Tacuba), invested Maxtla's capital from the opposite direction. This coalition between Tenochtitlan, Tetzcoco, and Tlacopan was to be formalized following their victory as the Triple Alliance. Other contingents from Xaltocan and Tlaxcala also joined the attackers, and after 114 days Atzcapotzalco's defenses were breached. According to the historian Fernando de Alva Ixtlilxóchitl, who wrote from the Tetzcocan point of view, Netzahualcoyotl himself led the final assault.[2] Maxtla was dragged from hiding in a ritual sweatbath by his own embittered countrymen and delivered to the official "captor," Netzahualcoyotl.

The sacrifice of Maxtla

Then followed a fearsome rite that dramatically shows how inseparable rulership, war, and human sacrifice were in ancient Mexican culture. It will be remembered that a primary objective of warriors was to capture an enemy in battle and to take him for sacrifice. This practice also applied to enemy rulers. Upon capturing Maxtla, Netzahualcoyotl had a platform built in Atzcapotzalco to perform this triumphal sacrifice. The victorious warriors were called to assemble in their finest panoply: jaguar warriors in black-spotted suits, peering out from snarling helmets, and eagle warriors with beaked helmets and feathered suits with talons. Standard-bearers were placed among the assembled companies, with wicker racks on their backs upon which emblems were tied: tall rectangular banners with geometric designs, great birds with spreading wings, tree-like forms with open flowers set with butterflies, and many other abstract devices arranged with tropical feathers. Many warriors held painted shields with heraldic designs – step-frets, concentric circles, stripes, bars, and animal and floral emblems. The commanders were distinguished by ear-plugs, nose-plugs, and lip-plugs of obsidian, jade, and crystal. Only the Tetzcocan contingents stood apart from this brilliant array, wearing simple white loincloths and mantles devoid of ornament. Presently, Maxtla was brought up stripped of all signs of rank and authority. He was then held down across a sacrificial block by four attendants. With a blow from an obsidian knife, Netzahualcoyotl himself struck open Maxtla's chest and tore out the heart, scattering Maxtla's blood to each of the four directions. The body was then disposed of with the full funerary honors accorded a *tlatoani*.

This ritual action brought to an end the power of the Tepanecs. On one level the performance may be seen as an expression of personal vengeance by Netzahualcoyotl and an assertion of his status as a *tlatoani* (although he would not in fact be crowned ruler of Tetzcoco until 1431). But the act of offering the vanquished king's blood to the four quarters had deeper implications, reaching to the very soil and its life-sources. Sacrificial human blood was regarded as the primary ritual fertilizing agent, ensuring the earth's regeneration in the planting cycle and the arrival of water, especially at the critical annual change from the dry to the rainy season. In a similar manner, war and sacrifice were linked to the renewal of the state in coronation rites, when society was transformed from dissolution to reintegration and production. Thus Maxtla's sacrifice transformed death into life. On another level, Maxtla's demise signaled the fertilization of captured alien land and joined it with the land of the victors. Finally, the sacrifice marked a major social turning point, because the formerly subservient city-states of Tenochtitlan and Tetzcoco now themselves became sovereign.

The Triple Alliance

The overthrow of Atzcapotzalco suddenly made land and tribute available in quantities hitherto beyond the experience of the victors, and triggered significant changes in social organization. After the troops from Huexot-zingo and other distant places went home, presumably pleased with their plunder, the three allied cities within the Valley divided the Tepanec land amongst themselves. Tlacopan, the junior associate, assumed control over the western side with its old Tepanec cities; Tetzcoco was allotted the eastern basin with its many old Chichimec towns; and Tenochtitlan and Tlatelolco were assigned control of extensive regions to the south and north. This pattern of distribution determined the future expansion of the empire in all directions. Although detailed information is lacking about the way the land was divided within the allied communities, the historian Fernando de Alva Ixtlilxóchitl mentions that Tlacaelel and Motecuhzoma each received ten parcels (units of land), while military commanders of lesser rank each received two, and the *calpultin* (tribal clans) each received one parcel for the upkeep of their temples. This information points to a dramatic change in the economic structure in favor of the rulers and the rising warrior class, who now found a personal source of prestige, rank, and wealth within grasp. As Nigel Davies has pointed out, "Private holdings of land had probably existed previously, apart from those controlled by the ruler himself – but on a relatively modest scale. Now, however, the conquest of the Tepanec and other territories radically altered the balance; the proportion that was individually occupied increased out of all proportion."[3]

A course of economic exploitation was set which was to last until the Spanish arrived a hundred years later. By that time, private land tenure was of two basic kinds. First came the largest holdings controlled by the *tlatoani* and a small class of nobles, the *pipiltin*, of whom many were directly related to the ruling dynasty. These lands were tended by serfs who were legally bound to the soil. The second form of tenure consisted of lands theoretically owned by the rulers, but awarded to leading warriors who held them in a manner similar to the way *calpultin* lands were held by individual families; thus, distinguished warriors were rewarded for their service, and in actual practice a warrior's tenure tended to become hereditary. Communal lands were held by royal palaces (*tecpantlalli*) and temples (*teopantlalli*), and the *calpultin* continued to be landholders at the base of the social order. These structural changes were almost surely already in progress by the time of the Tepanec war, based on the example of the Tepanecs themselves. The success of the war reinforced this tendency, and ensured the growth of a socio-economic organization with war as a principal means of acquiring land and tribute, and exerting internal social control.

Without the checks exerted by traditional forms of communal government, the rulers began to conduct ever more far-reaching campaigns. The pursuit of war, with its emphasis on discipline and the display of force, helped deter internal dissension and potential rebellion, assuring greater social cohesion and a shared sense of purpose. By the time Motecuhzoma II ascended the throne of Tenochtitlan in 1502, the office of *tlatoani* had become a locus of virtually supreme political, economic, and military authority. The custom of human sacrifice was to play an increasingly important role as an instrument of power, for the terrifying sights at the temples of Tenochtitlan, Tetzcoco, and Tlacopan hardened people to violence and bloodshed, while affirming the connection between the conquest of tribute-paying communities and the control of land as a source of life.

The war against Atzcapotzalco thus led directly to the rise of the Aztec empire during the 15th and early 16th centuries. We are speaking here of a confederation of independent city-states, Tenochtitlan, Tetzcoco, and Tlacopan, each with its own tributary domain; they were never to form a single politically unified or centrally managed state. The Mexica formed the largest and most powerful society, and Tenochtitlan was destined to become the dominant city. Tetzcoco, the Acolhua capital, was second in importance: under Netzahualcoyotl it would also be known as a center of learning and culture. Tlacopan was the decidedly junior partner: while retaining its hold on the old Tepanec heartland on the western side of the Valley, it was often assigned a primarily logistical role in campaigns of conquest.

From the reigns of Itzcoatl and Motecuhzoma I at Tenochtitlan, and Netzahualcoyotl in Tetzcoco, the course of empire-building began to evolve in the way of warrior-nations. Was this a repeat of Toltec history, a renascence of all that was meant by the heritage of Tula? Although the Aztecs revered the memory of the Toltecs, their endeavor soon began to assume a different character from that of Tula in fundamental respects.

The social and political make-up of the highlands reflected the existence of different polities: there were city-states and chiefdoms, small farming communities, and even semi-civilized hunting and gathering groups. Many communities had long histories, while others had been formed more recently; some were more powerful with networks of allies, others were small isolated settlements in remote mountain districts. None were strong enough to form a major unity except those of the Valley of Mexico. In the second quarter of the 15th century the Aztec confederation consolidated its hold within the Valley and began to reach beyond. As the campaigns unfolded it became apparent that coercion alone could not ensure the lasting success of imperial authority. The lesson provided by the fate of the Tepanec rulers was important to consider, for they had failed to build a broad base for social cohesion, and their essentially fragile empire quickly succumbed to rebellious associates and vassals. Instead, what was required was a more effective system for maintaining control. So new strategies were devised, and although a fundamentally military policy was retained, the Aztecs began to build a more complex administrative and religious infrastructure. These are the patterns of empire-building that will be discussed in Part III.

PART III

THE
CLIMAX
OF
EMPIRE

5 · New Conquests, New Strategies

The brief life of the Tepanec city of Atzcapotzalco was surely the subject of reflection among the Aztec victors, inviting comparisons with memories of Toltec Tula. There can be no doubt that such matters were considered in the Aztec councils of state, for a new tendency was soon to appear in which conquests and the threat of reprisal were accompanied by the building of alliances and networks of family connections, by the creation of a new legal system, by the organization of tribute and agricultural production, and by an imaginative effort to encourage religious rites and festivals as a means of incorporating and managing a multi-ethnic society. By the mid-15th century impressive monuments designed to manifest this movement appeared in fully developed form. The remarkable proliferation of symbolic sculptures, buildings, and ritual centers, designed as settings for agricultural festivals and state ceremonies, presents a most striking contrast to the limited vocabulary of art and architecture of the Toltecs. Indeed, such a project had not been seen in the Valley of Mexico since the centuries of Teotihuacan.

The chinampa district

Itzcoatl's first concern following the fall of the Tepanec empire in 1428 was to secure the political and economic success of Tenochtitlan by conquering the *chinampa* communities around the southern lakes. Enlisting the help of Netzahualcoyotl (the future *tlatoani* of Tetzcoco who, for the moment, still resided in Tenochtitlan) and Totoquilhuaztli, *tlatoani* of the allied Tepanec town of Tlacopan, the Mexica leader conducted successful campaigns against Culhuacan, Xochimilco, Cuitlahuac, Mixquic, and several smaller dependencies. Control of these prime agricultural centers would strongly contribute to the future ascendancy of the Mexica within the Triple Alliance itself.

Today, one may hire a flat-bottomed canoe and pole through the quiet narrow canals in the vicinity of Xochimilco, but few who visit the "floating gardens" are aware that these are only a fragment of the *chinampa* system that once covered miles of lakebed terrain. (Indeed, work continues on the ancient agricultural platforms, and vegetable and flower plantations still supply a measure of fresh produce and ornamental plants to the markets of the city.) Aerial photographs show the extent of the former cultivated area: a pattern of long, thin fossil fields covering the former

Chinampa plantations

38–40 ABOVE LEFT Aerial view of the Xochimilco basin, showing long, narrow agricultural plots which correspond to old *chinampa* plantations. ABOVE RIGHT A detail from the *Plano en Papel de Maguey*, dating to *c.* 1523–25, showing a *chinampa* district probably located in the outskirts of northwestern Tenochtitlan. Ownership is shown by houses crowned with heads and name-glyphs. BELOW Children poling a flat-bottomed scow in the *chinampa* district of modern Xochimilco.

lakebed between Chalco and Xochimilco. The regular plan of the fields, plus abundant 15th-century potsherds recovered from the surface, have suggested to archaeologists that the final conversion of the great marshland-lake into intensive agricultural lands was closely associated with the development of Tenochtitlan into a city of some 200,000–300,000 people. The chronology of this land reclamation has not yet been charted but it has been estimated that between the time of Itzcoatl's conquest in 1428 and the arrival of the Spanish in 1519, the *chinampa* zone was made to produce half if not more of the foodstuffs entering the capital.[1]

Itzcoatl now assumed the title *Culhua tecuhtli*, "Lord of the Culhua," a name carrying heavy Toltec associations; and the ruler of Tlacopan, Totoquihuaztli, became *Tepaneca tecuhtli*, "Lord of the Tepanecs," undoubtedly the title once held by Tezozomoc. The status of Netzahualcoyotl remained to be clarified, for he did not immediately return to Tetzcoco after Atzcapotzalco's defeat. Strongly independent-minded communities within his homeland had first to be defeated and incorporated in the larger domain he planned. With Itzcoatl's help he began by moving in force against Huexotla, an old Chichimec town, and followed this successful campaign with measures to secure the submission of nearby Coatlinchan. Gradually other towns along the northwestern lakeshore were also defeated. Netzahualcoyotl was crowned *Acolhua tecuhtli* and *Chichimeca tecuhtli* in Tenochtitlan in 1431, but he did not officially remove to Tetzcoco until 1433. Soon thereafter he led an army to capture Tollantzinco, beyond the traditional heartland, in a move that presaged a new phase of military expansion.

The allies now began to plan an ambitious joint expedition across the rim of the Ajusco mountains into the rich Tlahuica lands to the south. The Tepanecs had once extended their reach into this warm and productive basin, of which the town of Cuauhnahuac (modern Cuernavaca) was the principal center. The crossing of the Ajusco range was in many respects the crossing of a psychological as well as a political barrier, for the Aztecs were now determined to equal if not surpass the Tepanec achievement. Thousands of warriors were summoned and assembled in squadrons, each identified by tall feathered emblems borne aloft by their captains. The men wore only loincloths and sandals on the outward journey, carrying tumpline bundles with their weapons, battle-costumes, and jewelry, while porters bore tumpline baskets with heavier loads of food and provisions.

The trail led up from the Xochimilco littoral past the volcano Teuhtli, winding over terraced slopes with scattered towns and hamlets. The Ajusco escarpment is still covered today by cool forests of oak, pine, fir, and cedar, and at high elevations there are fields of grass growing on volcanic ash. Old contorted lava flows wind down among the trees from dozens of extinct cindercones along the spine of the sierra. The path descends from the divide through steep wooded canyons. Small streams cascade from pool to pool towards the valley, and a vista opens from the line of cliffs to the wide plain below. The surface of the spreading land is scored by deep ravines, and Cuauhnahuac itself was strategically perched between two of these canyons. The archaeological foundations of some of its buildings may be seen today in the plaza before the Palace of Cortes in downtown Cuernavaca. Low hills traverse the valley in the middle distance, beyond which appear the rich green bottomlands of agricultural districts. The horizon to the west and south is defined by pale blue ridges of the Sierra Madre. Access to that hinterland was another Aztec objective, for it had been known since Olmec times, 1,500 years earlier, as a source of rare stones and minerals.

Historical accounts of this successful campaign – and others that were to follow – were written by Fernando de Alva Ixtlilxóchitl and Diego Durán. Further information can be obtained from pictorial manuscripts, of which the Codex Mendoza is an important example. This extraordinary record of the growth of the Aztec empire was commissioned in about 1525 by the first Spanish Viceroy, Don Antonio de Mendoza. The Viceroy's purpose was to learn about the history, extent, and resources of the former Aztec dominions, as well as other matters concerning their life and culture. The Codex, painted by an anonymous Indian artist and annotated by a Spanish scribe, incorporated material from older native pictorial records, but it was designed in European book format instead of the traditional native screenfold. Using this Codex and the *Matrícula de Tributos* (another key pictorial document), as well as various ethnohistorical texts, the scholar Robert Barlow published in 1949 a classic study of Aztec networks of tribute.[2] This was the first comprehensive effort to map the towns named on the Aztec conquest- and tribute-lists. Barlow's study has since been expanded by the work of many other scholars, most notably by Ross Hassig who has mapped the routes of specific campaigns.[3]

Networks of tribute

The first section of the Codex Mendoza, which opens with the founding of Tenochtitlan with the eagle on the cactus, lists the rulers of Tenochtitlan, the years of their reign, and the names of the towns they conquered (ill. 41). Each ruler is identified by his name hieroglyph and has a speech-scroll in front of his mouth in sign of *tlatoa* ("speech" or "command"), and a shield with darts representing "conquest." The towns they conquered are identified by place-name hieroglyphs (and also noted by the Spanish scribe), while a picture of a burning temple by each show they had been captured. The second section concentrates on the tribute required from these towns, which are listed in different groupings according to the tribute-districts developed by the Aztecs by the time of the Spanish arrival. The places are again named by hieroglyphs, followed by a list of the goods they were obliged to send to Tenochtitlan on a regular basis. For example, Cuauhnahuac is shown at the top of a column of 16 towns that were

41 The conquests of Itzcoatl, depicted in the Codex Mendoza. The ruler is shown seated on a mat, with his name-glyph Obsidian Serpent. The shield with darts and spear-thrower is the sign for conquest; tributary towns are rendered as burning temples with place-glyphs.

required to send mantles, loincloths, and skirts; each "feather" above an object signifies the number 400. This tribute was exacted semi-annually. In addition, colorful shields and war-dresses were payable once a year. Other pages from the Codex depict similar lists from the conquests of later Aztec emperors.

While the Codex Mendoza is devoted to Tenochtitlan's imperial tribute, other texts account for the way the goods were divided among the three allies when working on joint expeditions. Generally speaking, Tenochtitlan and Tetzcoco each acquired 40 percent of the spoils, with Tlacopan receiving the remaining 20 percent. However, variations to this basic pattern evolved as the three cities gradually developed a complex network of tribute connections within and without their respective areas of direct influence.[4] Although the rulers of the three cities might participate in the conquest of towns in any of the three provinces, only the ruler in whose conquest-area the campaign was carried out was regarded as chief commander of that campaign. If only one ruler was involved in a particular conquest, he was entitled to retain all the booty and assigned tribute. But when joint expeditions were made, a ruler could actually be assigned

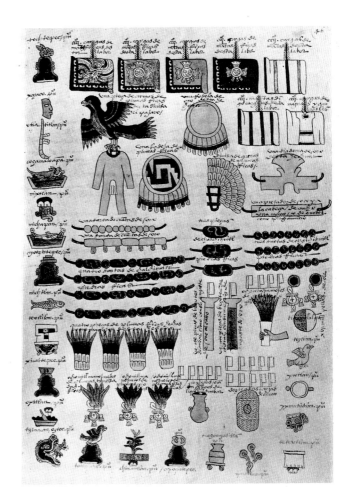

42 A page from the Codex Mendoza tribute list, showing towns on the left and bottom. The items exacted included mantles, war-dresses, shields, gold jewelry, jade beads, lip-plugs, bags of cacao, and bunches of feathers.

tribute-towns within another ruler's region. For example, Tenochtitlan received goods from towns within the Tetzcocan region in return for Mexica support during Netzahualcoyotl's campaign of reconquest in Acolhuacan. This is illustrated in the Codex Mendoza, which shows Tepetlaoztoc as a Tenochtitlan tributary, although the town is only a few miles from Tetzcoco itself. Similarly, Netzahualcoyotl, who participated in the conquest of Cuauhnahuac, received tribute from that town and others within the region.

In addition to the tribute divided among the allied city-states, individual rulers would assign income and lands to their personal allies and friends in reward for faithful service. Many lords from the principal towns thus enjoyed income from places far from their immediate territories. In terms of tribute-payment, this resulted in a system whereby some towns were obliged to pay tribute to one of the dominant Aztec cities, while a sub-section or estate within that town might also pay special tribute to a different individual.[5] It appears that in the case of joint conquests, it was customary (but not always strictly so) for the whole tribute to be sent to Tenochtitlan where it would be divided among the participants.

Jerome Offner's research has shown how the system of tribute worked at Tetzcoco.[6] Netzahualcoyotl created eight districts, and to each was assigned a tribute-collector charged with supplying the administrative palace in Tetzcoco with food and firewood. Some of these districts supplied the needs of the king's own apartment, while others were designated to provide firewood on a regular, rotating basis for the other royal residences or the temples of the city. Offner's research on the system of rotation developed in Tetzcoco has focused on a page from the early post-conquest pictorial manuscript known as the Mapa Quinatzin. This illustration depicts Netzahualcoyotl's administrative quarters within the Tetzcoco palace complex, whose foundations today lie beneath a downtown plaza in the middle of the modern town of Tetzcoco, spelled Texcoco. On the Mapa Quinatzin, the courtyard is surrounded by open porticoed rooms, in a plan similar to that of an Aztec residence excavated in 1938 at Chiconauhtla, near Texcoco. The leaders of major towns are shown seated around the courtyard, placed according to rank and age. The assembly is presided over by Netzahualcoyotl and his son Netzahualpilli, seated in a small chamber above and at center. The presence of Netzahualpilli reveals that this assembly was convened late in Netzahualcoyotl's life, probably in the 1460s; but the system of seating and the administrative organization it alludes to were established earlier.

The courtyard contains two flaming braziers, indicating the needs of the palace for firewood, which was supplied throughout the solar and ritual years by two sets of 13 towns whose chiefs were present at the meeting. As Offner points out, "this shows a type of rotational tribute that almost certainly varied in numbers and tributary towns over long periods of time, yet indicates a structure for the empire that effectively 'revolved' around Tetzcoco."[7] Among other important tribute obligations of the Tetzcocan provinces were service in time of war and labor for the construction and maintenance of temples. Since most towns had multiple tribute obligations at different times of year, there was a constant traffic of long trains of carriers, tribute collectors, and other people belonging to the administrative system traveling in and out of Tetzcoco. This lively coming and going brought news from the provinces into the court, and also duly impressed travelers with the culture, armed might, and political power of the capital city. The network of tribute thus provided a number of administrative, economic, and social ways to achieve a greater cohesion.

The income from tribute-districts allowed the Aztec rulers to develop impressive courts and palaces, and provided the labor and supplies to carry out building projects. By the time of the Spanish Conquest, Tenochtitlan had three royal palace-complexes, one of which was sufficiently large and well-provisioned by its system of tribute-towns to house and feed the whole Spanish and Tlaxcalan army. In sum, from at least the early reigns of Itzcoatl and Netzahualcoyotl, there developed a fabric of private and state-controlled land and tribute organizations which

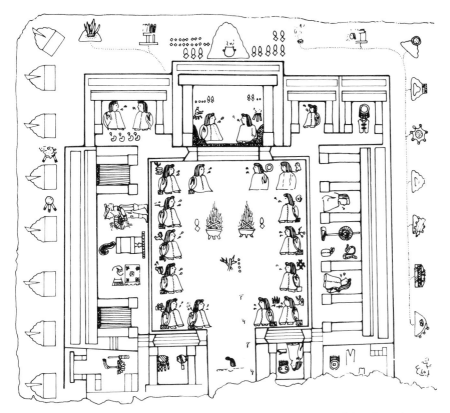

43 Netzahualcoyotl's palace at Tetzcoco, from the Mapa Quinatzin. Elders from the various Acolhuacan communities sit in council around the open patio. Netzahualcoyotl (right) and his son Netzahualpilli (left) preside from the raised porch of the main room (above center).

formed a criss-crossing web of economic and political relationships. The many levels of these connections enabled the *huey tlatoque*, "great commanders," to control the resources of a vast landscape, to distribute goods within their hierarchy, and to consolidate and expand their personal power as well as that of their nations.

Alliances, clients, and kinship connections

Motecuhzoma Ihuilcamina (Motecuhzoma I, "The Elder") succeeded Itzcoatl in 1440. This able ruler had a strong history of military accomplishment, yet he understood the need to postpone major armed adventures in order to attend to the pressing problems of administration within lands already subjected. Netzahualcoyotl became similarly engaged in consolidating his own web of connections between the heartland and outlying districts of Acolhuacan. This process was obviously closely tied to the system of tribute relationships. Again, the Mapa Quinatzin provides a reference for alliances developed by Netzahualcoyotl in the region of Tetzcoco. The hieroglyphs of 20 towns are painted around the damaged borders of the picture. Fifteen of these towns were especially important for they were the heads of districts with many other communities subordinate to them. Jerome Offner has shown that the seated figures around the courtyard were local rulers restored to office following conquest by the allies, or men especially installed by Netzahualcoyotl himself. In Tenochtitlan, Itzcoatl had first advised the Tetzcocan ruler against the restoration of existing local rulers. But Netzahualcoyotl's personal experience at the hands of the Tepanec tyrants had made him well aware of the ambitions, resentments, and dangerous intrigues that could be presented by dispossessed royal heirs. He decided to minimize these threats and proceeded with his personal strategy of making appointments. Itzcoatl became convinced by Netzahualcoyotl's success and soon restored nine rulerships in his own domains, while Totoquilhuaztli also acted on Netzahualcoyotl's advice and restored seven rulerships in the old Tepanec kingdom. At one point the Triple Alliance was governed by the three principal *tlatoque* and 30 lesser appointee rulers who commanded the different districts.

Research has yet to disclose fully the structures of government in the many lands conquered by the Aztecs. Various forms of organization were doubtless used among the peoples of diverse ethnic and cultural background in central Mexico. The 16th-century Spanish lawyer Alonso de Zorita, who traveled in the highlands and took a keen interest in recording previous systems of law and government, described the pattern of an administrative council in the Matlazinca capital of Malinalco before it was incorporated by the Mexica:

Before Axayacatl ... waged war on the people of Maztlalcingo, they had three lords. One was the principal lord, the second somewhat below the first, and the third of lesser rank than the first two. On the death of the principal lord, who in virtue of his dignity and lordship was named Tlatuan, his place was filled by the second lord, who was named Tlacatecatle, and in his vacant place entered the third lord, who was named Tlacuxcalcatl ... Each of these lords had assigned to him certain towns and barrios that they call calpules, which rendered service to their acknowledged lord. This lord had in each town or calpul a principal, or perpetual governor ... although each of the supreme lords had his particular towns, barrios, and jurisdiction, affairs of small importance were taken to the second or third lord, and dispatched by one or both of them. They referred a grave or important question to the principal lord, and all three resolved it jointly.[8]

This type of supreme council corresponds in essential outline to the system in Tenochtitlan itself. Below the *tlatoani* were two officers, the *tlaccatecatl* and *tlacochcalcatl*, and a third, the *etzhuanhuanco*, all senior commanders whose duties were largely of a military nature. A fourth office, the *tillancalqui*, is also named in some accounts. At Malinalco, there is concrete, archaeological evidence that the Aztecs took advantage of this compatible system by installing their own military government. A famous rock-cut temple at this site displays on a bench in the circular interior the stone-carved jaguar and eagle seats of the governing council (ills. 56–61). The men who sat in this chamber were governors and adjudicators of military background.[9] Whether they were retained local magnates or appointees of the Aztecs, these rulers were delegates of the great lord, the *huey tlatoani* of Tenochtitlan.

Netzahualcoyotl, Totoquilhuaztli, Itzcoatl, and later Motecuhzoma Ihuilcamina, also arranged marriages and required the attendance of the lesser lords or their children at the three principal courts. This was designed to prevent "thoughts of insurrection or rebellion." The lesser lords were also obliged ceremonially to pay homage to their ruler on major state occasions, and to assist him with men and supplies in war. It is also apparent that the leading families of the principal towns were bonded to Netzahualcoyotl through marriage to his numerous sons and daughters, and there is ample reason to believe that this was also the practice in Tenochtitlan. Considerable numbers of princes and princesses were produced in the royal "harems" to ensure that the offspring of the lords of the kingdom would be tied by blood relationships. Thus the Aztec rulers maintained their authority through extended family connections.

Netzahualcoyotl's division of resources in central Acolhuacan among his appointees, allies, children, and relatives is well-illustrated by an early 16th-century legal document known as the *Titles of Tetzcotzingo*.[10] This important text describes how Netzahualcoyotl grants water-rights to Lord Xochipanitzin, a relative by marriage. The ceremony took place at the Hill of Tetzcotzingo (a major ritual location with a view of Mt Tlaloc and its sources of water) where Netzahualcoyotl also had a villa and botanical plantations.[11] The *tlatoani* allots water-sources and aqueducts to specific towns and peoples:

> And from Mt Tzinacanoztoc [the water] goes straight to Tezontla and Ixcayoc.
> None shall take it from you, for it is my royal property
> In truth, [these waters] will serve all of my children
> who are there in the royal town of Tetzcoco.[12]

The act of assigning to kinsmen water from the site of a royal residence and a pivotal ritual place is another example of the tendency towards the centralized distribution of resources. This tendency also stemmed from ancient beliefs concerning the relations between society and the cosmos. As will be seen in Chapter 7, this notion of unification between humankind and nature found its most visible forms of expression in myths, rites, and the symbolism of sacred places in the highland landscape.

Netzahualcoyotl's "legalist" system

The centralization of power in Tetzcoco and Tenochtitlan was further consolidated by the promulgation of a "legalist" system, designed to ensure government by severe but standardized laws that favored the rule of the state. Netzahualcoyotl is credited with the creation of this remarkable system, which ordered the empire by defining behavior and responsibilities, with punishments to be meted out with strict impartiality. Rules prescribed exclusive and concrete solutions to specific types of dispute, and these rules were mechanically applied, with no regard to mitigating circumstances.

Jerome Offner, whose research has brought to light the essential outlines of this system in operation in Tetzcoco, has called attention to two pages from the Mapa Quinatzin. The first of these pages depicts a series of crimes (thefts) and their corresponding punishments (strangulation). The second column on the page shows punishment meted out to the son of a lord for the careless handling of property. Below, another crime against the rulers is depicted in which a rebellious lord is dealt with: first, a Tetzcocan representative speaks to older (and presumably wiser) members of the rebellious community. Then the dissident leader himself is warned by being presented with a particular symbolic headdress. Finally, after conferring with warriors, the representative has the dissident chieftain executed. The second page from the Mapa Quinatzin shows punishments for other sorts of crime such as adultery (jailing, burning, strangulation, and stoning). The trials of corrupt and incompetent judges are also portrayed, in which the judges are shown in buildings with the hieroglyphs of Netzahualcoyotl and Netzahualpilli. The judges then appear below, strangled, for having tried cases in their houses (implying that they had accepted bribes) instead of in the royal rooms as decreed by law. These pictures indicate that certain crimes were given certain prescribed punishments, but the law did not always extend to crimes committed by judges themselves, and in these instances decisions were made on a case by case basis with precedents taken into account.

The second section of the Codex Mendoza shows how a similar system operated in Tenochtitlan (ill. 46). It cites a case in which Aztec traders are mortally wounded by the subjects of a distant ruler, so Aztec representatives arrive to reprimand the chieftain and deliver the dreaded headdress. Finally an Aztec constable delivers judgment (a "thorn word") and the ruler is strangled while his wife and child are tied by slave-collars about their necks.

Although there were 80 laws in the Tetzcocan legal code, not everything could actually be judged in a strictly "legalist" manner. Indeed, there was an entirely different aspect of law which stemmed from tribal traditions established long before the Aztec state was formed. This aspect of justice centered on the concept of "the reasonable man," under which there were no rigid prescriptions for crime and punishment but judgments were

44 Drawing from the Mapa Quinatzin illustrating
Netzahualcoyotl's rules for punishing crimes.

instead made according to general, culturally accepted notions of reasonable behavior. Thus the "reasonable man" element of Tetzcocan law mitigated to a certain extent the severity of the imperial legalist system.

In considering these aspects of Aztec jurisprudence, Offner has pointed out that legalist systems have arisen very rarely in the history of the world, other principal examples being in Europe and under the Ch'in Dynasty in China.[13] Legalism appears to develop in times of turmoil and change, when different ethnic groups and societies come into contact during war, migration, and urbanization. Although the rise of harsh legalism in the Aztec system may have had its roots in some older Mesoamerican tradition, it is clear that as Netzahualcoyotl reorganized the political system within the empire, he perceived the need for a legal code with severe sanctions and uniform applications in order to incorporate all the different tribal and urban peoples. As well as standardizing laws governing these diverse groups, the new code was important because it controlled judges (curbing corruption and other abuses of power), increased the efficiency of law courts, and limited the influence of distant dissident lords. In these respects the legalist system not only contributed greatly to the breakdown of old tribal society, it also helped to build greater regimentation and submission to central authority.

6 · The Great Expansion

The reign of Motecuhzoma I

The first task of Motecuhzoma Ihuilcamina following his coronation in 1440 was to assert Aztec rule by consolidating claims on towns already conquered by Itzcoatl in the Valley of Mexico. Having received assurances of their submission, he then used the rebuilding of the Great Pyramid as a pretext for soliciting help from additional cities. Those who acquiesced tacitly agreed to Tenochtitlan's domination, for "contributions" to the pyramid construction in the form of labor or materials was in effect an expression of tribute. Only Chalco refused, and this precipitated a long intermittent series of hostilities that were to last until the mid-1450s. Motecuhzoma's next step was to send an expedition to secure towns in Morelos and Guerrero which had for the most part already been tribute-payers in the old Tepanec domain.

It was not until surprisingly late in his career that Motecuhzoma initiated systematic campaigns of conquest into more distant regions. During the first 18 years of his reign he had effectively strengthened the cohesion of the alliance with the rulers of Tetzcoco and Tlacopan, and established firm foundations for an ambitious expansionist policy. Because of the unresolved war with Chalco and its allies, and because of the effects of a great famine in 1452–54, this move towards conquest had been delayed. Motecuhzoma's first step, then, was to subdue Chalco and its allies once and for all. The defeat of Chalco opened the way finally for a series of extraordinary campaigns that were to take the army far from the mountains rimming the Valley of Mexico. The sequence of Motecuhzoma's campaigns is disputed today among scholars. Here we follow the sequence of events outlined by Ross Hassig in his book, *Aztec Warfare*.[1] The Huaxtec region of north-central Veracruz was the first to be visited for the stated purpose of avenging the mistreatment and murder of Aztec merchants in Tochpan and neighboring towns. In part, the choice of this theater of operations was determined by the fact that Netzahualcoyotl of Tetzcoco had previously conquered a series of towns leading towards the Huaxtec region, thus providing the allied army with a firm logistical base for the advance. The Huaxtecs were successfully defeated by the Aztec warriors in a well-planned feigned retreat and trap. The subjugation of this rich coastal area secured new sources of tribute and made allies and enemies alike recognize that much larger and longer military enterprises

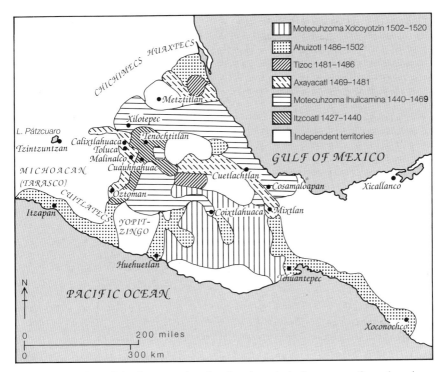

45 The expansion of the Aztec empire, showing the principal conquests from the reign of Itzcoatl.

than those previously experienced could be successfully organized and launched.

The allies' next move was into the rugged Mixtec country. The target was Coixtlahuaca, an old trading center commanding major routes and resources, and with important connections to the rich lands of Oaxaca and further south. The campaign probably took place after the onset of the dry season in autumn 1458, when the time for war was traditionally proclaimed. Although the motive was to obtain plunder and tribute, the pretext was again supplied by merchants who reported themselves attacked at Coixtlahuaca. Following what was becoming standard procedure (Chapter 5), emissaries were sent to demand redress, and war was declared.

More is known about the Mixtecs than any other group conquered by the Aztecs at this time in their history.[2] They were – and still are – a people inhabiting ancient communities scattered in valleys separated by mountain ranges. In the 15th century each valley was organized as an autonomous "kingdom" under the rule of a local lord, who maintained his lands by force and intrigue against neighboring rivals. The Mixtecs periodically feuded amongst themselves. There are also records of longer, short-lived confederations that mounted military expeditions into more distant lands, and in case of foreign attack the Mixtecs could assemble considerable defensive forces on an *ad hoc* basis. But no Mixtec lord had ever been able to establish ascendancy over any large district for a long period of time.

The most populous and powerful Mixtec towns such as Coixtlahuaca were organized in a class-system comprising the ruler and his extended family; a small stratum of hereditary nobles who functioned as administrators, advisors, and entrepreneurs; a broad class of farmers, tradesmen, and artisans; and at the bottom of the social order the tenant farmers, servants, and slaves who cared for the lands and households of the nobility. The region was famous for its craftspeople, and many of the finest "Aztec" goldsmithing, lapidary work, weaving, manuscript-painting, and ceramics, were actually manufactured by Mixtec artisans brought to Tenochtitlan. Despite their considerable sophistication, Mixtec towns had not the complexity, social organization, or population density of cities in the central basin. The Mixtecs had never achieved the degree of political unification that might have led to a state-like society. There is little evidence of a professional warrior class like that of the officers directing the Aztec army. The Mixtecs now faced a threat greater than any they had yet experienced in their long history.

In Tenochtitlan, the first step in the campaign against Coixtlahuaca was to send out the call for warriors to the four wards of the city and to the allied rulers and client chieftains. Large numbers of supplies were requisitioned, and long strings of porters began to arrive with foodstuffs, arms, and equipment. Warriors assembled in their own districts and towns, and moved towards areas of concentration. The maintenance of a large body of troops during the time of inactivity before marching, and the need for a regular supply of provisions, presented a major logistical task which proved again the efficiency of Aztec tribute-gathering and administration.

The Aztec order of march will be discussed in greater detail in Chapter 11, but we will describe here the prescribed sequence of units, beginning with special squads of scouts or advance raiding parties, each consisting of some four to eight warriors. The larger formations then began to depart at intervals, in an army totalling about 200,000 men, supported by 100,000 porters. The route they took to the Valley of Puebla probably passed by the town of Itzyocan (modern Izucar) before crossing the expanse of the plain and following the old trade route into the mountainous land to the south.

Intelligence of the Aztec advance was supplied to the Mixtec ruler Atonal by his Huexotzingan and Tlaxcalan allies, who had arrayed themselves against their common enemy. Messengers began to arrive with descriptions of the stupefying sight of squadron after squadron followed by porters, marching hour upon hour in a seemingly endless flow towards the Coixtlahuaca Valley. First came the scouts in their short white cotton xicolli shirts and yellow ocher on their faces, with their long black hair tied in a topknot with stiff red ribbons. Their legs were bare, and every man was girded by a loincloth. Each man carried a spear, some set with blades of obsidian, while others bore feathered fans and high-backed sandals indicating their rank and authority. Conch-shell trumpets were also carried to signal back to the main army. Then came the warriors, still dressed lightly for the trail. The rank and file carried tumpline bundles that held their weapons and battle-dress: darts, slings, clubs, and painted shields and feathered devices, while the commanders had porters carrying their leather or feather-woven body-suits in green, red, or yellow, some spotted or striped as animals, others woven or painted with abstract heraldic patterns. As this force spread out in the fields before Coixtlahuaca, Mixtec warriors hastened up from outlying districts and towns. Even with the support of the Tlaxcalans and Huexotzingans, it was not easy for the Mixtecs to improvise an effective defense against an invader who had successfully brought thousands of fighting men across the broken land-scape. For although it is not inconceivable that the invading army was smaller than the defending host, it was led by more experienced and purposeful commanders, accustomed to obedience and discipline.

Few details are available concerning the following battle, but enough can be gleaned from various other campaign accounts to characterize the fighting. The basic concept of battle was strongly characterized by man-to-man combat, desperate sorties, and duels between individual champions, recalling the wild melee beneath the walls of Troy. The assembled ranks confronted each other across open ground. All were now dressed in their flashing plumes, animal helmets, and body-suits, and the captains bore insignia waving in the bright mountain sunlight. Taunts, boasts, and challenges were flung across the field; and here and there daring youths would jump out to strike insulting or indecent postures to belittle the enemy and show bravado to their fellow warriors. As tension built the voices of thousands of men rose in a deep wave of sound. The conch-shell trumpets were blown with full force, and suddenly the air was filled with the din of whistling, shrill war-cries, whoops, and howls, as the lines charged towards each other in the rising dust. Volleys and counter-volleys of stones were hurled with stunning effect, and at closer range rattling clouds of darts were cast from atlatls. The formations met with a shock as men swung their heavy obsidian-bladed clubs, seeking to cut down or capture opponents as trophies for sacrifice.

Although the Aztecs were not practiced in the close-formation drill of Roman or Spanish legions, the impact of the Aztec onslaught and the fearful sense of their discipline and fighting spirit was something the Mixtecs had not previously encountered. The Aztec force broke through the defenders' ranks and a running battle developed as the Mixtecs and their allies fell back through the town, fighting between the houses. The Aztec warriors were urged on by their captains towards the principal pyramid where, sensing victory, they broke through again and ran up the stairs to set fire to the thatch roof of the temple. This was the traditional signal of victory, and as the column of smoke and flames rose up, the remaining defenders were pursued in a rout through the dry corn-fields and into the hills. Captured, wounded, and dead warriors were stripped of their battle-finery as the Aztec victors turned to pillage. Soon the streets and lanes of Coixtlahuaca were strewn with broken household wreckage – pottery, boxes, and pieces of cloth – as dogs and turkeys ran about, chased down by hungry warriors.

That the Mixtecs and their allies had been defeated was clear to the women, children, and elders witnessing the battle from their retreat in the mountains. The Mixtecs were now obliged to buy peace. A delegation of Coixtlahuaca magnates approached the Aztec commanders and terms of submission were bargained. According to established practice the defeated chieftains were allowed to retain their positions on condition that they provided regular tribute from their respective districts. Only the ruler Atonal's life was forfeited to the Aztecs: he was strangled, and his family taken as slaves. The Codex Mendoza shows the tribute exacted from Coixtlahuaca and its environs: 2,000 finely woven blankets, 2 splendid military outfits, an unspecified number of string collars of greenstone beads, 800 bunches of green feathers, another feathered emblem such as worn by Aztec chieftains, 40 bags of prized red cochineal dye (made from the dried bodies of the insect *Coccus cacti*), and 20 bowls of gold dust. Other accounts mention loads of cotton, chile, and salt. To ensure the

46 The attack on Aztec traders near Coixtlahuaca, and the subsequent judgment and execution of the Mixtec leader, Atonal. From the Codex Mendoza.

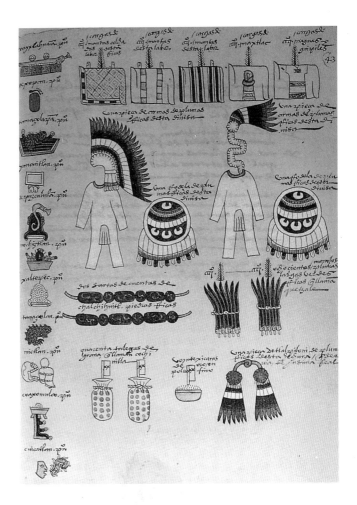

47 The tribute list of Motecuhzoma I from the Codex Mendoza. Coixtlahuaca is depicted top left.

arrival of these goods on a regular basis, the Aztecs appointed a tribute-collector. In addition, the Mixtec chieftains were obliged to present the Aztecs with a magnificent feast, and were forced to listen to their boasts and humiliating insults. The Aztec army departed with heavy loads of tribute and plunder, including important Mixtec religious paraphernalia taken from the burnt temple. The latter objects were destined to be held as spiritual hostages in a special building, the *coateocalli*, within the main ceremonial enclosure of Tenochtitlan. The departing army was also accompanied by a long line of dispirited captives, destined for ritual sacrifice.

In the cities of the Aztec homeland, the returning warriors were welcomed by jubilant crowds. Their triumph was celebrated in Tenochtitlan, where the exultant Aztecs presented their captives at the landing of the Great Pyramid. The victims were led up the stairs through thick clouds of incense, to be stretched over the sacrificial block for the rite of heart-excision. Blood ran down the pyramid steps and the bodies of victims were flung down to be decapitated and dismembered in a ritual carnage, enacting the myth of Huitzilopochtli's defeat of Coyolxauhqui and the

Four Hundred Huitznaua (Chapter 3). The heads of the victims were strung up on the skull rack as public trophies, while the captor-warriors were presented with a severed arm or thigh. Sahagún says that these gruesome joints were taken home amid much jubilation, to be prepared in a savory stew with chiles and tomatoes for a ritual meal. Yet it must not be imagined that human flesh was a primary way of satisfying hunger among the Aztec populations. Rather, it remained an essentially sacramental act, for by ingesting the flesh and blood of the enemy, the warrior participated in the offering made to Huitzilopochtli at his shrine on the living pyramid-mountain. These celebrations were accompanied by displays of wealth and gift-giving designed to exalt the victors' status and to impress the representatives of foreign communities.

The pattern of the Coixtlahuaca campaign was to be repeated elsewhere, as Motecuhzoma directed the victorious army to Cosamaloapan in 1459, and then again on a lengthy expedition to Ahuilizapan (modern Orizaba) and Cuetlachtlan (Cotaxtla). These were hard-fought, complex campaigns for, as Hassig has pointed out, the native communities were assisted by considerable military units from Tlaxcala, Huexotzingo, and Chololan.[3]

Under Motecuhzoma I the Aztecs had won a decisive series of conquests. These set a course of military expansion that was to dominate Aztec policy until the Spanish arrival. By the time of Motecuhzoma's death in 1469 and the death of Netzahualcoyotl in 1472, the lands paying tribute to the Aztecs reached south to Oaxaca, east from Totonac Cosamaloapan to Tuxpan in the Huaxtec country, and another large segment of the highlands northeast to Xilotepec. An unimaginable wealth from tropical lowlands and the upland plateaus now poured into the imperial cities on a regular basis, guaranteed by tribute-gatherers and the threat of armed retribution. Gradually, the Aztec system of marriage-alliances and political clients would be extended into the conquered regions, but it would always be the fear of punitive force that ensured the flow of tribute.

Early imperial monuments

As the Aztec armies reached further afield the idea of empire was given powerful ritual and artistic expression. In Tenochtitlan, a singular monument was commissioned in the form of a cylindrical stone, with a diadem of the sun carved on its upper surface. A stone handle was carved in the center, to which sacrificial warriors were tethered. A picture from Diego Durán's *Book of Rites* illustrates how an enemy warrior captured in battle would be tied by an ankle upon such a monument, and given a club pasted with feathers with which to defend himself. It was the task of the victim to stand and duel with a series of Aztec champions armed with deadly clubs set with obsidian razors. The enemy warrior was thus sacrificed to the sun. The monument was an altar for the sun cult, which was the special responsibility of the Aztec military orders.

Ɒxxi ꝗmarço ꝺia ꭗsant
ꝺenịto. tlaca ꭗi peualị tli
es gran fiesta

48 Scene of gladiatorial sacrifice from the Codex Magliabechiano. A prisoner of war dressed as the deity Xipe Totec (left) – armed only with a feathered club, and with one leg tethered to the round stone – confronts an Aztec jaguar-warrior wielding an obsidian-bladed club.

The sun-altar was a forerunner of two other famous cylindrical commemorative sculptures. The first was recently excavated beneath the patio of the old Spanish Archbishop's Palace, immediately south of the ruins of the Great Pyramid. This monument was probably made late in Motecuhzoma Ihuilcamina's reign or during the reign of his successor Axayacatl (1469–1481). It is still being deciphered, but its iconography has been resolved through analysis of a similar design on the second sculpture, discovered beneath the Plaza Mayor in 1790. This was one of the first and most important finds to be regarded as "archaeological" in the late Spanish colonial period. The much-studied monument was carved during the reign of Tizoc (1481–1486). The Tizoc Stone (ills. 49,50) shows the empire of Tenochtitlan in the form of a cosmic diagram. The flat upper surface of the cylinder is carved with a sun-disc, whose four main rays point to the cardinal directions. A band of stars, the "eyes" of the night, surround the disc on the upper rim, completing the celestial level. Another band frames the bottom edge, carved with flint points and four abstract Tlaltecuhtli masks, corresponding to the earth. Between the heavens and the earth a series of Aztec warriors are shown in identical poses, grasping the representatives of foreign towns by their hair. The names of these towns are indicated by hieroglyphs above each figure. The *tlatoani* Tizoc appears at the beginning of the sequence, dressed in the sacred regalia of the gods Huitzilopochtli and Tezcatlipoca. The foreign figures who bow in submission are the deities of their respective communities. The capturing Aztecs all face to the right, and move around the perimeter in counter-clockwise procession, enclosing the world and claiming it as sacred territory. The Aztecs portrayed their conquests in terms of ritual events unfolding around the rim of a cosmological diagram.

The reign of Axayacatl: expansion and defeat

The expansion during the reigns of Motecuhzoma and Netzahualcoyotl began the conquests that were to absorb the energies of the following *tlatoque*, with greater or lesser degrees of success.

Following Motecuhzoma's death the 19-year-old prince Axayacatl was elected *tlatoani*. Though hardly more than a youth, he had already proved himself a brave soldier and an able leader, who held important commands in the expeditions of Motecuhzoma. He was to reign for 13 years, from 1469 to 1481. Ross Hassig describes his principal military accomplishments in a chronological sequence beginning with his coronation-war in the Isthmus of Tehuantepec, followed by a succession of expeditions in the Puebla Valley, the Gulf Coast, the Toluca Valley, Guerrero, and north of the Valley of Mexico.[4] Axayacatl's successes were marred, however, by a disastrous defeat at the hands of the Tarascans in 1479. During his reign, long-standing tensions between the "sister" cities of Tlatelolco and Tenochtitlan erupted in what amounted to a brief civil war on the island, and ended with the subjugation of the Tlatelolcans in 1473.

The troubles with Tlatelolco stemmed from old resentments and rivalries which were brought to a new pitch of tension by the intrigues of the Tlatelolcan *tlatoani*, Moquihuix. In the wake of Netzahualcoyotl's death in 1472, and disagreement among the nobility as to his successor, and also due to the death of the *tlatoani* of Tlacopan, Axayacatl faced a serious threat of political instability at the heart of the Triple Alliance. At this juncture Moquihuix opportunistically sought support from Tenochtitlan's traditional enemies, the Chalcas, Tlaxcalans, Huexotzingans, and Cholollans, as well as other communities in the Valley of Mexico. The plot was disclosed and men from both sides began to fan the embers. According to one account, Moquihuix attempted to gain advantage by sending a force of warriors by canoe at night, after letting it be known that a hunt for aquatic birds was at hand. The ruse was reported, and Axayacatl blocked the entrances to Tlatelolco to prevent reinforcements from arriving before sending in a ferocious attack. The action culminated when the outnumbered Tlatelolcans were massacred in the plaza near the

The Stone of Tizoc

49,50 ABOVE and CENTER On top of the stone, the sun-disk and a band of stars represent the heavens, while pointed stones and four "earth-monster" masks on the bottom (not shown) symbolize the surface of the earth. BELOW The sides of the stone depict Aztec conquests as a series of ritual "captive" scenes, with Tizoc (extreme left) and his minions grasping the deities of enemy towns.

market. Moquihuix was killed by Axayacatl himself, according to one account, or cast himself from the high pyramid, according to another. Axayacatl then ordered the killing of all the rulers of towns thought to have conspired with the Tlatelolcans, including the ruler of Xochimilco who had not promptly come to his aid. Thus Tenochtitlan secured the loyalty of the survivors. Tlatelolco was sacked, her lands were appropriated, and rubbish was cast in the burned temples. Tribute was also levied, and as a final humiliation Tlatelolcans were requisitioned as porters for future Aztec campaigns.

An early victory brilliantly won by Axayacatl against Toluca in 1475–76 led to further campaigns on the western marches in 1476–77 and 1477–78. These gains provided the logistical base for an Aztec thrust against the Tarascan dominions, probably in the dry season of 1478–79. The Tarascans still inhabit their ancestral homeland, centered in the modern state of Michoacan. The archaeological ruins of their ancient capital, Tzintzuntzan, may be seen on a bluff above the colonial town of that same name overlooking Lake Pátzcuaro. In the 15th century the Tarascans were organized as a confederation similar to those elsewhere in Mesoamerica. Some scholars have seen them as a power that rivaled the Aztecs. This, however, is largely unsupported by facts other than their successful resistance to Aztec military aggressions. The historical descriptions of Axayacatl's invasion vary greatly, but all agree that the Aztec force suffered an unprecedented defeat. In the vicinity of Taximaloyan (modern Charo) the Aztecs assembled some 32,000 warriors against an enemy host of about 50,000. Although Axayacatl sought to call off the battle he was persuaded to press the attack. The Aztec squadrons broke and fled, but their commanders rallied and again asserted their will to confront the enemy. The next day they were catastrophically defeated. Of their great army only 200 returned to Tenochtitlan, Axayacatl among them; and 400 Tetzcocans, 400 Tepanecs, 400 Chalcas, and 400 Xochimilcas as well as 300 Otomies (elite soldiers) are said to have survived. Axayacatl's reign concluded with yet another expedition back to the Gulf Coast region, to reconquer rebellious towns. This pattern of conquest and reconquest was to remain a feature of the empire until the Spanish arrival.

Failure and rebellion under Tizoc

When Axayacatl died in 1481 he was succeeded by his brother Tizoc, who had served as a member of the highest military council. From the outset his reign was marked by misfortune in battle, experienced first in his coronation war. As we shall see in Chapter 11, the long process by which the *tlatoani* was installed in office demanded that he lead a battle to bring back captives for sacrifice at the confirmation ceremony. The Aztecs chose Metztitlan as their objective, located in mountainous country some 125 miles to the northeast. Much to their surprise they found the enemy defending a narrow valley, where maneuver was limited and any numerical advantage held by the Aztecs was correspondingly reduced. The day was saved only when a formation of teenage boys rose in the face of an impending rout and succeeded in capturing 40 prisoners. This was meager by all precedent, but it was to be the only visible token of victory brought home by the humiliated Aztecs. The coronation was concluded, but Tizoc's poor performance was perceived as an unfavorable omen.

Thereafter Tizoc's wars aimed to suppress rebellions in areas previously conquered, mostly within territories where the Aztecs could draw upon logistical support. No significant ventures were extended to regions beyond the limits achieved by his predecessors. Tizoc had lost the offensive, and the longer his reign continued, the more the empire disintegrated. Because the tribute-system was essentially controlled by threat of violent reprisal, internal revolts became more of a danger than ever before. Tizoc's failure as an aggressive commander led to his death by poison in 1486, perhaps by order of his brother Ahuizotl, who held a post (known as the *tlaccatecatl*) on the high military council normally reserved for the "heir apparent." Four days after Tizoc's death the elective council met formally and indeed appointed this ambitious young prince to the office of *tlatoani*.

Ahuizotl's reign: expansion and renewal

Ahuizotl was to prove Tenochtitlan's most extraordinary military leader. He was a born warrior and adventurer-conqueror: tough and fearless, he lived and fought with his army and inspired the men with his personal valor. His campaigns were marked by swift, murderous action and ruthless retribution against his enemies. His first action – his coronation war – was to lead the allied army on a circuit into the Toluca Valley and northward to Xilotepec before turning back into the northern Valley of Mexico. This foray had the desired effect of putting down rebellious communities while reasserting strong leadership for the demoralized army. The successful fulfillment of these two aims was underlined by the booty and prisoners obtained. The triumphant conclusion of Ahuizotl's coronation saw unprecedented gift-giving and feasting on a scale said to equal the tribute of an entire year. As was customary, the prisoners were sacrificed in the final act of the confirmation rite.

The clear expression of Ahuizotl's aims was followed by another punitive campaign to the Gulf Coast where many towns had refused to send tribute. Once again the Aztec army returned victorious, this time with the intention of staging another grand ceremony to rededicate the Great Pyramid of Tenochtitlan. As we shall see in Chapter 8, the Pyramid was continually being enlarged during the reigns of successive rulers, for the leaders of Tenochtitlan were concerned with constructing the ritual center to match the grandeur of other highland cities of centuries past. Renovation of this building had been started during Axayacatl's reign and now, in 1487, the

51–53 Sacrifice was both a means of nourishing the deities and an instrument of political power. ABOVE A captive's heart is ripped from his body on the steps of a temple; from the Codex Magliabechiano. RIGHT Sacrificial knife, with a handle shaped as an eagle warrior and inlaid with turquoise, jade, and shell. BELOW Jaguar-shaped receptacle in which the hearts of sacrificial victims were placed.

Within the illustration: *Templo del ydolo Vitzilo puestli.*

Human sacrifice and the skull rack

54,55 ABOVE The skull rack or *tzompantli* in the ritual precinct of Tenochtitlan, with the twin temples of Tlaloc (left) and Huitzilopochtli (right) on the platform atop the Great Pyramid. From Diego Durán's *Historia de la Nueva España*. BELOW The excavated base of a small skull rack by the foundations of the Great Pyramid in Mexico City.

expansion was complete. The rededication of the looming structure was seized by Ahuizotl as an opportunity to reaffirm the imperial mission, staging a sacrifice that would forever remain the most terrifying occasion in the ritual life of Tenochtitlan. Prisoners of war were lined along the length of the causeways into the city, and in numbers entirely unprecedented the sacrifices continued for four days. Appalled ambassadors from foreign nations were summoned to witness the dreadful slaughter, and the population of Tenochtitlan stood in awe in the plazas facing the pyramid. Streams of blood poured down the stairway and sides of the monument, forming huge pools on the white stucco pavement. The accounts of the Aztec elders still conveyed a sense of horror 50 years later, when their descriptions were recorded by Spanish historians. Ahuizotl had turned the image of sacrifice into an overtly political lesson, to instill terror in the hearts of enemies and to inure the sensibilities of his own population to new thresholds of violence. The renewal of the building and the idea of ritually nourishing the sun and the earth were now used to affirm the renewal of Tenochtitlan's warlike intentions.

The shock of the calculated carnage and the sight of the blood-covered pyramid and skull racks strung with gory trophies of thousands of victims marked a turning point in Aztec rulership under Ahuizotl. As he turned away from the model of Motecuhzoma I, the administrator-warrior, he assumed more the role of Huitzilopochtli, the deified mythical warrior-chieftain. By such methods Ahuizotl instilled the will to conquer. The expansion of the empire continued without let-up. Year after year the Aztec armies departed to subdue the peoples and claim the riches of mountainous lands in Guerrero, Oaxaca, and down to the Isthmus of Tehuantepec. Yet as Nigel Davies has observed, this empire was more of an armature of lines and strongpoints in a vast terrain, for the Aztec armies hardly had time to penetrate the hinterlands.[5] Moreover, the Aztecs had not developed a centralized administrative bureaucracy in the Mesopotamian or Chinese sense. The hegemony established by the network of marriages, alliances, and political relationships always remained unstable; and long distances, broken topography, and the policy of leaving local chiefs in authority as long as the tribute flowed remained sources of weakness and potential rebellion. But the Aztecs under Ahuizotl did develop other effective means to consolidate control, as we shall now see.

Temples and public works
The program of state-supported construction of public works and temples was extended to the provinces during Ahuizotl's reign. Several of these sites were excavated and restored during the 1930s and 1940s. Tepoztlan, Malinalco, and Calixtlahuaca provide valuable archaeological information that complements the written sources, supplying another kind of information about the role of religion, the resettlement of peoples, and permanent occupation of conquered land.

At Tepoztlan, a mountain community high on the cliffs overlooking the Valley of Morelos, a new temple was commandingly sited upon a crag. Within this temple chamber, a hieroglyphic inscription includes the name of Ahuizotl. The site was part of an Aztec effort to establish a permanent presence in the area and to link local cults such as the Tepozteco pulque deity to the larger cycle of agricultural festivals celebrated in Tenochtitlan.[6]

The site of Malinalco is located in the high forested mountains to the southwest of Mexico City, in what is still Matlazinca Indian territory. The original town of Malinalco lay on a high, easily defended promontory above the small valley where the colonial town was later built. Excavations by José García Payón in the 1930s disclosed an Aztec ceremonial center on a steep flank of the hill, partly carved from living rock and partly built up with platforms.[7] New excavations at the top, carried out in the late 1980s by the Instituto Nacional de Antropologia e Historia, are revealing the extent of the original Matlazinca settlement and ceremonial center. Malinalco and other towns in the Matlazinca region were originally subjected by Axayacatl in 1476. Several rebelled under Tizoc's rule, but Malinalco was not among them. Although the rebellions were suppressed, it remained for Ahuizotl to return and reassert Aztec control. His ruthless campaign against nearby Oztoman and Alahuistan, where wholesale slaughter of the population took place, successfully re-established the imperial presence. In addition to having strategic importance as a base for operations and logistic support, Malinalco had historical significance for the Aztecs, for it was there that the dissident Malinalxochitl was said to have settled after being abandoned by Huitzilopochtli's band during the legendary time of migration. Ahuizotl visited Malinalco in the first year of his reign where he received the allegiance of local chieftains, but it was not until the final year of his life that the Aztec buildings were begun. Pages from the Codex Aubin specifically mention the project and the use of forced labor in 1501. The site is again mentioned as a place where "they went to excavate rock" in 1503, and it appears again in the year 1515, when people were brought from Huexotzingo to work, construction thus continuing into the reign of Motecuhzoma II.

The circular rock-cut temple at Malinalco (Chapter 5) is one of the most impressive Aztec monuments to have survived the Spanish Conquest. The entrance to the chamber was a carved mask in the form of the open jaws of a serpent, a symbol for "cave." Within, a semicircular bench around the back wall was sculptured with the pelts of eagles and a jaguar or mountain lion. Another eagle was carved on the floor. These were the seats of Aztec authorities – the "eagle chair," and "mountain-lion-skin seat." Indeed, the four seats correspond to the positions of *tlatoani*, *tlaccatecatl*, *tlacochcalcatl*, and *etzhuanhuanco* (or tillancalqui), whose offices tended to be replicated on the local, provincial level. The men who occupied this chamber were military governors from Tenochtitlan, or members of the local nobility appointed by the supreme *tlatoani*. The

56,57 ABOVE The site of Malinalco overlooks the Valley of Mexico. The original settlement is located at the top of the hill, while the thatched roof of the reconstructed temple halfway down the slope on the right marks the site of the Aztec monuments. RIGHT Plan of the excavated Aztec monuments at Malinalco; the circular rock-cut temple (labeled I) is to the left.

Opposite:
58–61 CENTER LEFT Facade of the rock-cut temple. CENTER RIGHT Detail from the Codex Borgia depicting the deity Tepeyollotl (Mountain Heart) approaching a circular earth temple similar to that at Malinalco. BELOW LEFT and RIGHT Interior chamber of the temple showing the eagle and feline seats of Aztec military governors. An orifice in the floor behind the central eagle was for receiving ceremonial blood-offerings.

The ceremonial center at Malinalco

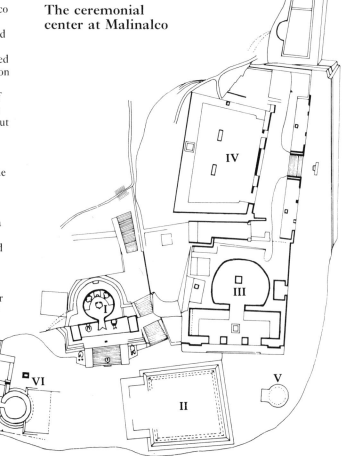

rock-cut temple did not therefore have an exclusively religious function as an earth-cult temple, but was a place where religious and state concerns were brought together to serve the royal representatives. The primary function of the building is revealed by a small circular hole cut down into the floor in the back of the central eagle pelt. This was a ritual place for offerings to the "heart of the earth" or "the heart of the mountain," the location of the earth's life force. When any ruler acceded to power, he was obliged to offer drops of his own blood – taken from the ears and the legs – as a sign of truth and a bond with the land he was to govern. As we shall see in describing Aztec coronation rites in Chapter 11, this ceremony was performed in another architectural "cave" in the ritual precinct of Tenochtitlan. The temple and other Aztec buildings at Malinalco were a permanent center of Aztec rule, and expressed a validation of that rule by the sacred earth itself.

The archaeological zone of Calixtlahuaca is located a few miles north of Toluca, at the base of a low hill rising from the floor of the Valley of Toluca. This was originally an ancient Matlazinca settlement, part of an occupation that may date as far back as the 8th century AD. It was taken by the Aztecs during Axayacatl's campaign in the region in the 1470s and, during Ahuizotl's reign, was turned over to colonists brought from the Valley of Mexico as part of a project of resettlement and consolidation. Like Malinalco, the buildings extended the architectural language and symbolic code of the metropolitan area in order to indicate imperial possession. José García Payón's excavations during the 1930s revealed a ritual center, including a structure assumed to be a priestly school (*telpochcalli* or *calmecac*), and a circular platform connected with the cult of Ehecatl, deity of wind or storm associated with the more well-known Quetzalcoatl.[8] The effigy of Ehecatl recovered from the ruins is one of the masterpieces of Aztec sculpture, representing a standing male figure clad in a loincloth and sandals, and wearing the bird-bill mask of the deity. The basalt effigy would have been ritually dressed in the elaborate paraphernalia of the cult on appropriate occasions. The importation of such high quality figures from the metropolitan workshops and the construction of the ritual buildings reinforce the conclusion that Aztec intentions were to establish a permanent, territorially-based presence in conquered territories.

Archaeological evidence thus suggests that in addition to controlling the empire through political connections, marriage relationships, and the patronage of client chieftains, the Aztecs also developed, during Ahuizotl's reign, a concept of territorial possession extending into provincial regions hitherto belonging to other peoples.

This tendency towards the claiming and holding of territory may be linked to a unique development along the Tarascan frontier. A series of forts was constructed by the Tarascans from north to south along their border with the Aztecs. The archaeological sites identified by Dan Stanislawski in his 1947 study of Tarascan political geography provide another body of evidence that complements the written sources.[9] The forts were strategic strongpoints placed at locations commanding the valleys along which an invading force was likely to march.[10] The Tarascans also improved their defenses in this borderland by replacing local Matlazinca chieftains with their own rulers. The Tarascan answer to the Aztec threat was unique in Mesoamerica where fortifications were only rudimentary, as in terraced hilltop sites, in settlements placed on easily defended natural promontories or islands, or in urban areas where palaces or ritual precincts might be strengthened against assault. The Tarascan fortifications provided intelligence of enemy advances, acted as bulwarks to detain or hamper an invading force, and deterred the Aztec practice of encroaching on enemy territories by capturing a series of frontier towns. The line of forts assured the Tarascans of a greater degree of stability along a fixed frontier. Control over territory was thus asserted by permanent military installations, as opposed to the traditional reliance on political and dynastic relationships.

There is additional archaeological evidence, supported by historical texts, that the Aztecs themselves were building fortified sites at Alahuistan and Oztoman to the south of this frontier. Oztoticpac, another Aztec conquest, was partly surveyed and explored by Moedano in the 1940s.[11] Both sites had been decimated by Ahuizotl in his campaign of 1488–89, when all adults were killed and some 40,000 children were taken from the region and redistributed throughout the empire. The towns were subsequently resettled by about 9,000 married couples from Tenochtitlan, Tetzcoco, Tlacopan, and neighboring cities.

Ahuizotl's campaign of 1490–91 into Guerrero and northward along the Pacific coast may in part have been an initial effort to establish a series of tributary towns that would eventually have lent logistical support for an envelopment of the Tarascan region by outflanking the line of forts. The last conquests of this formidable *tlatoani* brought the Aztec armies far to the south, first to Tehuantepec and the Isthmus around 1497, and again in 1499 or 1500 as far as Xoconochco on the marches of the rich cacao-producing provinces of the Pacific coast of Guatemala. The latter expedition was led by Motecuhzoma Xocoyotzin, who would be the new *tlatoani* within two years.

It has sometimes been asked why the Aztecs did not advance in another direction, towards the lands of the Maya and Toltec-Maya in Yucatan and Guatemala (although by the time of the Conquest there *was* an Aztec presence at Xicallanco in the southern Gulf Coast region, which could be interpreted as a presage of impending conquests into the Yucatan). Nigel Davies ventures an opinion that the established, far-reaching network of trade based at Xicallanco on the Gulf Coast at Laguna de Términos, which brought much-prized jade and jadeite from highland Guatemala and beyond, would have been interrupted by outright conquest, and that Ahuizotl chose not to jeopardize this source of a most highly valued material.[12] By the end of his life, Ahuizotl's campaigns had regained the lost imperial initiative, stabilizing the dominions and achieving impressive new conquests.

Motecuhzoma II, the last independent ruler

The final Aztec reign opened with Motecuhzoma Xocoyotzin's coronation in 1502. Following religious tradition, his first military expedition was to procure prisoners for sacrifice at the ceremony. Soon thereafter the new ruler began a concerted effort to woo the nobility, since the threat of intrigues was always present (as demonstrated by the conspiracy of Moquihuix and the demise of Tizoc). Strictly enforced sumptuary laws were proclaimed that further distinguished the nobles from the lower classes. Accomplished warriors among the commoners were no longer permitted to wear insignia or clothes different from those of inferior rank. At the same time Motecuhzoma took care not to strip away the prerogatives of commoners who had attained noble standing, but made the attainment of such rank more difficult. Within the palace, elaborate court etiquette was enforced to affirm the new hierarchy, surrounding the new *tlatoani* with layers of ceremonial procedure. Many of the elaborate obeisances and expressions of extreme respect observed by the Spanish in the court of Motecuhzoma Xocoyotzin had their origin in his first years of tenure.

The new *tlatoani* also doubted the continued loyalty of Ahuizotl's supporters, and moved rapidly to replace these men with followers of his own. According to some accounts the former were put to death. At the same time he replaced all the existing servants in the palaces with junior members of the nobility from provincial towns. The young nobles thus brought into the palaces not only served, but were indoctrinated and kept as quasi-hostages to ensure the cooperation of their parents and relatives.

Motecuhzoma II was a notable warrior and his campaigns systematically enlarged the tribute domain and consolidated the network of conquests made by former rulers. Only the stubborn Tarascans and Tlaxcalans remained undefeated. The Aztecs under Motecuhzoma Xocoyotzin were involved in no less than four wars against the Tlaxcalans and Huexotzin-gans, the last of which in 1515 proved most disastrous. By the time Cortés arrived in 1519, a bitter, entrenched, and irreconcilable hatred existed between the Aztecs and Tlaxcalans which the Spanish invaders quickly learned to exploit. Yet Motecuhzoma's campaigns reached into Oaxaca, Puebla, Guerrero, the old Chichimeca, and south again to Xoconochco and the Isthmus, substantially advancing the Aztec position on all fronts. The empire was dynamically expanding and there is little evidence that the energy of Tenochtitlan and her allies was on the wane. The spectacular ritual life of the Aztecs was one of the principal integrating forces behind this economic, social, and ideological cohesion, and it is to the Aztec symbolic world that we turn in Part IV.

PART IV

AZTEC RELIGION AND BELIEFS

7 · The Aztec Symbolic World

Since remote times the rhythms of life in highland Mexico had been deeply embedded in the land and the changing seasons. The annual alternation of rain and drought – periods of life and death – determined the cycle of farming peoples and hunter-gatherers before them. The pragmatic business of obtaining food went hand in hand with a sense of periodicity, rhythm and cyclic recurrence, and with the notion of belonging to the land. To the Aztecs, this interaction of humankind with nature was of profound significance, and was affirmed through a calendar of cyclic festivals performed at a network of sacred places in cities and throughout the natural landscape. The religious status and functions of rulers were critical in these relationships, for the Aztec *tlatoque* and their priestly minions were obliged to ensure, by means of traditional rituals, the regularity of the seasons, the productivity of the land, and the fertility of crops and animals.

The Aztec deities

When the Chichimec tribes first entered the Valley of Mexico, each town already had its own religious cults centered on nature-deities, deified ancestors, and legendary heroes. There was no concept of a "family of gods" as in ancient Mediterranean civilizations, but a host of deities each identified with the various spheres of the universe. The 16th-century Spanish historian Juan Bautista Pomar remarked that "they had many idols, and so many that almost for each thing there was one." As the Aztec empire expanded, the principal deity of a conquered community was incorporated into the Aztec pantheon. Indeed, the very process of conquest could be represented as the "capture" of the tutelary deity of an enemy town: as we have seen (ills. 49,50), the Stone of Tizoc portrays Aztec *tlatoani* Tizoc wearing the emblems of Huitzilopochtli and Tezcatlipoca and leading his minions in the capture of deities, each identified by the place-glyph of a particular town. In Tenochtitlan, a special building in the great ceremonial precinct – the *coateocalli* – was assigned to house the captive cult paraphernalia and fetishes of conquered communities. The deities thus captured were extraordinarily diverse, but their fundamental characteristics often show strong similarities, for they were ultimately linked to the land and the sky. When the Spanish friars called a meeting with the leading Aztec priests to inform them that their

old religion was to be renounced, the leading priest responded with words
that characterized their most basic perception of these deities:

> They [the ancestors] said
> That it is through
> The sacred spirits
> That all live...
> That they give us
> Our daily fare
> And all that we
> Drink, all that
> We eat,
> Our sustenance,
> Maize, beans,
> Amaranth, chia.
> They we supplicate
> For water
> For rain,
> With which
> Everything flourishes
> On earth.

An exhaustive study of the Aztec religious system has not yet been
undertaken, but Henry Nicholson's research has greatly illuminated the
worship of the Aztec deities. Nicholson pointed out that most, if not all,
the cults can be grouped in basic clusters, which can be named for the
dominant deity of that complex (see list of principal gods and cults).[1] The
following discussion represents a modified version of Nicholson's approach.

Tezcatlipoca, "Smoking Mirror" (obsidian), is often characterized as
the most powerful, supreme deity of the ancient pantheon, and was
associated with the notion of destiny or fate. He probably embodies the idea
of a mana-like numinous power inherent in all things. His quintessential
emblem, an obsidian mirror, was an implement associated with divination
and may ultimately reflect shamanistic origins, but there can be little
doubt that this cult was particularly identified with royalty, because
Tezcatlipoca is the object of the most lengthy and reverent prayers in the
rites of kingship.

Tonatiuh, the sun, was another of the supreme forces worshiped in
ancient Mexico. The emblem of Tonatiuh was the solar disk, sometimes
worn on the back of ritual impersonators, but more often carved on
sculptural monuments. The sun was perceived as a primary source of life
whose special devotees were the warriors. The warriors were charged with
the mission to provide the sun with sacrificial victims. A special altar to
the sun was used for sacrifices in coronation-rites, a fact which signifies
the importance of the deity.

Principal Gods and Cults of the Aztecs

	NAME	TRANSLATION	MAIN ATTRIBUTES
PRIMORDIAL CREATORS	**Ometecuhtli** **Omecihuatl** also known as **Tonacatecuhtli** **Tonacacihuatl**	Two Lord Two Lady Lord and Lady of Sustenance	Primordial male-female creative principle
FATE, DESTINY	**Tezcatlipoca**	Smoking Mirror (Obsidian Mirror)	Omnipotent deity, associated with fate, both beneficial and destructive. His other metaphoric titles include **Moyocoyani** (Maker of Himself), **Titlacauan** (We His Slaves), **Yaotl** (Enemy), **Ipalnemoani** (Lord of the Near and the Nigh), and **Tloque Nahuaque** (Night, Wind). **Tezcatlipoca** figures prominently in coronation speeches and prayer and must be considered especially associated with rulership
SKY	**Tonatiuh** **Metztli** **Tlahuizcalpantecuhtli**	He Who Makes the Day Moon Dawn Lord	The sun Venus (the Morning Star)
WIND	**Quetzalcoatl** **Ehecatl**	Quetzal (feathered) Serpent Wind	Windstorms that bring rain (see also deified heroes and ancestral deities)
FIRE	**Huehueteotl** **Chantico** **Xiuhtecuhtli**	Old, Old Deity In the House Turquoise Lord	Fire The hearth fire Fire
EARTH	**Popocatepetl** **Ixtaccihuatl** **Mt Tlaloc** and **Tlalocan** **Tetzcotzingo** **Matlalcueye** **Tepeyollotl**	Smoke Mountain White Woman Place of the Rain (God) Honorable Place of the Bald Rock (?) Blue Skirt Heart of the Mountain	Sacred mountains whose cult embraced various others associated with the earth, rain, ground water, and vegetation Locus of the earth's regenerative powers
	Toci **Teteoinnan** **Tonantzin** **Coatlicue** **Itzpapalotl** **Tlaltecuhtli** **Tlazolteotl** **Ilamatecuhtli**	Our Grandmother Mother of the Deities Honored Mother Serpent Skirt Obsidian Butterfly Earth Lord or Lady Sacred Filth Eater Old Mother Deity	} Female deities variously associated with the earth and its fertility

Principal Gods and Cults of the Aztecs

NAME	TRANSLATION	MAIN ATTRIBUTES
Tlaloc	That Which Lies Upon the Surface of the Earth (referring to clouds forming around the mountaintops)	The rain deity, also associated with the earth's fertility
Tlaloque	Little Tlalocs	
Tepictoton	Little Old Hills	
Chalchiuhtlicue	She of the Jade Skirt	Deity of springs, rivers, lakes, and the sea
Huixtocihuatl	Huixtotin Lady	Deity of salt
Xilonen	Young Maize Ear	Deity of first tender maize
Centeotl	Deified Maize *or* Divine Maize Ear	Late-ripening maize
Chicomecoatl	Seven Serpent	Seed corn
Xipe Totec	Our Flayed Lord	Vegetation deity (especially seeds)
Mayahuel	Maguey Plant	Maguey plant deity
Octli Deities		Variously named deities of pulque (fermented drink of maguey juice)
Xochipilli	Flower Prince	Deity of flowers, plants, and patron of song and dance
Xochiquetzal	Flower Quetzal	Goddess of flowers, grains, patroness of weavers
Macuilxochitl	Five Flower	Deity of flowers, plants, song, dance, and games
Mictlantecuhtli	Lord of Mictlan (land of the dead)	Deity of death, darkness, the subterranean regions
Mictlantecacihuatl	Lady of Mictlan	Female counterpart of **Mictlantecuhtli**
Huitzilopochtli	Hummingbird on the Left	Mexica-Aztec ancestral tutelary deity, patron of war, associated with the sun
Quetzalcoatl	Feathered Serpent	Ancient wind and storm deity. His name also a title of rulers; historically associated with a celebrated ruler of Toltec Tula. At time of Spanish Conquest, this cult was seated in Cholula
Yacatecuhtli	Lord of the Nose	Tutelary deity of traders
Mixcoatl	Cloud Serpent	Ancient tribal deity of the hunt. Especially revered in Tlaxcala, Huexotzingo, and other communities in Puebla Valley
Camaxtli	Lord of the Chase	Chichimec deity whose cult was centered in Huexotzingo

Row groups (left margin labels):
- **RAIN, WATER** — Tlaloc through Huixtocihuatl
- **MAIZE, VEGETATION** — Xilonen through Macuilxochitl
- **THE LAND OF THE DEAD** — Mictlantecuhtli, Mictlantecacihuatl
- **DEIFIED HEROES AND ANCESTRAL DEITIES** — Huitzilopochtli through Camaxtli

The Aztec pantheon

62–64 LEFT The "old, old deity" Huehueteotl (god of fire), recovered from the Great Pyramid. BELOW LEFT Quetzalcoatl; the green, iridescent feathers of the quetzal bird were an ancient symbol of royalty and of the sky. BELOW RIGHT The base of the coiled Quetzalcoatl portrays the rain god Tlaloc. The entire sculpture represents a great windstorm rising out of the mountains bringing the seasonal rain.

65–68 TOP LEFT An impersonator of Tlaloc, from the Codex Ixtlilxóchitl. TOP RIGHT Mayahuel, female deity of the maguey cactus, a plant highly prized for its fiber and juice. ABOVE Huitzilopochtli, the deified Aztec warrior-hero and patron of Tenochtitlan, shown with his hummingbird headdress, shield, and darts. LEFT The sculpted mask of Xipe Totec (god of vegetation), representing a flayed human skin sewn over the head of a living impersonator. The mask alludes to a dry husk enclosing a living seed.

Huehueteotl, the "old, old deity," was one of the names of the cult of fire, which was among the oldest in Mesoamerica. The idea of sacred fire stems from its most basic function in the domestic hearth. Ceramic and stone effigies of an old man bearing a brazier on his back have been found at Teotihuacan, and were also excavated from the circular pyramid of Cuicuilco, dating from c.300 BC. Among the Aztecs, the maintenance of sacred fires in the temples was a principal priestly duty, and as we shall see, it was only during the last hours of the old year that the flames were extinguished. The renewal of fire was identified with the renewal of time itself.

The cult of Tlaloc, the rain deity, was another of the oldest and most universal cults in ancient Mexico. Although the name itself may be Aztec, the idea of a storm god especially identified with mountaintop shrines and with life-giving rain was certainly as old as Teotihuacan. The goggle-eyed mask of Tlaloc was as ubiquitous in that ancient city as it was at Tenochtitlan, 1,000 years later. The name Tlaloc derives from the word *tlalli*, "earth," and the suffix *oc* which implies "something lying upon the surface." This alludes to the familiar sight of clouds welling up from canyons and collecting around mountaintops during the rainy season. Impersonators of Tlaloc would wear the distinctive mask and heron-feather headdress, and often carried a cornstalk or a symbolic lightning-bolt wand; another symbol of Tlaloc was a ritual water-jar. Tlaloc was manifested in the form of boulders at shrine-sites, and in the Valley of Mexico the primary shrine to this major deity was located atop Mt Tlaloc.

Chalchiuhtlicue, "she of the jade skirt," was the deity connected with the worship of ground water. Her shrines were therefore by springs, streams, irrigation ditches, or aqueducts, the most important of these shrines being at Pantitlan, in the center of Lake Tetzcoco. Sometimes described as the "sister" of Tlaloc, Chalchiuhtlicue was impersonated by ritual performers wearing the green skirt that identified the deity. Like that of Tlaloc, this cult was intimately linked to the earth, fertility, and the regeneration of nature.

The name Quetzalcoatl, "quetzal (feather) serpent," had dozens of associations. It was the name of a nature-deity; it was a royal title; it figured in Toltec times as a military title and emblem; it was the name of a legendary priest-ruler; it was a title of high priestly office; and it was the patron cult of the *calmecac* schools described in Chapter 9. Without attempting to review the complex manifestations of this major cult, we may point to an image that perhaps best explains its most fundamental significance. This is the sculpture of a plumed serpent coiled in conical form, rising from a base whose underside is carved with the symbols of the earth-deity and Tlaloc (ills. 63,64). The image of the serpent rising from the earth and bearing water on its tail is echoed by a description of Quetzalcoatl from a text by Sahagún which describes the rise of a great thunderstorm with wind sweeping down, raising the dust before the rain.[2]

The cults of the earth were as protean as those of the sky. In its most basic form the earth was referred to as Tlaltecuhtli (earth-lord or earth-lady) and was represented as a crouching figure with an upturned, grinning mask, often wearing sacrificial symbols and a skull as a symbol upon its back. Serpents, spiders, and centipedes were also depicted as creatures close to the earth. The earth was not only a giver of life, it was also the ultimate recipient of all that grows and moves on its surface. Other images alluding to the earth's regenerative powers depict the earth-womb, as in the famous Chicomoztoc page from the Historia Tolteca-Chichimeca (ill. 33). Ritual impersonators of the earth-mother were especially identified with procreation and agricultural fertility. Their names, Teteo-innan, Tlazolteotl, Tonantzin, Itzpapalotl, Cihuateteo, and others, described the earth's various powers as portrayed in its many cults. There were also many links between the costume and other symbolic elements associated with the earth-mother and those of the maize deities.

Maize was portrayed in feminine terms, and three deities were especially important. Xilonen, "young maize," was portrayed as an adolescent girl with the first tender corn of the rainy season harvest worn on her headdress. Chicomecoatl, "seven serpent," was the title given to dried seed corn, which was harvested and kept for the next year; priestesses bearing ears of this seed corn appeared at the onset of the planting season. Cinteotl, "sacred maize-ear," was the more general term for corn eaten after the fall harvest season.

Other important cultigens were represented in the Aztec pantheon, amongst which the maguey agave was particularly important. In central Mexico these great cacti are still to be seen bordering the corn fields. They were the source of octi (pulque), a mildly fermented beer-like drink which, consumed in moderate amounts, was a staple of highland diet. The plant is also a source of fiber and was used to make cloth, netting, ropes, bags, and many other useful products.

Among the cults of deified ancestors, that of Huitzilopochtli was pre-eminent in Tenochtitlan. We have already recounted the story of this legendary hero, and discussed the possibility that he was actually a composite entity, fabricated by the primitive Mexica from other such figures identified with older towns in the Valley. In any event, the custom of deifying heroes or outstanding rulers can be seen in Tetzcoco, where the ruler Netzahualcoyotl was worshiped posthumously at Tetzcotzingo, his effigy having been carved in the rock among other shrines to nature-deities. This is an instance of a "founder-father" figure gradually attaining the status of a deity among the local population.

The concept of teotl

A basic concept of Aztec religious thought was expressed by the word-root *teo*, often written with the *tl* suffix as *teotl*. Difficult to translate, the word was recorded by the Spanish as "god," "saint," or sometimes "demon." Studies of the word *teo* show that it appears in Nahuatl texts in a variety of contexts. Sometimes it accompanies the names of nature-deities, but it was also used in connection with human impersonators of those divinities, as well as in association with their sacred masks and related ceremonial objects, including sculptured effigies of wood, stone, or dough. Such words as "mana," "numinous" or "sacred" have been used to suggest its significance. But the word *teo* may similarly be used to qualify almost anything mysterious, powerful, or beyond ordinary experience, such as animals of prey, a remote and awe-inspiring snowcapped mountain, a phenomenon of terrible power such as the sun or a bolt of lightning, or the life-giving earth, water, and maize, or even a great *tlatoani* at the time of his coronation. Nor was its application restricted to good or ethical things, for malign phenomena might also be designated by *teo*.

The diverse contexts of the word *teo* suggest that the Aztecs regarded the things of their world – both transitory or permanent – as inherently charged to a greater or lesser degree with vital force or power. This reflects an outlook widespread among peoples of the "pre-modern" world, in which the things of the physical environment were endowed with wills of their own, and even given, on occasion, a sense of personality. Aztec rituals offer many examples of this mode of perception. For example, during Ahuizotl's reign in the late 15th century, he inaugurated a new aqueduct bringing water from Chapultepec to the center of Tenochtitlan. On that occasion his priests were dressed as the female water-deity Chalchiuhtlicue, "jade skirt." Attired as the deity, the priests waited by the channel to welcome the first flow of water. As the water rushed in they reached down to present incense, turquoise, and sacrificed quail to the life-giving element, and spoke to the water itself as the living object of the offering. This rite illustrates the curious, inextricable equivalence of the deity, deity-impersonator, priest, and the natural element – an association utterly alien to modern Western thought.

The myths of creation

The Aztec myths of creation were gathered in variant but related versions by the 16th-century Spanish friars, who worked in different locations within the Valley of Mexico and neighboring regions. The cosmogonic myths describe the primordial beginning of the world and the ensuing sequence of eras whose transformations led to the present earth and its animal and human inhabitants. An understanding of the myths helped to explain the origin of the earth and the regularity of such phenomena as the sun, the moon, the rainy season, as well as the cycle of vegetation and human beginnings. It also provided a way of learning sacred history and the principles governing cosmic and social existence. On many transmutable levels of meaning, the myths established themes by which

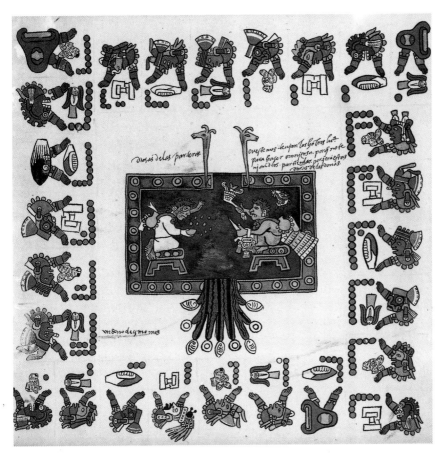

69 One of the central pages of the Codex Borbonicus, showing the creator god and goddess, Ometecuhtli and Omecihuatl. They sit in a sacred enclosure from which water flows, surrounded by day signs and a series of associated ruling deities.

The primordial male and female force

According to one important text, before the world appeared there were primordial masculine and feminine creative forces, named *ome tecuhtli* "two lord" and *ome cihuatl* "two lady." They resided in *omeyocan*, "the place of two" (this is often mistakenly translated as "the place of duality;" but as will be seen on the following pages, the concept of dual *opposing* forces was not a strong feature of Aztec cosmological thought). The masculine and feminine forces were also known as *Tonacatecuhtli* and *Tonacachuatl*, "Lord and Lady of our flesh and sustenance," names which show their close connection to the creation of food. A page from the Codex Borbonicus depicts the primordial couple seated within a rectangular

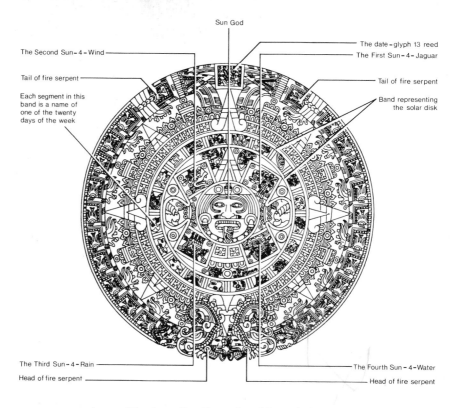

Sun God

The Second Sun – 4 – Wind

Tail of fire serpent

Each segment in this
band is a name of
one of the twenty
days of the week

The date – glyph 13 reed

The First Sun – 4 – Jaguar

Tail of fire serpent

Band representing
the solar disk

The Third Sun – 4 – Rain

Head of fire serpent

The Fourth Sun – 4 – Water

Head of fire serpent

70,71 ABOVE and RIGHT The Aztec Sun Stone, found beneath the central plaza of Mexico City in the last decade of the 18th century. Carved at its center is the face of the sun, or perhaps the earth monster, Tlaltecuhtli. The monument is not a fully functioning calendar, but commemorates the five mythic world-creations ("suns"). The date-glyph cartouche 13 reed at the top denotes the mythical beginning of the present sun, but also marks the calendrical year 1427, when Itzcoatl rose to power. The conjunction of a sacred date and the historical year sanctified the authority of the Aztec rulers and established a vital link between the cosmos and human society.

precinct surrounded by calendrical glyphs; they speak about time to each other. The two personified primordial forces had four sons, each of which was identified with one of the cardinal points. They were respectively colored red, black, blue, or white according to direction. Thus, the horizontal plane of the world was defined as having a living creative center around which the quadrants were symmetrically placed. Other cosmogonic accounts describe the vertical dimension of space, conceptually defined by an axis connecting the center of the plane of the earth to the celestial sphere above and the world below. The heavens were divided into a series of layers – thirteen by some descriptions, nine according to others – and the underworld was similarly arranged. There was no juxtaposition of heaven versus hell in this cosmological schema, for the levels of the sky and those of the lower world carried no moral value. The outer perimeter of the world was conceived as a circle (or sometimes a square), where the surrounding sea, *ilhuica-atl*, met the inverted bowl of the sky. One of the most ancient cosmological beliefs preserved by the Aztecs likened the

earth to an alligator floating in the primeval sea, with the scales and corrugations of its back corresponding to mountains and valleys.

The five ages

The original creation of the earth was followed by its destruction, and a succession of four imperfect creations leading to the present fifth era.[3] (The idea of multiple, imperfect creations was very old and widespread in Mesoamerica, for it is recorded in the sacred book of the Quiché Maya, the *Popol Vuh*.)[4] In the Aztec texts each of the five creations formed an age called a "sun." The sequence of eras officially accepted in Tenochtitlan is recorded on such famous sculptural monuments as the "Stone of the Five Suns," formerly known as the "Aztec Calendar," and the Coronation Tablet of Motecuhzoma II (ills. 104,105). Among the Aztecs the first era was called "four jaguar." At that time, giants walked the earth but did not till the soil or sow maize, only living by gleaning wild fruits and roots. This imperfect era ended when a jaguar devoured the giants. The hieroglyphic sign for the era was therefore a feline head. The second era, "four wind," was also flawed, and was destroyed by hurricanes that magically turned the existing men into monkeys – humanlike, but not fully human creatures. The sign of this era was the mask of Quetzalcoatl, lord of the winds. The third imperfect era ended in a rain of fire, and its people either perished or were changed into birds. This happened on the day "four rain," therefore the sign of this sun was the mask of Tlaloc, lord of the rain. The fourth era was one of rains so abundant and frequent that the earth was deluged and people were changed into fish. This was the reason that its sign was the head of Chalchiuhtlicue, "jade skirt," deity of lakes, rivers, springs, and seas. The fifth, or present era, was prophesied to end in earthquakes, and its sign was the hieroglyph *Ollin*, "movement" (of the earth). It was at the beginning of this era that the actual sun, moon, and human beings were finally created.

As the eminent Mexican scholar Alfonso Caso originally pointed out, this succession of ages is quite unlike the Judeo-Christian concept of an original paradise, followed by the fall and expulsion of the first human beings.[5] Instead, the image of the Aztec creation myths is of a progression of worlds, as the creator-forces and deities strove to find a formula for a more perfect world and humanity. There is also the sense of a search for progressively better foodstuffs: in the first era the giants ate roots and wild fruits; the second era lists *acocentli*, pine nuts; the third era names *ace centli*, millium; and the fourth names *cencocopi*, or *teocentli*, a wild grasslike plant with seeds similar to that of primitive maize.

The creation of the sun and moon
An account of how the sun was created at the beginning of the fifth era was recorded by Bernardino de Sahagún:

> It is told that when yet [all] was in darkness, when yet no sun had shone and no dawn had broken, it is said – the gods gathered themselves together and took counsel among themselves there at Teotihuacan.
> They spoke; they said among themselves: "Come hither, O gods! Who will carry the burden? Who will take it upon himself to be the sun, to bring the dawn?[6]

In answer to this question, two gods volunteered to sacrifice themselves to become the sun. In preparation, the one named Tecuciztecatl laid out a sacrificial kit of the most costly materials. His fir branches were of quetzal feathers; his grass balls were of gold; his maguey spines were of greenstone; while the reddened bloodied spines were of coral. His incense, moreover, was of the best kind. The other volunteer, an impoverished deity named Nanauatzin, could only afford green rushes, pine needles, actual maguey spines, and his own blood; and for incense, the scabs from his sores. Four nights of penance were spent atop the Moon Pyramid and the Pyramid of the Sun at Teotihuacan. On the fifth night the two volunteers were ceremonially dressed and brought before a great hearth where a bonfire was blazing. It was midnight and the assembled gods said to Tecuciztecatl: "Take courage O Tecuciztecatl; fall – cast thyself – into the fire!" But the immense heap of glowing coals and the furious flames cast a heat so unbearable that four times he tried to throw himself in, only to turn away. Then Nanauatzin was called and, gathering his courage, he quickly cast himself in; then Tecuciztecatl took courage and followed.

> After this, when both had cast themselves into the flames, when they had already burned, then the gods sat waiting to see where Nanauatzin would come to rise – he who fell first into the fire – in order that he might shine [as the sun]; in order that dawn might break.[7]

In all directions the gods looked, and kept turning about, until those who looked east saw the first sunrise. The poetic parallel with the heat of the sacrificial bonfire the night before is especially striking:

> And when the sun came to rise, when he burst forth, he appeared to be red; he kept swaying from side to side. It was impossible to look into his face; he blinded one with his light. Intensely did he shine. He issued rays of light from himself; his rays reached in all directions; his brilliant rays penetrated everywhere.[8]

Then, afterward, Tecuciztecatl rose as the moon, and to darken its first brilliance one of the gods threw a rabbit in his face – which is why in ancient Mexico the moon was perceived as having the imprint of a rabbit. But the sun and moon were still stationary: and it was only after all the gods had sacrificed themselves and Ehecatl (another name of Quetzalcoatl, the lord of the wind) blew and blew, that the sun and the moon were sent on their paths by day and night respectively.

The creation of humankind
The final episode of the creation myth was preserved in yet another account by Fray Gerónimo de Mendieta.[9] This describes Quetzalcoatl descending to the underworld regions of the dead, where he gathered a great heap of bones from past generations. These he sprinkled with his own blood and ground them up to create a new humanity.

It must not be imagined that myths such as these were told to provide entertainment or to exercise personal fantasy. Much less were they intended as rationally consistent and objective explanations of cosmic or human happenings. The stories provided a metaphoric expression of the truths and principles that formed an underpinning to life and experience. The image of primordial male and female figures seated within an enclosure, suggests a duality which arises from a primal unity of equally necessary generative forces. The myths describing a succession of cycles of creation and destruction show that death was but a condition for the inevitable rebirth. The deities that offer themselves to the raging bonfire to be transformed into the sun and moon speak of the necessity of sacrifice to bring forth new forms of life. Similarly, the creator-god who offers his blood to be mingled with bones from the ancestors shows how something of value had to be offered to make something of greater value. These mythic events took place in a hallowed time when models were established for subsequent actions. Thus the rising of the sun was seen as a sacred event because it was identified with the original sacrifice. And just as darkness was transformed into daylight, so too countless other changes experienced in the natural world could be traced to prototypes described in the mythic creation-time. The annual change from drought to rain, and the rebirth of vegetation; the passage of one stage of human life to the next, as in birth, puberty, marriage, and death; or the accession of a great chieftain, passing from a lower social role to a higher one – all reflect a basic aspect of the Aztec world view, which was marked by a tendency to focus on things in the process of becoming another.

Aztec cosmogony stands in contrast to that of ancient Mesopotamia, which stresses the struggle of dual powers of light versus dark, order versus chaos, life versus death, or good versus evil. In ancient Mexico by contrast, the myths seem not to lose sight of the observable seasonal process of birth, growth, maturity, and death, followed by sacrifice to ensure rebirth and renewal. As we shall see, it was the kings who were ritually responsible for making the offerings essential to bring about new life: in the vast schema of cosmic events portrayed in Aztec myths, humankind was only a small part, yet it played a critical role in ensuring the progression of the seasons, the movement of heavenly bodies, and the periodic regeneration of nature as well as communal life. Whatever cosmic dualism existed in Aztec thought, it was a dualism of complimentary forces in continual process of change, not a dualism of opposing forces struggling for each other's destruction.

The ritual calendar

Before describing Aztec religious festivals and buildings, it is important to discuss their calendar system. The arrangement of time governed all important activities of individual life as well as the scheduling and performance of state-organized events. Like many other peoples of antiquity in the New World and the Old, the Aztecs did not experience time as a succession of uniform movements, stretching monotonously from the indefinite past into the indefinite future. Nor was their time of indifferent, uniform quality. It would be impossible to overstress the fact that time for the Aztecs was full of energy and motion, the harbinger of change, and always charged with a sense of miraculous happening. The cosmogonic myths reveal a preoccupation with the process of creation, destruction and recreation, and the calendrical system reflected these notions about the character of time.

There were two aspects of Aztec time-counting, each with different functions. The first was the curious *tonalpohualli* "counting of the days," a 260-day cycle used for the purpose of divination. This repeating round of days formed a sacred almanac, widely used among Mesoamerican peoples long before the Aztecs. It is speculated that the *tonalpohualli* may have originated as far back as the Olmec period in the first millennium BC, or even further. The second division of the calendrical system was a 365-day solar count, known as the *xiuhpohualli*, "counting of the years," which regulated the recurrent cycle of annual seasonal festivals. These two counts were simultaneously in operation. They have often been explained as two engaged, rotating gears, in which the beginning day of the larger 365-day wheel would align with the beginning day of the smaller 260-day cycle every 52 years. This 52-year period constituted a Mesoamerican "century." The change from one 52-year period into the next was always the occasion of an important religious festival.

The 260-day count
It is thought that the 260-day *tonalpohualli* count originated in an observed astronomical phenomenon. Archaeoastronomers today have noted that the sun, on its annual passage from south to north and back again, crosses a zenith point at a latitude near the Classic Maya city of Copán, in modern Honduras, at a 260-day interval. Did this interval determine the original planting-to-harvest season at an unknown time in history? Did it acquire a prestigious significance, hallowed from antiquity and preserved by custom as a time-count in later religious traditions? Answers to these questions are beyond our present purpose, but what may be described in greater detail is the organization of the *tonalpohualli* and some of the functions it served in ordering the lives of Aztec people.

The 260-day cycle was composed of 20 groups of named and numbered days. Each day received a name, such as rabbit, water, flint knife, alligator, jaguar, etc, which was visually represented by a hieroglyphic sign of the particular animal or object. The cycle of 20 days intermeshed with a rotating cycle of numbers, 1 to 13, each number denoted by dots. After every complete rotation, each number was engaged with a new day. Thus, within the 260-day period each day was identified by the combination of one of the 20 day names with one of the 13 numbers (20 × 13 = 260).

The sacred 260-day cycle was then divided into 20 "weeks" of 13 days each, called *trecenas* by the Spaniards. Every *trecena* began with the number 1 and the day-name which came up in the sequence of rotation. Thus, each combination was unique within the *tonalpohualli* cycle, for no day in any one week could be confused with that of another.

The *tonalpohualli* counts were kept in screenfold books called *tonalamatls*. The books were made from a long strip of *amate* bark paper, from which the word tonal*amatl* derives. This paper was coated with white gesso upon which the fine drawing and brilliant painting were done. One

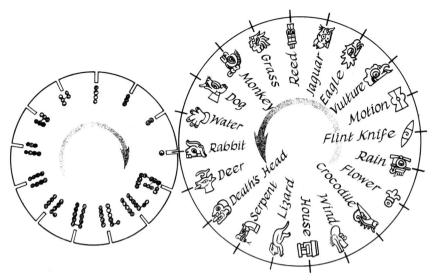

72,73 ABOVE Schematic representation of the 260-day Aztec *tonalpohualli* calendar. The 20 named days intercalate with the numbers 1 to 13. RIGHT The first page of the ritual almanac, the Codex Fejervary-Mayer, shows Xiuhtecuhtli (god of fire) in the central panel as the vertical axis mundi. The East lies at the top, where the sun-disk rises; West is at the bottom, shown as an earth-monster where the sun sets. The unbroken outer border consists of the 260 positions of the Calendar Round: the 20 day signs appear at intervals of 13.

of the most famous of these screenfold books is the Codex Borbonicus. The Codex was made in Tenochtitlan or in the vicinity of Ixtapalapan-Culhuacan, very soon after the Spanish Conquest. At some time during the colonial period it was taken to Spain, where it rested in the library of the Escorial Palace, near Madrid. It was removed to France probably around 1823 and bought by the Library of the Chamber of Deputies in the old Bourbon Palace in Paris: hence the name Borbonicus. The Indian artist worked in a virtually pure pre-Hispanic style, but spaces were ruled off to receive commentary written by the Spanish using Roman script.

Each of the screenfold pages in this Codex is devoted to a 13-day *trecena*, and is also divided to show a dominant deity or regent presiding over the *trecena*. The individual days are shown in rectangular subdivisions, each with its own associated deity: there were 13 Lords of the Day, each with a particular bird or butterfly, and 9 Lords of the Night. These deities recur throughout the *tonalpohualli* in independent, repeating cycles. The *tonalpohualli* is thus revealed to be more than a system of numbers and days, for each *trecena* was influenced by a dominant deity, and each day was influenced by its own day-lord and night-lord.

It is clear from the writings of the Spanish chroniclers that the influences displayed by the *tonalpohualli* were interpreted by professional diviners. These specialists were called upon to make prognostications for newborn

children, to give advice for different endeavors according to auspicious or inauspicious days, or to determine the best days for planting and harvesting.

These characters [of the *tonalamatl*] also taught the Indian nations the days on which they were to sow, reap, till the land, cultivate corn, weed, harvest, store, shell the ears of corn, sow beans and flax seed. They always took into account that it had to be in such and such month, after such and such feast, on such and such a day, under such and such a sign. All this was done with superstitious order and care. If chili was not sown on a certain day, squash on another, maize on another, and so forth, in disregard of the orderly count of the days, the people felt there would be great damage and loss of any crop sown outside of the established order of the days. The reason for all this was that some signs were held to be good, others evil, and others indifferent, just as our almanacs record the signs of the zodiac.[10]

We may suppose that such prognostications were made in conjunction with known weather patterns and other environmental conditions, as well as social and economic factors. Unfortunately, most of the immense accumulated body of orally-transmitted knowledge that accompanied the *tonalpohualli* was lost or diffused amid other recorded information during the Spanish colonial period. Nevertheless, Bernardino de Sahagún's Book

Four, *The Soothsayers*, and Diego Durán's *Book of Gods and Rites and the Ancient Calendar* contain valuable records.[11]

Divination, the art of foreseeing future events or discovering hidden knowledge through supernatural means, was a standard feature of official and private life in many other ancient civilizations. All peoples seek to know the unknowable, to control the uncontrollable, or to make a confident choice about a difficult decision, and divination has been one of the mechanisms by which this is attempted. Like the Greeks, the Romans, and the Chinese, the Aztecs believed in the portentous meaning of omens and auguries in the natural world. The pattern of diverse hidden phenomena which appear to coincide were perceived as highly meaningful – auguring good or evil, success or failure for a proposed endeavor. In Greece, no king or commander would dare take a major course of action without consulting one of the many famous oracles, such as that of Delphi; Alexander's career was deeply affected by the Libyan oracle at Siwah. Roman generals regularly sacrificed bullocks in order to read, from the configuration of their livers, the supernatural circumstances foretelling triumph or defeat in an impending campaign. Similarly in Shang China, oracle-bones of tortoise shell or the shoulder-blades of buffalo were carefully prepared, inscribed, and exposed to heat, so that cracks developing on the surface would reveal a hidden pattern of cosmic phenomena that could be interpreted. Another analogy to help understand the divinatory functions of the *tonalpohualli* is provided by the ancient Chinese *Book of Changes*, also known as the *I Ching*.[12] This book of wisdom was already old when Confucius wrote his commentaries on it around 500 BC, yet it continues to be widely consulted in the present day. To use the book, a question is posed and yarrow stalks (or coins) are thrown, to produce a pattern which is recorded as a linear diagram. This in turn is interpreted according to the *I Ching* texts. The texts present a series of images describing changes and relationships observed in natural forces, interpreting them in terms of social circumstances. Thus, when a question is posed, those forces affecting the question at the moment it was formed can be taken into account in deciding a course of action. The *I Ching* texts, which reflect knowledge accumulated since great antiquity, are not intended to foretell fate as in ordinary soothsaying or fortune-telling. What they offer the questioner is a picture of the cosmic circumstances surrounding a particular problem, and counsel for what may be done to arrive at the right course of action.

Another avenue to understanding the possible uses of the Aztec *tonalpohualli* is presented closer to Central Mexico. Today, a traditional form of calendrical divination is still practiced by Maya Indian diviners, called "daykeepers," at mountain shrines in Guatemala.[13] At such sacred places, candles are lit and copal incense is burned as an offering. Using coral seeds and crystals the daykeeper will make arrangements in lots of

74 Four of the eight year signs: 1 house, 2 rabbit, 3 reed, and 4 knife. From the Codex Magliabechiano.

four, counting out the days of the 260-day calendar. One day is assigned to each lot, starting from the current day or the day the client's problem began. This is the beginning of a complex process of interpretation, through which the daykeeper's client will receive counsel on the course of action revealed by the time-count and the pattern of seeds and crystals.

Did the lost oral tradition accompanying the Aztec *tonalpohualli*, which was probably rooted in a very old agricultural cycle, have similar functions to those presented by these analogies? At present it is possible to say only that as a sophisticated system of divination, the *tonalpohualli* was undoubtedly the carrier of tradition and authority, a system woven into the fabric of Mesoamerican thinking. The *tonalpohualli* played an especially important role in the daily lives of the Aztecs, from the solving of personal perplexities, and serving the needs of rulers searching for counsel in matters of state, to prescribing the appropriate times for carrying out planting and harvesting.

The 365-day count

The annual ceremonial calendar of the Aztec state was governed according to the 365-day solar count, the *xiuhpohualli*. This period was divided into 18 "months" of 20 days each, called *veintenas* by the Spanish, plus a 5-day period between the old year and the new. The latter was a dangerous and inactive time of transition called *nemontemi*. Each *veintena* had its own special festival, closely correlated to the agricultural year. The years were named after the "year bearer," one of four possible day-names of the *tonalpohualli* which could begin a new year with its accompanying number, according to the system of rotation. The possible year-names were rabbit, reed, flint knife, and house. The years were distinguished by their numbers – thus 1 rabbit, 2 reed, 3 house, 4 flint knife, until the 13 numbers and the 4 day- and year-names began to repeat themselves every 52 years (13 × 4).

Curiously, the succession of 52-year cycles was not calendrically differentiated. It is as if our centuries were not distinguished as being before or after Christ. Thus the voyage of Columbus would have been recorded as '92, or the meeting of Cortés and Motecuhzoma as '19, or the end of the Second World War as '45. In the Aztec system, only a knowledge of historical events would allow one to place them in the appropriate 52-year cycle. It was customary in writing, or in sculptured inscriptions, to indicate year-names and their numbers by enclosing them

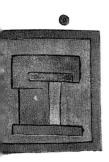   

in a square cartouche, as may be seen on the Coronation Stone of Motecuhzoma II. Day-names were ordinarily left unenclosed.

The conclusion of a 52-year cycle and the beginning of a new one was the occasion for special ceremonies. At that time the "binding of the years" took place, marked by the ceremonial tying of a bundle of 52 reeds, the *xiuhmopilli*. Stone sculptural representations of one of these objects have been recovered from Aztec ruins in the vicinity of the cathedral in downtown Mexico City. One example in the National Museum is carved with its date-hieroglyph corresponding to the year 1508, when a New Fire ceremony was also celebrated to ensure the beginning of a new cycle (see Chapter 8). Special importance was placed on the completion of two cycles (104 years), for at such times the solar count, the *tonalpohualli*, and the 52-year cycle coincided.

As mentioned above, there was an annual cycle of 18 festivals associated with the eighteen *veintena* "months" of the 365-day solar year. These festivals were basically of three types: those directed to mountains and water in order to ensure rain; those directed to the earth, the sun, and maize, to ensure fertility and an abundant harvest; and those directed to special deities, particularly those identified as patrons of different community groups or of the community as a whole. The latter festivals usually had various purposes, among which the particular historical and cultural identity of a given group might be a special concern.

Just as the *tonalpohualli* seems to have functioned in a similar way in all areas, so too the same order of *veintena* festivals has been recorded in the ethnohistoric texts. Nevertheless there was great variation in the local practice of these festivals, due to different geographical and cultural conditions. For example, in the Valley of Mexico and its environs there are many micro-environments where rain may arrive at somewhat different times and with different intensity, or where the time for harvest may be subject to variation due to altitude, local frosts, and so on. Such environmental factors would affect festivals concerned with agriculture. In addition, political factors and cultural change strongly affected ceremonial events, as the rulers of empires adapted old practices or invented new variations to express the new political, religious, and social needs. In this way, traditional agricultural ceremonies were often invested with new military and imperial themes. Old myths were thus fitted with new rites, and new myths might be created to accommodate old ritual procedures. Many such changes were occurring in the Valley of Mexico at the time of the Spanish arrival. But no uniform practice of the festival cycle had yet been devised, hence the variety of descriptions recorded by the Spanish.

The chart of festivals found at the end of the book outlines the principal cult themes and local deities. But the festivals are best understood in the context of the landscapes, temples, or urban settings where they were celebrated. For this reason we shall now turn to the Aztec ordering of space, to see how the land was organized and equipped with monuments.

8 · Sacred Landscapes

It is difficult for many who live in large cities today, removed from the natural environment that supports us, to grasp the interconnectedness between ourselves, the land, and the seasons. But among Amerindian peoples there was a strong tendency to see the forms of the land as primary, sacred entities that came before the historic forms of their many deities. In central highland Mexico the most significant places were identified with some special spiritual presence. Many such places used by the Aztecs had already accumulated mythical and historical meanings from centuries of earlier occupations. Topographical features and man-made symbols were joined at certain points to form a ritual network for religious communication between the people who embodied the social order, and the natural forces, deities, and ancestral heroes. This was the structure of a sacred geography. As we will see below, the hill named Huixachtlan, the great urban pyramid of Tenochtitlan, the ritual Hill of Tetzcotzingo, and the shrines upon the heights of Mt Tlaloc and at Pantitlan in Lake Tetzcoco were principal icons of Aztec sacred geography, designed to manifest the inherent power of things seen and unseen in the natural environment.

The need to develop a system of sacred places was given impetus by an unprecedented natural disaster that affected the highlands between 1452 and 1454. This period marked the end of the 52-year cycle begun in 1402. The calamity began in 1450, when a four-year sequence of frosts and droughts produced a terrible famine. In those years the clouds that usually appear on mountaintops failed to form and to bring summer rain and renewal. The long dry season that begins in late September and lasts until mid-June stretched into July and August. In the withering heat of the sun, most of the scanty showers evaporated before reaching the ground, and maize fields yellowed soon after sprouting. The dry season continued through the following year, and was repeated the year after that. At first, stocks of food were sufficient to ameliorate the worst effects, but soon the disproportion between reserves and the prolonged demand for them became frighteningly evident. The drought affected a large highland region and tribute alone could not feed the entire population. The unfruitfulness of the earth forced farmers and their families away from the desolate fields into the mountains in search of game, or to the lakeshores where they might find fish, birds, or other aquatic life. As maize, amaranth, and beans grew scarcer, market stalls were abandoned and the streets and canals of the cities became a dwelling-place for those who could no longer move on. The country trails were also scenes of bitter desolation as men, women and children, weakened by hunger, were forced to lie by the wayside. Languor and exhaustion were followed by sickness, and thousands of starving and bewildered people slowly began to die.

The scale of the calamity grew in the third year because the last reserves of maize had disappeared and even the seed-corn was eaten. Parents sold their children into slavery for a few ears of maize, to Huaxtecs and Totonacs from the rich eastern coastland unaffected by the drought. At least the children would be fed and might therefore survive. In the atmosphere of corruption and despair suspicion abounded, and soon it was widely imagined that witches were abroad in the land. Some were seen by people in dreams, others were witnessed by victims predisposed to believe in them, while others actually confessed to witchcraft. The fear of those terrible years, like 20th-century memories of the great economic depression in the 1930s, was indelibly impressed on the Aztecs. The Codex Telleriano-Remensis, recording principal historical events, illustrates the year 1454 with the sign of diseased, famine-struck victims.

As the end of the old 52-year cycle drew near, preparations took place for the New Fire rites to bring in the new cycle. This was always a time of tension, for who knew what the future might bring when at present all seemed dark and uncertain?

The New Fire rites

The last five days of the year were, as we have seen, known as *nemontemi* and were considered a time of transition. People let their fires go out,

75 The year 1 rabbit (1454) was an unforgettable time of famine, as symbolized by the sick and starving people on this page from the Codex Telleriano-Remensis.

76 The New Fire rites are celebrated at Tenochtitlan. Above right, the hill Huixachtlan
is depicted with a fire-drill. Footprints indicate the route taken by the torch-bearers to
the fire-temple. Representatives from the four wards of the city light torches from the
flaming hearth, and deities from all the other temples arrive with their own torches.
Above center right, Huitzilopochtli presides over the city. From the Codex Borbonicus.

fasting and abstinence were observed, silence was kept, utensils were
broken, and all normal daily activities ceased. *Nemontemi* was a time of
ritual death, in preparation for renewal. During the last day, pregnant
women were enclosed in granaries to signal the hope for new life by
associating them with life-giving maize. When the sun disappeared over
the rim of the western sierra and darkness filled the Valley, a long line of
fire-priests departed from Tenochtitlan across the causeway to Ixtapalapan.
Their destination was an ancient shrine on the hill named Huixachtlan,
"thorn-tree place," an extinct volcano commanding the headland between
lakes Tetzcoco and Xochimilco. The summit is centrally located and
visible from almost everywhere in the basin. This was the site of a temple-
platform, hallowed long before the Aztecs had arrived in the region. All
fires were now extinguished in every town and city. No one set forth, and
a primeval silence reigned as thousands of people stood hushed on the
rooftops or in open yards and patios. All looked towards the dark shape
of Huixachtlan, and up to the millions of stars whose soft light was
reflected in the wide sheet of water covering the floor of the Valley.
Meteors were seen to glance over in random flitting patterns against the

gauzy belt of the Milky Way stretching across the heavens. Perhaps in whispers the people would name the constellations: "the s-shaped stars;" "the scorpion stars." But the most anxiously awaited "fire-drill" had not yet risen over the western horizon. This would be the first sign of the beginning of the new cycle, and of the renewal of time suspended in the *nemontemi* transition. When the first point of the "fire-drill" (probably Orion's belt) emerged from behind the black wall of the western sierra a man was immediately sacrificed upon the platform at Huixachtlan. A fire-drill was then placed upon his chest. The new cycle was proclaimed as the first sparks were drawn from the drill-board on the body of the sacrificed victim. A great bonfire was lit from this sacred smouldering tinder, and as flames flared on the mountain, waiting runners crowded in to light their pitch-pine torches. Soon they were seen as points of light moving quickly down the trails to carry new fire to the fire-temple hearths in every waiting community. From Tenochtitlan the runner's torch could be seen coming across the long causeway and on to the center of the city. A page from the Codex Borbonicus (ill.76) shows the spectacular conclusion to the ceremony as the new fire blazed in the fire-temple altar, and four priests lit brands to carry the flame to the four wards of the city. The cult of fire, whose antiquity was denoted by the name *Huehueteotl*, "old-old teotl," was thus linked to the idea of the renewal of time and the rising constellation.

The mountains of life: Mt Tlaloc and Tetzcotzingo

As the new year wore on and the season for rain drew closer, rites were carried out in other places to bring forth the life-giving water. This time the drought was broken, and as fallow fields turned green again, a new program of temple building was begun in conjunction with agricultural production. In the Tetzcocan heartland Netzahualcoyotl had several temples refurbished or reconstructed, among which the Hill of Tetzcot-zingo was especially important. Located at the base of the Mt Tlaloc foothills to the east of Tetzcoco, this hill is a major archaeological site, surrounded by agricultural terraces. Another extraordinary ritual place that figured in rain-making rites is located on the summit of Mt Tlaloc, the highest point of the sierra on the eastern side of the Valley of Mexico. These heights are primary sources of rain and springwater for central Acolhuacan.

The temple on Mt Tlaloc was maintained by the allied nations, but the history of this location as a place of offering goes back for many centuries. There has been little archaeological excavation at Tetzcotzingo and Mt Tlaloc, but survey plans, aerial views, and surface explorations reveal their design, and the remains can be interpreted with the help of 16th-century texts. Conversely, the monuments and their natural contexts reveal meanings and functions that texts alone do not mention. Tetzcotzingo and Mt Tlaloc disclose the essential religious role of Aztec rulers as priestly rain-makers responsible for the change of the dry to the rainy season. At these two sites the combination of architecture, sculpture, landscape, and ritual disclose how the Aztec rulers enacted a creation myth that the Spanish friars never recorded. Like the platform at Huixachtlan – site of the New Fire ritual – the temple on Mt Tlaloc and the Hill of Tetzcotzingo are key archaeological sites, for they show how religion, economy, and history were linked to the land in the Aztec world-view.

The temple on Mt Tlaloc stands far above the tree-line at the 4000 m level. The cold height affords a splendid view of the snow-capped volcanoes Popocatepetl and Ixtaccihuatl, and the valleys of Puebla and Mexico. In 1989 a detailed map of the temple was prepared by the present writer and Felipe Solís of the National Museum of Anthropology, and a team from the Mexican National Institute of Anthropology and History. The entrance to the temple is from the west through a long corridor-like processional way, enclosed by parallel walls of dry-stone masonry. These walls formerly rose to a height of approximately 3 m. The approach leads to an open quadrangle enclosed by walls of similar height. Originally the visitor would have seen nothing of the spectacular view after entering the corridor. The surface of the enclosed yard contains no building remains and is overgrown with mountain grass. Several basalt boulders project upwards, and at the eastern side of the quadrangle a rectangular shaft, measuring approximately 1.5 × 2 m, was cut down into the solid bedrock to a depth of over 3 m.

The chronicler Diego Durán describes the temple as the place of an annual royal pilgrimage made by the kings of Tenochtitlan, Tetzcoco, Tlacopan, and Xochimilco.[1] The pilgrimage was made in April or May at the height of the dry season, to perform a ceremony to call forth rain from within the mountain. This was a seasonal rite of passage, to initiate the transition from the time of death to the time of rebirth. Durán says that the quadrangle originally contained a finely-made temple of impermanent materials – probably a simple houselike structure with an elegant thatched roof. He also mentions "idols," the principal of which was named Tlaloc. This was surrounded by others named after other peaks of this range of mountains. These rocks and the Tlaloc idol were the focus of the annual rites.

No trace of the Tlaloc sculpture remains today, although a fragment of the idol was photographed in the quadrangle in the 1920s and again in the 1950s. The location of the upthrust boulders shows that they were undoubtedly part of the symbolic layout. Allowing for a certain irregularity, four of the large rock clusters rise at the intercardinal points. Another rises to the east, and yet another (enclosed by a recently constructed shrine) is at the center. Other rocks and quantities of earth were doubtless removed when the site was constructed to leave these particular stones in place. This arrangement clearly obeys a cosmological geometry. Similar

The temple at Mt Tlaloc

77–79 ABOVE Access to the rectangular Temple of Tlaloc was through a long, narrow processional way. The volcanoes Ixtaccíhuatl and Popocatepetl can be seen in the distance. BELOW The stone walls enclosing the processional way and ritual precinct once rose to a height of *c.* 3 m. RIGHT Tlaloc stands in the central panel of this scene from the Codex Borgia, between the cloudy sky and the cultivated earth. Four other Tlalocs are placed at the intercardinal points, indicating "rain in the four directions." The format of this illustration echoes the design of the temple.

four-part cosmic plans governed cities and ritual centers, and they were also often used in the design of painted manuscript pages. For example, the Codex Borgia contains a page depicting four Tlalocs at the intercardinal points and another Tlaloc standing in the center. Each figure rests upon a female form symbolizing mother earth. The similarity between this illustration and the layout of the Tlaloc temple supports the notion that the quadrangle formed a symbolic landscape, a microcosm of Mt Tlaloc and its adjacent peaks. In keeping with this abstract schema, the shaft on the eastern side of the enclosure corresponds to an "omphalos," or earth-navel, leading down to the mountain interior.

During the course of surveying the temple the question of the original height of the enclosing walls emerged. Why was it important for these walls to have been built up to 3 m? Once inside the visitor would have seen nothing but the symbolic landscape and the empty void of the sky. Only upon re-emerging from the long narrow corridor would the outside world be seen again. This separation of exterior and interior space was clearly intentional. Similarly, what was the purpose of the long processional way? Why were the kings, as chief ritualists of their nations, required to parade down this narrow corridor to reach the precinct interior? Diego Durán describes the royal processions in detail. The assembled kings first entered with gifts, following strict rank order, and then proceeded to dress the stone idols in Tlaloc's splendid regalia. Then they withdrew from the temple, but soon re-entered with sacrificial offerings. These included the blood of a male child and magnificent dishes of food. It is said that during the famine of the early 1450s, the children of royal houses were offered on mountaintops. Lengthy prayers were spoken during all stages of these acts. The rite concluded as the feast was spread and the kings withdrew to attend another feast outside the sacred precinct.

Considering the form of the temple-enclosure in the context of the landscape, and the movement of ritual processions, the enclosure and the processional way may be seen as a symbolic womb of the mountain (the womb of mother earth), entered by the Aztec kings on their fertilizing mission. The well-known page from the Historia Tolteca-Chichimeca (ill.33) – an early 17th-century Spanish colonial document – depicting the mountain Culhuacan helps us to understand this concept. The caves are drawn in a womb-like form, and a priest stands outside striking the entrance with his staff to summon the tribes from inside. The temple on Mt Tlaloc may similarly be considered a symbolic earth-womb built upon the summit of the mountain, where water-rocks were honored with Tlaloc's sacred regalia and fertilized by ruler-priests with human blood and food. At this place of meeting between inside and outside, where the underworld meets the sky, the Aztec kings recycled energy between the social and the natural orders. Afterwards, in weeks to come, the first clouds of the rainy season would be seen to collect around the mountain and dark thunderstorms would form. Quetzalcoatl would then blow down the storm with lightning and peals of thunder, bringing rain and renewing life in the Valley. No one who has ever lived in this part of the world will forget the dramatic seasonal change from the dry to the rainy season.

The Aztec rulers were not abject supplicants, fearing a punitive deity, but active agents performing an essential role in the change of seasons. The long pilgrimage had brought the kings from the floor of the Valley, across the lake, and up through chasms to the zone of ritual danger on the mountaintop. In this sacred, womb-like enclosure above the zone of forest-life, the rulers entered the place of contact between the earth and the heavens. Offerings were made and the kings returned home as bringers of life-giving water. This ritual process has the structure of a mythical happening. In some distant time of genesis, a hero emerges from a dry land – the earth still incomplete. He undertakes an arduous journey in quest of a supernatural boon. The place is found, offerings are made, and he returns to the point of departure bearing the gift of life. Rain arrives, plants spring forth, and the fruits of the earth are given. Such a myth was never recorded by the Spanish friars, but its "text" may be read in the rites, the topography, the design of the temple, and in the seasonal change.

As the rites on Mt Tlaloc were taking place, another rite was unfolding in the main ritual center of Tenochtitlan. A large tree, specially cut and transported in a sacred manner, was erected in the courtyard on the Tlaloc side of the Great Pyramid. This tree was named Tota, "father," and was surrounded by four smaller trees, forming a symbolic forest. A young maiden, attired as Chalchiuhtlicue, "jade skirt," the deity of ground water, was brought to sit within this arbor as a living personification of the lake. A long chant was begun to the rhythm of drums, until news was received that the lords had completed the rites atop Mt Tlaloc and had returned to assemble at the eastern shore of Lake Tetzcoco. In Tenochtitlan the Tota-tree was taken up and carefully bound on a raft. It was then rowed out into the lake to a place called Pantitlan, accompanied by musicians, priests, Chalchiuhtlicue, and a vast crowd of singing people in a fleet of canoes. Pantitlan was the site of a great spring (according to some accounts) or a sump-hole (according to others), surrounded by banners attached to poles stuck into the muddy bottom of the shallow lake. At this place in the middle of the water, the kings returning from Mt Tlaloc met the procession in their own fleet of canoes. As the assembled nobility and populace watched, the Tota-tree was unbound and set up by the spring or sump-hole as a new "tree of life" – the symbol of plant regeneration. The Chalchiuhtlicue-child was then sacrificed and her blood poured on the water, along with as much greenstone jewelry as had been offered to the rocks on Mt Tlaloc. The rite concluded, everyone departed leaving the tree standing along with others that remained from previous years.

While the rites performed on Mt Tlaloc acknowledged male water (clouds and rain), the sacrifice of Chalchiuhtlicue was addressed to the female water of springs, streams, lakes, and the distant seas. Indeed Lake Tetzcoco was spoken of as Tonanhueyatl, "mother great water," a provider of moisture to *chinampas*, teeming with edible plants and algae, and the home of fish and myriad creatures of aquatic and avian species. The lake was a sustainer of life, and was regarded as a mother by the peoples of the Valley of Mexico. The rites at Pantitlan expressed their perception of water as the element that precedes solid form, and is the support of all earthly creation. The structure of the highland landscape, with its mountains, clouds, springs and lakes, was thus the setting for dramas recalling the mythical time of creation.

Following this model, other temples of the city and country were designed as symbolic landscapes. The Hill of Tetzcotzingo is one of the places where a new ceremonial center was built. During the 1450s, following the famine, Netzahualcoyotl (the ruler of Tetzcoco) designed – or redesigned – Tetzcotzingo, with works of art and architecture. The site was probably already a place of worship, for it had been a stopping point when the Chichimecs first settled. A system of farming terraces extended around a huge natural amphitheater formed by foothills to the northern

The ritual hill of Tetzcotzingo

80–83 ABOVE Tetzcotzingo overlooks the terraced hillside and fields of central Acolhuacan. LEFT The rock-cut bath on the south side of the hill, used in ceremonies of ritual purification. BELOW The Tlaloc mask petroglyph at the summit of the hill. OPPOSITE Plan of the ritual zone at Tetzcotzingo.

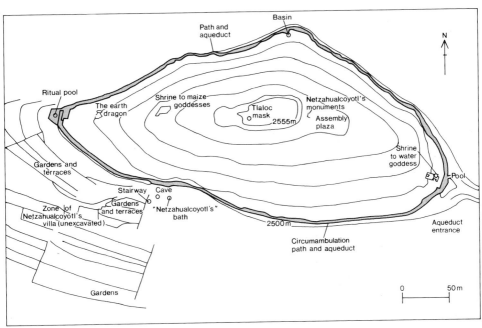

Path and
aqueduct

Basin

N

Ritual pool

The earth
dragon

Shrine to maize
goddesses

Tlaloc
mask

2555m

Netzahualcoyotl's
monuments

Assembly
plaza

Gardens and
terraces

Shrine
to water
goddess

Pool

Stairway   Cave

Gardens
and terraces

Zone of
Netzahualcoyotl's
villa (unexcavated)

"Netzahualcoyotl's"
bath

2500 m

Aqueduct
entrance

Circumambulation
path and aqueduct

Gardens

0   50 m

Earth deities

84–86 LEFT Jade sculpture of the earth deity Tlazolteotl giving birth. RIGHT Scene from the Codex Borbonicus depicting the same goddess Tlazolteotl. FAR RIGHT An earth deity squatting in a parturition position, with a stylized upturned mask and open jaws. The earth was not only the giver of life, it was also the eventual receiver of life, hence the skull and crossbone skirt and clawed hands and feet.

side of Tetzcotzingo. The towns and villages of this district still bear their Nahuatl names, and were supplied with water by aqueducts from springs high on Mt Tlaloc. The rights to this water were assigned by Netzahualcoyotl in the *Titles of Tetzcotzingo* (see Chapter 5). Although the monuments at Tetzcotzingo were almost entirely destroyed by the Spanish in 1539, texts, pictorial manuscripts, and related works of sculpture and architecture provide the information to decode what remains at the site.

Tetzcotzingo was mapped by the writer in 1979.[2] The plan reveals how the upper hill was organized in a cosmological design. The ritual zone is demarcated by a walkway cut around the hill about 55 m below the summit. Four baths or shallow basins are still seen on this path at points corresponding to the cardinal directions. As manifestations of Chalchiuhtlicue's aquatic domain, these receptacles were for purposes of ritual purification, and were supplied with water by an aqueduct built on the path. The path itself was for processional circumambulation, and divided the upper sacred zone from the space below. Another sequence of shrine stations was aligned on the east–west axis, following the natural ridge of the hill. This alignment reflects the path of the sun, suggesting that Tetzcotzingo had astronomical and calendrical functions at equinoctial and solstitial times. The summit shows traces of foundations of a demolished temple; and a goggle-eyed mask of Tlaloc is engraved on a bedrock boulder, revealing the cult once housed in this location. Another

important shrine was a cave located immediately below the circumscribing path and near a system of lower terraces where Netzahualcoyotl's villa and botanical plantations once stood. Although the cave has now lost all trace of its original sculpture, it can be assumed to have had a specific religious purpose. The ritual use of natural caves (or architectural temple-caves such as Malinalco) as places of communion with the earth is well known in Mexico. Such names as *tlalli yiollo*, "earth-heart," or *tepe yiollo*, "mountain-heart," speak of beliefs concerning the earth as a center of life. In seasonal festivals, impersonators of the earth deities donned masks, insignia, and other sacred paraphernalia to manifest the earth's fertility as well as its terrifying and destructive powers. Throughout the centuries, diverse languages in Mexico had developed a wide range of metaphors to name the properties of the earth, several of which were incorporated in the ritual speech of the Aztecs. Toci "our grandmother," Tlaltecuhtli "earth lord (or lady)," and Coatlicue, "serpent skirt," are some of the figures of speech that were also the names of earth deities. Aztec sculptors often portrayed the earth deities in seated or squatting parturition positions, with grinning upturned masks (the face of the earth, turned to the sky), skulls and crossbones on their skirts (the earth's role as eventual devourer of all that grows or walks upon its surface), and other symbols such as animals and insects that live close upon or beneath its surface.

Caves also had historical associations, as illustrated by a page from the Mapa Tlohtzin showing Chichimec chieftains within a cave identified with Tetzcoco. These are the immigrant ancestors who established Netzahualcoyotl's lineage. Although the picture records an historical event, it also recalls the genesis theme of the first emergence of people from the womb of the earth. The cave, thus depicted, calls attention to the legitimacy of Netzahualcoyotl's title by alluding to the time of creation. Similar themes and uses are implied by the cave on the side of Tetzcotzingo.

Another shrine on Tetzcotzingo is placed high on the western axis. Two effigies are carved in the living rock, with a view of terraces and planted fields below in the agricultural crescent. Both sculptures are severely damaged, yet fragments of a headdress and the outline of their shape show that they were female divinities connected with the cycle of maize. The Codex Borbonicus depicts such figures holding multicolored ears of maize and wearing others as emblems in their headdresses. Sahagún's *Book of Ceremonies* and Durán's *Book of the Gods, Rites, and the Ancient Calendar* describe a sequence of three festivals in which these deities appeared.[3] The first was *Huey Tozoztli*, celebrated at the height of the dry season, when dried seed corn was consecrated by Chicomecoatl priestesses for the coming planting. Chicomecoatl, "seven serpent," was the Aztec deity of dried seed corn. The second festival was *Huey Tecuilhuitl*, which took place towards the middle of the rainy season. Attention centered on the female deity named Xilonen, whose named derived from the word *xilotl*, "corn silk." The term was also given to the first tender sweet maize to appear in the growing period. The young girl who impersonated Xilonen was the focus of a first-fruits offering. The last of the maize festivals was *Ochpaniztli*, involving a sequence of ceremonies which featured the deities of earth and maize, signaling the harvest and the onset of the dry season. They also heralded the time for war that was fast approaching. The last four days of this festival were especially dramatic, when a series of agricultural and military analogies were skillfully interwoven. The deity Toci, an earth-mother, scattered cornmeal as she took annual leave of the marketplace. Human sacrifices were then made, in which the skin of Toci was displayed to hail the coming of the dry season, along with a mask that proclaimed the period for war. Presents and insignia were distributed by the *tlatoani* to his warrior-chiefs, officially commissioning the army for the coming campaigns. The final episode was marked by the return of the Chicomecoatl priestesses, who flung out seed corn – white, yellow, black and red, mixed with the seeds of squash. Everyone scrambled for these grains to keep for next year's planting, just as the army would soon fight to glean tribute on the fields of battle.

The last of the shrines at Tetzcotzingo were Netzahualcoyotl's personal commemorative monuments, located below the summit on the eastern slope of the hill. A broad assembly ground was constructed facing an exposed rock-face where the sculptures were carved. The monuments are completely destroyed and only texts from Fernando de Alva Ixtlilxóchitl survive to describe what was once there. The first monument was of

Maize deities

87–89 ABOVE Destroyed figures of maize deities on a rock face at Tetzcotzingo. The fragment of a headdress is visible in the foreground. LEFT A maize goddess with a headdress akin to that found at Tetzcotzingo. BELOW Detail of a maize and earth deity, from the Codex Borbonicus.

circular design and is said to have recorded the principal deeds of Netzahualcoyotl as a hero-king, the founder of the imperial Tetzcocan nation. Next to this sculpture stood a seated stone coyote, which was the hieroglyphic name of Netzahualcoyotl himself. These two vanished historical monuments were seen against the backdrop of Acolhuacan, and they faced east to the rising sun, linking the memory of the great *tlatoani* with the daily appearance of heat and light, and with the eternal renewal of the seasons. Although Netzahualcoyotl was an historical person he became deified after death, and was enshrined in a hero-cult at the top of his sacred mountain.

The Great Pyramid at Tenochtitlan

The final site to be discussed is an urban center, where the sacred landscapes at Mt Tlaloc and Tetzcotzingo were replicated in the architecture of the Great Pyramid of Tenochtitlan. Continuing a project begun by his immediate predecessor Itzcoatl, Motecuhzoma Ihuilcamina enlarged the central precinct and Great Pyramid with building materials and labor supplied from tribute communities. This work was apparently continued even in the worst years of the great famine, 1452–1454. The approach to the precinct was by way of a long avenue, leading east–west through the city. The pyramid rose in the middle of the sacred enclosure, as the social and geographical center of the Aztec universe. This configuration echoes that of the Tlaloc temple on the mountaintop as well as the design of Netzahualcoyotl's mountain. Hernán Cortés and Bernal Diaz describe the looming pyramid with four superimposed platforms rising in stepped-back tiers and a pair of steep stairways on the west facade; the fourth platform formed a broad ceremonial level at the top of the building, upon

90 Reconstruction model of the ritual precinct at Tenochtitlan.

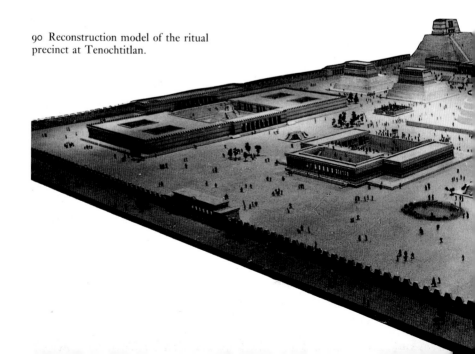

which the dual temples of Tlaloc and Huitzilopochtli were built. These twin temples faced west. Tlaloc, on the northern side, was painted with blue and white symbols of rain and moisture. Huitzilopochtli, to the south, was colored with red and white symbols of war and sacrifice. By the time the Spanish arrived the entire pyramid rose some 60 m, offering a sweeping view of the city, the lake, and the surrounding countryside.

The location of the pyramid foundations in downtown Mexico City was long known, and small-scale archaeological excavations began during the early 20th century. But in 1978 a worker for an electrical company was digging beneath Guatemala Street when he made a chance discovery of an extraordinary sculpture. Further investigations, this time by a team of archaeologists, revealed that the sculpture was a huge monolith, 3.25 m in diameter, of a decapitated and dismembered female deity (ills. 98–100). This was the goddess Coyolxauhqui who, it will be remembered, was killed by her brother Huitzilopochtli on the hill at Coatepetl according to the migration legend. This discovery led to the excavation of the Great Pyramid foundations in one of the most unusual archaeological projects in the history of Mexico. The project, directed by Eduardo Matos Moctezuma, presented an unprecedented opportunity to answer questions about the nature of the pyramid and the dynamic role it played in the development of the imperial state.[4] The first phase of the project was to demolish and remove the 19th-century buildings and colonial remains superimposed on the site. Gradually, the Aztec foundations appeared. The structure seen by Cortés, razed soon after the Conquest, was revealed to have been constructed in a succession of layers. Each of these layers completely enclosed an earlier version of the pyramid. As excavations continued to disclose the concentric foundations, vast quantities of offerings buried in foundation-caches were also unearthed.

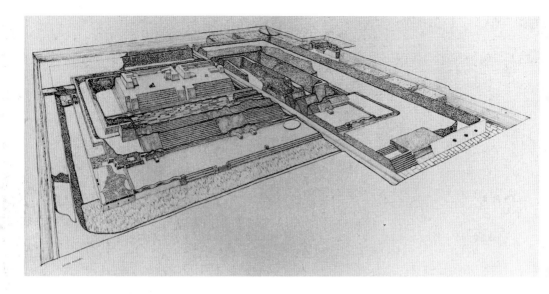

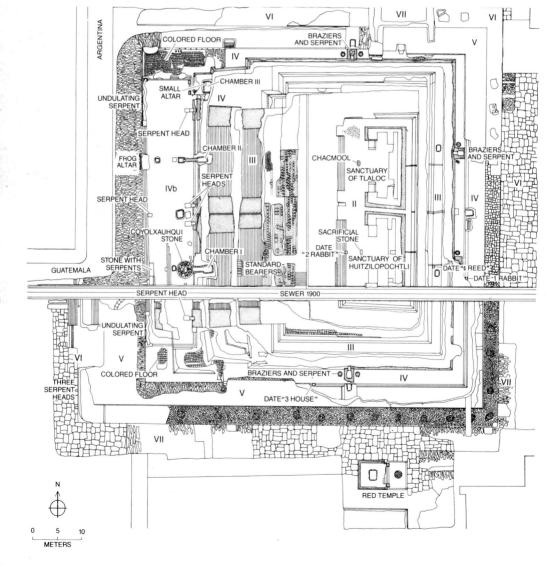

ARGENTINA

COLORED FLOOR

BRAZIERS
AND SERPENT

VI

VII

VI

V

IV

UNDULATING
SERPENT

CHAMBER III

SMALL ALTAR

IV

SERPENT HEAD

CHAMBER II

IV

CHACMOOL

SANCTUARY
OF TLALOC

BRAZIERS
AND SERPENT

FROG
ALTAR

III

SERPENT
HEADS

IVb

SERPENT HEAD

VI

III

IV

COYOLXAUHQUI
STONE

II

SACRIFICIAL
STONE

GUATEMALA

STONE WITH
SERPENTS

CHAMBER I

DATE
"2 RABBIT"

SANCTUARY OF
HUITZILOPOCHTLI

DATE "1 REED"

STANDARD
BEARERS

DATE "1 RABBIT"

SERPENT HEAD

SEWER 1900

UNDULATING
SERPENT

III

VI

V

COLORED FLOOR

BRAZIERS AND SERPENT

IV

THREE
SERPENT
HEADS

V

DATE "3 HOUSE"

VII

RED TEMPLE

N

0   5   10
METERS

Excavating the Great Pyramid

91–93 OPPOSITE ABOVE Drawing of the excavated foundations of the Great Pyramid. OPPOSITE BELOW Plan of the foundations, showing the successive enlargements. ABOVE View of the excavations in progress. The earliest dual pyramid-platform (Temple II) lies under the temporary protective roof on the right, and the Coyolxauhqui Stone (ills. 98–100) is beneath the scaffolding near the center of the picture.

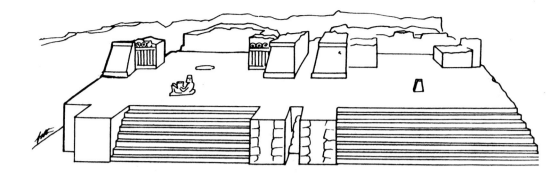

The dual shrines of the Great Pyramid

94–97 ABOVE Sketch of the summit of Temple II, with the recumbent chacmool figure in front of Tlaloc's shrine and a sacrificial stone at the entrance to Huitzilopochtli's shrine. LEFT The chacmool sculpture found by Tlaloc's shrine. Dating from about 1390, this crude, polychromed figure strongly echoes Toltec prototypes (see ill. 25). BELOW General view of the summit of Temple II. RIGHT The pyramid of Tlaloc and Huitzilopochtli in Tetzcoco followed the style of the Great Pyramid in Tenochtitlan; from the Codex Ixtlilxóchitl.

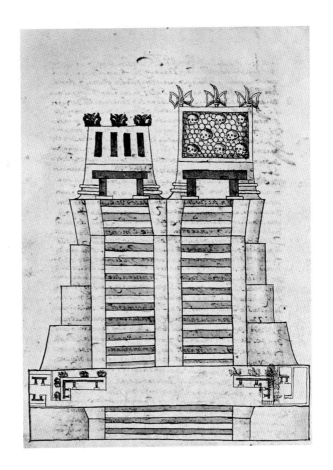

The central problem of interpretation was to understand the pyramid in symbolic terms, particularly its function in enhancing agricultural stability and military expansion. Three related themes have emerged in considering this problem. The first theme concerns state patronage as revealed by the growth of the pyramid during consecutive reigns, and particularly during the time of Motecuhzoma Ihuilcamina and his successor, Axayacatl. The second theme concerns the symbolic organization of the pyramid as a man-made mountain. The third theme concerns the pyramid as a stage for mythic drama, expressed in rites offered to Tlaloc (similar to those at the distant mountain, but also performed in the city at various times of the year); in sacrificial triumphs devoted to Huitzilopochtli, especially at the successful conclusion of a war; and in the coronation rites of the Aztec *tlatoque*.

One of the unique features of Mesoamerican pyramids is that they were frequently built in enveloping layers over decades or centuries. In this way an original sacred place, marked by a small construction, would later be completely enclosed – together with its sculptures, offerings, and related artifacts – by new superimposed structures. Containing vast accumulations, such buildings became living architectural fetishes in the minds of their makers. The Tenochtitlan pyramid reflects this tradition of construction. The most primitive foundation thus far unearthed probably dates from the reign of Acamapichtli, as suggested by the stone date-glyph 2 rabbit, which would correspond to the year 1390. This date-marker was found embedded in the stairway of the Huitzilopochtli side. Another earlier platform, perhaps dating from the time of the founding of Tenochtitlan, in the first half of the 14th century, has been located within this structure. A sacrificial block in the platform in front of the Huitzilopochtli temple, and a crude but colorful recumbent sculpture found on the Tlaloc side, confirm that the two deities were already being worshiped at this early time. Pyramids with a dual-shrine format had a long history prior to the Aztecs in the Valley of Mexico. The earliest example, at Cuicuilco, dates from *c*.300 BC, although the nature of the cults at its two shrines has not been clearly established.

Few changes were made to the Tenochtitlan empire during the reigns of Huitzilihuitl (1390–1417) and Chimalpopoca (1417–27), when the Mexica were still paying tribute to the Tepanec city of Atzcapotzalco. It was after the formation of the Triple Alliance in 1428 that Itzcoatl commissioned a more ambitious temple for the Aztec capital. A date-glyph of 4 reed (1431) marks this phase of construction. The pyramid grew in size and was equipped with imposing sculpted stone figures in the form of standard-bearers, reflecting Itzcoatl's concern to express the rising status of Tenochtitlan. The next layer of additions corresponds to the reign of Motecuhzoma Ihuilcamina, as indicated by the date-glyph 1 rabbit (1454) incorporated in a new structure on the rear of the Huitzilopochtli temple. At this time the pyramid was embellished with large-scale incense braziers and offering-cysts on all four sides, and a new grand stairway was added over the old one on the west facade. The next excavated date-glyph 3 house (1469) corresponds to Axayacatl's coronation year. It is almost certain that during his reign (1469–81) a platform was extended in front of the stairway, set with one of the most powerfully expressive sculptures of Mesoamerican art. This is the disk of Coyolxauhqui discovered by the electricity workers, carved in high relief with an assurance of design and a technical virtuosity not previously seen at the pyramid (ills. 98–100). Although the Coyolxauhqui Stone probably dates from Axayacatl's reign, the theme had already appeared by the time of Motecuhzoma Ihuilcamina – as shown by another, stylistically more primitive Coyolxauhqui carved on a greenstone slab buried beneath the new larger Coyolxauhqui disk. A third Coyolxauhqui, the famous greenstone head in the Museum of Anthropology (ill. 142), was carved at a later date.

The disk of Coyolxauhqui is carved with her dismembered limbs displayed in a dynamic pose, and her ritual attire is outlined in meticulous detail. This fearsome image shows the Aztec genius, developed by the middle of the 15th century, for translating traditional two-dimensional forms seen in manuscript paintings into an extraordinarily effective sculptural medium. As Eduardo Matos Moctezuma first noted, the placement of the sculpture at the foot of the stairs was to commemorate the legend of Huitzilopochtli defeating Coyolxauhqui in the battle on Mt Coatepetl. (As we learned in Chapter 3, Huiztilopochtli was magically born as a warrior and attacked the enemy army led by his sister Coyolxauhqui. She was cut to pieces and rolled down the sides of the mountain.) Positioned at the landing of the stairway leading up to Huitzilopochtli's temple, Coyolxauhqui lay as a forbidding sign to the enemies of Tenochtitlan. Sacrificial victims brought home by warriors were paraded across this terrifying monument on their way up the stairway to the block in front of Huitzilopochtli's grim shrine. In remembrance of the legend, the pyramid was named Coatepetl. Yet the north side of the pyramid supported the Temple of Tlaloc, and the structure was therefore also identified with Tlaloc's mountain of life. Within this temple chamber there stood an effigy filled with seeds of all the important cultivated plants. The pyramid foundations on both sides contained offering-caches with thousands of artifacts. Tlaloc-masked pots and ceramic vessels with the image of the water-deity Chalchiuhtlicue were used as containers of ritual water, and hundreds of seashells, different coral species, and a splendid necklace of mother-of-pearl and jade carved with figures of aquatic animals, similarly alluded to these cults. Also recovered were miniature fish of mother-of-pearl, model canoes of greenstone with implements of a lacustrine economy, as well as the skeletons of water-birds and fish. The crocodile skeleton found brings to mind the ancient mythic image of the earth floating in the sea. The skeleton of a jaguar alluded to rulership, for

The Coyolxauhqui Stone

98–100 OPPOSITE ABOVE Placed at the foot of the Huitzilopochtli stairway, the huge disk represented the defeat of the Aztecs' enemies. OPPOSITE BELOW and ABOVE Details of Coyolxauhqui's right foot and severed head.

the jaguar was "lord of the forest." Trophy objects from conquered regions, antiquities such as an Olmec mask, and another mask carved in the manner of Teotihuacan, alluded to the pyramid as an imperial symbol and to the Aztec nation as the heir to the past. The pyramid was therefore at once a replica of Huitzilopochtli's mountain and Tlaloc's eternal mountain of life. In the heart of Tenochtitlan the pyramid rose as an architectural fetish, charged with the powers of all the offerings, and the blood from thousands of sacrificed human beings. The structure was the terrifying center of the Aztec world, and an architectural hieroglyph of the term *atl tepetl*, "water mountain," the Nahuatl word for "city." The human habitat was thus defined in terms of those aspects of the land upon which all life depended.[5]

The New Fire platform at Huixachtlan, the urban pyramid of Tenochtitlan, the Hill of Tetzcotzingo, and the shrines on Mt Tlaloc and at Pantitlan in Lake Tetzcoco were all designed to manifest the eternal power of things in the natural environment. Aztec religion was an outgrowth of the recognition of these natural elements and of the conviction that humankind was an integral part of the larger cosmic system. The fundamental purpose of elaborate rites and blood sacrifices was to fulfill an obligation to return food and energy from society to the earth, the sky, and the waters. The Nahuatl word for sacrifice is *uemmana*, composed of the term *uentli*, "offering," and *mana*, "to spread out," as has recently been pointed out by the historian, Kay Reed.[6] The Aztec rulers and priests played an essential role in renewing the cycles of time and ensuring the rebirth of life.

101,102 Olmec mask (LEFT) and Mixtec mask (RIGHT) recovered from the foundations of the Great Pyramid. Both are symbolic of conquered regions incorporated into the Aztec empire.

PART V

THE AZTEC WAY OF LIFE

9 · The Family and Education

Birth and childhood

The Aztecs were devoted to children, and parents were expected to take special responsibility for their discipline and instruction. From the day of birth, children were brought up to respect their elders, to revere the deities, and to be obedient, well-mannered and productive. While Aztec society offered opportunities for individuals to rise socially and profession-ally, especially in the military and priesthood, children tended to inherit the profession and status of their parents. Education did not emphasize individualism as it is understood in Western culture. Rather, the individu-ality of a person was always subordinate to the life of the family, the school, the *calpulli*, the professional organization, and society as a whole. In this respect Aztec culture more closely resembled that of traditional China or Japan.

The arrival of a newborn child was a special occasion. Upon delivering the baby, the midwife shouted war cries to honor the mother for having fought a good battle, for having become a warrior who had "captured" a baby. The midwife then spoke to the baby, as if addressing an honored but tired and hungry traveler, exhorting it to rest among its parents and grandparents, and telling it of the transitory nature of life. The umbilical cord of a male child was kept and eventually taken by an adult warrior to be buried on a distant battlefield; the female cord would be buried by the hearth. The ceremonial cutting of the cord was also accompanied by formal speeches describing the roles of men and women and exhorting the infant to work hard and do its duty. Then followed the child's first bath, during which the midwife spoke in a low voice to the baby about the purifying water deity, Chalchiuhtlicue:

> Approach thy mother Chalchiuhtlicue, Chalchiuh Tlatonac! May she receive thee! May she wash thee! May she remove, may she transfer, the filthiness which thou hast taken from thy mother, from thy father! May she cleanse thy heart! May she make it fine, good! May she give thee fine, good conduct![1]

More speeches were given by the midwife as she proceeded with the first ritual cleansing, and then she spoke to the mother as many guests from the extended family arrived. Aunts and grandmothers would speak in turn, honoring the midwife, and the midwife would reply. In these speeches there is always a sense of reverence for the mother and especially for the infant. Such speeches were an essential aspect of the midwife's professional training and qualifications.

Among the nobles or wealthy merchants, the arrival of a child was the occasion for even more elegant speeches and visits. Many pages from Bernardino de Sahagún's texts are devoted to these ceremonial addresses, which often include admonitions to the baby as a responsible member of the ruling classes.

The most powerful families would receive visitors – even ambassadors – from near and far, sometimes for as long as 20 days after the birth of a child. The most important guests would be greeted with gifts of fine clothing – beautifully woven capes, skirts, or shifts, as many as 20 or 40. And even the most humble visitors would be given food, drink, or pulque (a mildly alcoholic drink made from the fermented juice of the maguey cactus). But at all levels of society, the hosts would provide for visitors in proportion to their economic status.

One of the most important events after childbirth was the visit of soothsayers, who would be summoned with their Book of Days, the *tonalamatl*. They were responsible for reading favorable or unfavorable day signs, and for determining the configuration of cosmic forces that would affect the child's life. It would be important to know the very instant in which it was born; the books would be opened and, if it were a bad day, perhaps the dominant ill effects would be modified by other, more beneficent signs associated with that moment. The soothsayer would then assign a time four days hence for the baptismal rite to take place. But if that time also had bad auguries he would skip to find another day. In this way the soothsayers sought to ameliorate adverse conditions and to exert a measure of control over the hidden forces affecting each child's destiny. In the readings it would be pointed out that unfavorable signs could be compensated for by the child through hard work and dedication. The *tonalamatl* was thus regarded not so much as a book of fate or predetermination, but rather as a guide to action.

The final episode in the new-born's rite of passage was the formal baptism. This differed from the first washing mentioned before. The baptismal ceremony was prepared by placing a basin of water upon a reed mat, and by laying out instruments appropriate to the sex of the baby. If male, there would be a miniature bow and arrow laid upon a "shield" made from a tortilla of amaranth-dough; or there would be the tools of the carpenter, featherworker, scribe, goldsmith, or potter, according to the family profession. If a girl was to be bathed, they laid out a spinning wheel, a batten, a reed basket and spinning bowls, and other weaving instruments, as well as a miniature skirt and shift. The Codex Mendoza depicts this layout and other aspects of the baptismal rite. The midwife is shown walking counterclockwise around the basin, talking to the child. The child was bathed, massaged, and presented four times to the sky and to the cleansing water. Older children would then run through the streets crying out the name of the new child; and the baby was returned to the cradle. A great feast and gifts were then offered by the parents to the assembled relatives.

The Codex Mendoza also shows that between the ages of three and four, children were introduced to basic household chores. Boys carried light loads of water and girls were given elementary instruction in weaving or the preparation of food. Later, boys carried heavier bundles, and by the age of six or seven they were involved in activities outside the home, such as practicing with fishing nets or gathering reeds. Knowledge of specialized crafts such as pottery, metal-working, and basketry was transmitted from father to son and mother to daughter, beginning between the ages of eight and ten. Disobedient or recalcitrant children were not (in theory) severely punished until this time. The Codex Mendoza depicts pinching the arms or ears, or more unusually, pricking with maguey thorns. In extreme cases children could be spanked, held over a fire of roasting chile peppers, or bound and left to lie outside in the cold or on muddy ground.

Schools and education

Children were promised to schools when they were still infants, but the formal entrance and presentation did not take place until they were of age (variously estimated to have been at seven, ten, or fourteen). Both the promising and the actual entrance ceremonies were marked by lengthy admonitory speeches, in which the children were urged to obedience, deportment, diligence, humility, self-discipline, and cleanliness. There were two types of school, neither of which was co-educational, for they were designed to perpetuate sexual and social distinctions. The first type of school was the *telpochcalli*, "youth house." Each ward or *calpulli* had its own *telpochcalli* attached to the local temple. These schools were for the education of commoners. Emphasis was placed on basic moral and religious training, knowledge of history, ritual dancing and singing, as well as rhetoric. Public speaking was very important in Aztec life, and both men and women were expected to be proficient in this art. Boys entering the *telpochcalli* would be given military training, while girls would learn to participate in the religious cults they would serve in later life.

The second type of school was known as the *calmecac*. Its purpose was to train the most promising boys and girls from the nobility for leadership in religious, military, or political life. Rarely, some of the most intelligent children of the lower classes were chosen for this school. There was only one *calmecac* for boys and another for girls in each city. Discipline was strict, obedience was enforced, and students underwent periods of rigorous abstinence with penances, prayers, and ritual baths. The atmosphere was akin to that of a military academy or a monastery. Since religion was a

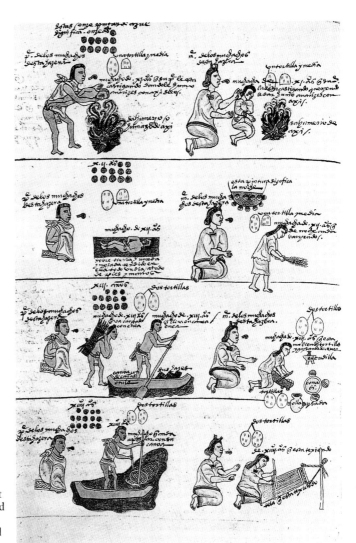

103 The upbringing of Aztec children emphasized discipline and hard work. This page from the Codex Mendoza shows how children between the ages of 11 and 14 (signified by the rows of dots) endured such punishments as inhaling the fumes of roasting chiles; on the left boys are taught by their fathers to carry loads and fish, while on the right girls are trained in the arts of cooking and weaving.

pervasive force in all aspects of Aztec life, the curriculum included basic calendrical calculation and the use of the *tonalamatl*; the significance and timing of the annual *veintena* festivals were taught, and students were expected to learn a range of ritual performances and how to address the deities. History, arithmetic, architecture, astronomy, agriculture, and warfare were also part of the curriculum. Since *calmecac* graduates were to be appointed as judges and to other key administrative posts, instruction included knowledge of the law.

The art of speaking was interwoven with the teaching of all these subjects, because the learning of technical skills, accounts of history, the reciting of stories and poetry, the conduct of lawsuits, and bargaining, were all primarily accomplished through oral means. To be educated was to be a master of expression, a dialectician, and an orator. An educated person had to be able to deliver artful or moving speeches on a diversity of occasions with all the etiquette prescribed by the highly formalized pattern of Aztec life.

There were no books in the sense of today's textbooks, no manuals, no histories or novels. Aztec hieroglyphic writing had a restricted field, where individual glyphs appear embedded in large pictorial compositions, communicating names, places, dates, and tallies. We have seen examples of this form of writing on pages of the Codex Mendoza, and on the relief sculpture of the Tizoc Stone. The viewer's ability to read the complex messages encoded by such combined graphic elements depends on an ability to grasp the interrelationships between all components. The Coronation Stone of Motecuhzoma II provides a clear example of this interconnectedness of hieroglyphic, figural, and sculptural forms. The rectangular block of basalt is carved on all sides. It was originally placed flat upon a floor and the composition was developed accordingly. The bottom was carved with the day sign 1 rabbit, alluding to the first day of the origin time. The sides depict squatting earth deities. The top face of the rectangle features the well-known hieroglyphs of the five "eras" or "suns," plus the year-cartouche 2 reed, and a day-sign 12 alligator. In the Christian calendar this date corresponds to 11 June 1502. The coronation of the emperor Motecuhzoma II was the principal event of that year, and this monument is a commemorative marker. The monument may be paraphrased as follows: "On 11 June 1502, when Motecuhzoma II was crowned, he became the ruler of the four quarters of the world in the time of the 'earth-movement sun', which was created on the day 1 rabbit, having been preceded by the four earlier eras, jaguar-sun, wind-sun, rain-sun, and winter-sun; thus Motecuhzoma's title stems from the time of origins and is legitimized by the sacred earth itself." To a certain extent such "texts" on monuments and in painted manuscripts had a mnemonic function, for their complex messages were meant to be filled out, amplified, or otherwise qualified by knowledge transmitted orally.

Memorization played a critical role in this oral mode of learning. It was facilitated by repetitive rhythms and the percussive beat of musical instruments as well as by the meter and cadence of poetry and song. Such devices also helped to recall this information during delivery of a speech. To be thoroughly literate also implied knowledge of hundreds of metaphors, set phrases, and sequences of repetitive verses or strophes.

Poetic language, music, and dance

Metaphors had a mnemonic function as well as being the very substance of Nahuatl poetry. The Nahuatl language employed a particular form of extended metaphor which has been curiously likened to the "kennings" of old Norse poetry.[2] An example of this convention is the term Chalchiuhtlicue, "jade skirt," which we have already seen as the name of the deity of lakes, springs, and rivers. If we say "the lake's water is

104,105 The Coronation Stone of Motecuhzoma II, proclaiming the ruler's title to the earth. LEFT Glyphic signs of the five cosmogonic ages appear in counter-clockwise order. The square cartouche contains the date 2 reed (1502), year of Motecuhzoma's coronation. ABOVE The rear, originally face down, is carved with the sign 1 rabbit, the mythical date marking the beginning of the present era.

like jade," we are making a simile or direct comparison; if we say "the lake's jade water," we are making an implied comparison, or metaphor, by not likening the water to jade, but calling it jade; however if we say "jade skirt" without mentioning either the lake or the water, then we are making a comparison by substitution, or kenning: the water *is* "jade skirt" and by implication it is personalized as "she." To understand the meaning of this extended form of metaphor the listener must know that in ceremonial or courtly language it is customary to refer to the water of lakes, rivers, or springs as "skirts of jade." Among the Aztecs, the names and attributes of deities and heroes were expressed in many such extended metaphors and were often translated into plastic form as hieroglyphic or figural elements. Thus, sculptural effigies of Chalchiuhtlicue would be shown wearing a jade-covered skirt or, as in the Codex Borbonicus, the skirt would be painted jade-green. When a ritual performer appeared as the personification of lake water and the female deity, their skirt would thus visually name Chalchiuhtlicue. In Aztec society everyone witnessing the performance would know how to "read" the element of ritual costume.

In his book on the life of Netzahualcoyotl, ruler of Tetzcoco, Jose Luis Martínez points out that Nahuatl poetry routinely used extended metaphors, not only for the names of deities but also for places, actions, heroes, and objects or concepts of special significance.[3] Thus, Tenochtitlan was variously known as "the place where darts are made," "the place of the white willows," or "the place of the eagle and the cactus." Warfare was "the song of shields," "where the smoke of shields diffuses," or "flowers of the heart upon the plain." Huitzilopochtli was spoken of as "the blue heron bird," "the lucid macaw," or "the eagle." Something precious or valued was "precious stones, gold, jade, flowers, fine feathers." Poetry was "flowers and song." The place where poetry was recited was "the house of flowers," "the house of springtime," "the flowering patio," and so on. Scores of other metaphors were employed in ceremonial speech and in the visual metaphoric language of manuscripts, sculptural monuments, and ritual costumes.

Many of the hymns and speeches recorded by Bernardino de Sahagún have archaic and hermetic forms of metaphor that seemed so unclear that he commented, "they would sing without understanding what was said." Durán, on the other hand, recognized that these forms of expression masked age-old mysteries and had a liturgical purpose:

All the songs of these [Indians] are composed of metaphors so obscure that there are only few who understand them, without taking pains to study and discuss them to grasp their meaning. I have given myself the purpose of listening with great attention to that which is sung, and between the words and terms of the metaphors, while they may first seem nonsense, but afterward, having spoken and conferred, they are admirable sentences, as much in the divine ones they compose as in the human songs composed.[4]

It would be difficult to underestimate the importance of music, song, and dance in Aztec society, and the *telpochcalli* and *calmecac* took pains to instruct students in these subjects. Everyone from the *tlatoani* down to individual family members took part in dances held on all festival occasions. The Spanish friar Gerónimo de Mendieta attests:

One of the principal things that was in all this land were the songs and dances, both to solemnize the feasts of their demons which they honored as gods and for private enjoyment and solace. Each lord had in his house a chapel with composer-singers of dances and songs, and these were thought to be ingenious in knowing how to compose the songs in their manner of meter and couplets that they had. Ordinarily they sang and danced in the principal festivities that were every twenty days, and also on other less principal occasions. The most important dances were in the plazas; on other occasions in the houses of the lords, as all the lords had large patios; they also danced in the houses of the lords and magistrates. When there had been some victory in war, or when a new ruler was assigned, or when a marriage was made with a high-ranking lady, or for any other novel event, the master would compose a new song, in addition to the general ones they already had for the festival of the demons and the deeds of antiquity and of past lords.[5]

Music and dance

106–108 ABOVE The Lordly Dance, from the Tovar Manuscript. LEFT
A carved wooden *panhuehuetl* drum, similar to that being played in
the picture above. BELOW A two-note *teponaztli* drum, carved in the
shape of a coyote, which would have been struck with rubber beaters.

Mendieta also refers to the careful rehearsals of songs and dances, and Durán describes the trouble taken in giving instruction to girls and young ladies. Teachers would set their drums in the center of the patio and the children, often paired, would dance around them. Extra instruction was given to those who could not follow the steps or body movements. The dancers were simultaneously required to sing, and rhythms and speech were guided both by the percussion and the tones of the singing. The Aztec songmasters modeled themselves on the Toltec ideal: artists who knew that the most creative levels of expression welled up from the deepest personal sources:

> The Toltecs were truly knowledgeable,
> they knew how to speak to their own hearts...
> they sounded the drum, the rattles,
> they were singers, they composed songs,
> they made them known,
> they learned them by memory,
> they made divine with their hearts
> the marvellous songs they composed.[6]

In the *telpochcalli* schools, which were located by the *calpulli* temples, a special patio with surrounding rooms was designated as the *cuicacalli*, "house of song." Here were taught the songs of heroes, elegies to princes, lamentations, war songs, love songs, and all that might fall under the classification of "profane." In the *calmecac* schools, on the other hand, emphasis was placed on songs and dances of a ritual nature. The role of music, dance, and ritual performance was to become increasingly important as adulthood and marriage approached.

Marriage

Marriage took place in the late teens or early twenties. When a youth arrived at the marrying age, his parents looked about for a suitable partner. A meal was prepared and the young man's schoolmasters were invited, to be told that his schooldays were over. Then another council was called and the assembled kinsmen decided which young woman was the most eligible – perhaps indeed someone who had already taken the youth's fancy at one of the great public festivals. Matchmakers were sent to the parents of the maiden to solicit her hand in marriage. The next day they would go again, and so on until the fourth day when her parents would give an answer.

As in all other rites of passage the marriage ceremony was preceded by elaborate preparations: cacao was bought, smoking tubes were prepared, flowers were secured, sauce bowls and pottery cups were purchased. Then maize was ground and tamales (corn husks filled with a mixture of meat and corn dough) were made, sometimes over two or three days, and honeyed

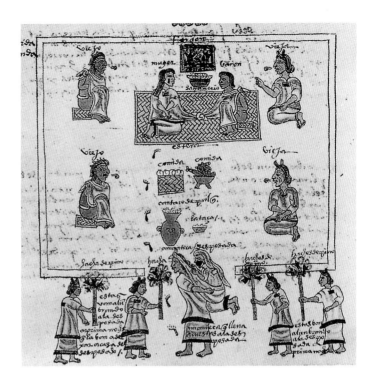

109 A marriage ceremony, from the Codex Mendoza. The bride is carried to the groom's house (bottom), and (above) the garments of the couple are knotted to signify union.

pulque was bought for the elders. As the evening of the appointed day approached, the bride was ceremonially bathed, dressed, and pasted with red feathers on her arms and legs; her face was painted with glittering pyrites. She was then counseled by her kinswomen and one of the strongest bore her on her back in a torchlight procession to the house of the groom. The Codex Mendoza depicts the arrival of the bride. Once inside, the bride and groom were seated upon a mat. A fire was lit in the hearth and copal incense laid out. After gifts of fine clothing were given by the mother of the groom, the elder matchmakers tied the groom's cape to the shift of the bride. Then the groom's mother fed the bride four mouthfuls of tamales in a special sauce, and another four mouthfuls to the young man. After that the bride and groom were led into their bedchamber. Four days of feasting followed, at the conclusion of which the elder women of the groom's family admonished and counseled the bride as to diligence, humility, and trust, and the bride's mother spoke to the groom of his duties and obligations, exhorting him to hard work, conscientiousness, and self-sacrifice. These speeches, preserved in the writings of Bernardino de Sahagún, provide us with an admirable picture of the ideals of an Aztec upbringing, if not always of the reality.

10 · Farmers, Traders, and Artisans

An ancient agricultural tradition

In his Nahuatl text, *General History of the Things of New Spain*, Bernardino de Sahagún distinguished between "farmers" and "horticulturalists." Farmers are described as general field workers charged with preparing the soil, weeding, breaking up clods, hoeing (with the *coa* digging stick), leveling, setting boundary markers, planting, and irrigating, as well as winnowing and storing grains. Horticulturalists were more specialized, with knowledge of the planting of trees and transplanting, as well as seeding These specialists would have needed a detailed understanding of the crop sequences and rotations necessary to ensure continuing high levels of production. Horticulturalists are also known to have played a managerial or supervisory role, for they were expected to read the *tonalamatl* almanacs to determine the best times for planting and harvesting.

Cultivation of the soil was the basis of life. It will be recalled from previous discussions of land tenure in the Valley of Mexico that the *calpultin*, at the base of the Aztec social order, held communal land that was assigned to individual families. But in the new *chinampa* zones, considerable numbers of farmers were not *calpultin* members but resident tenants tied to the land of estates, who paid "rent" in kind to owners residing in Tenochtitlan. These laborers were essentially dependent on the state and were supervised by state-appointed administrators. The estates were owned by the *pipiltin* (nobles) or the *tlatoani* himself, and were also awarded to distinguished warriors whose tenure tended to become hereditary. Food was thus supplied to Tenochtitlan by tenant farmers living outside the traditional *calpultin* framework, and additional food was acquired from non-tenant *calpultin* farmers who brought their surplus to market. A third source of food was provided by the tribute exacted from conquered communities.

But Tenochtitlan was growing, and these three sources of food were becoming increasingly inadequate. By the middle of the 15th century the city had a population estimated between 150,000 and 200,000, five times larger than Tetzcoco (with its population of 20,000 to 30,000). Yet it lacked a *chinampa* zone immediately attached to the city. It was therefore acutely important for its inhabitants to acquire new land and for this reason Itzcoatl led the conquest of the *chinampa* district around the southern lakes. Under Motecuhzoma I these conquests were consolidated, and agricultural production developed as new lands were reclaimed in the lakebed and brought into cultivation. Similarly, Netzahualcoyotl continued the project of agricultural terracing in central Acolhuacan. Additional lands were expropriated by conquests pursued abroad. The increased production provided food for thousands of non-food producing people working in a multiplicity of professions in the teeming urban centers.

Chinampas, terraces, and experimental gardens

Archaeological evidence of *chinampa* farming has been found in surveys of the Chalco-Xochimilco valley carried out between the 1950s and early 1970s, and is supported by data from 16th-century ethnohistoric sources.[1] The origins of *chinampa* agriculture in the Valley of Mexico remain unclear, but the archaeological surveys suggest that during the 13th and 14th centuries *chinampa* zones were restricted to islands within the lakebed, and to ground around the edges of the lakeshore. At that time, a large tract of the lakebed was essentially a wetland. By the 15th century, especially during the reign of Motecuhzoma I, older *chinampa* zones were incorporated in larger drainage and water-control systems that included large-scale construction of new *chinampa* fields. Aerial surveys show an overall uniformity in *chinampa* size and orientation, indicating a planned program of construction probably carried out over a short period of time.

Plots were constructed by staking out a rectangular enclosure approximately 30 m in length by 2.5 m wide, into the swampy lakebed. The stakes were joined by wattles and the fence thus formed was filled with mud and decaying vegetation. Another plot was then constructed parallel to the first, leaving a narrow canal in between for the passage of canoes. In this way, long lines of *chinampas* could be extended in a regular pattern. The Chalco-Xochimilco basin was watered by great springs along the base of the Ajusco mountains, and a sophisticated drainage system was installed including dams, sluice gates, and canals. This water-control system was interconnected throughout the *chinampa* zone, another factor suggesting central state management. Central control of the water supply was essential to ensure good harvests throughout the year. It was important to control the level of water in order to avoid flooding during the rainy season, and to maintain moisture during the dry season. In the dry months, irrigation of plants was done by hand, water being carried in containers from the canals to the seedbeds on the *chinampa* platform. To stabilize *chinampa* plots, tall slender willows were planted around the perimeter. In time these willows developed a dense root system that anchored the retaining walls, and constant pruning kept the trees from casting excessive shade. *Chinampa* gardens were fertilized with human excrement, collected in canoes from Tenochtitlan and transported to the field. Excrement was also sold in pots in the Tlatelolco market.

Chinampa development during the reigns of Itzcoatl and Motecuhzoma I was paralleled in central Acolhuacan by the construction of terrace systems during the long reign of Netzahualcoyotl. The large concentrations of potsherds and traces of domestic refuse found during archaeological surveys disclose that the piedmont and foothills of the Mt Tlaloc range were becoming heavily populated by the early 15th century.[2] It will be remembered that prior to that time, and continuing into the period of Netzahualcoyotl's "imperial" consolidation, the history of the Acolhua domain was characterized by a tendency to intensify food production. The early Chichimec leaders had directed – perhaps even forced – immigrant tribespeople to adopt "Toltec" ways that included agricultural practices and settlement in nucleated villages. Continuing this trend in an effort to extend control over the central region, Netzahualcoyotl encouraged the construction of an extensive system of aqueducts to bring water from mountain springs to the towns and agricultural terraces of the piedmont and foothills. Springs in the high vale named Tlalocto, below the temple on Mt Tlaloc, were channeled to supply Netzahualcoyotl's ritual palace and villa on Tetzcotzingo, as well as five other nearby towns of this central region. Another major spring near Santa Catarina del Monte supplied the towns around a terraced agricultural crescent running between Tetzcotzingo and La Purificación. A third source rises north of San Gregorio Amanalco, running northwest before branching down to the towns of the north-central district.

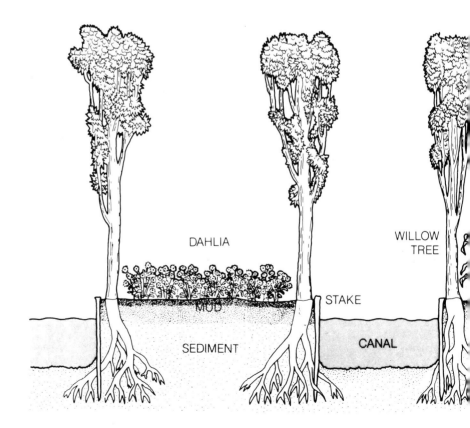

Aztec horticulture

110,111 ABOVE Planting, cultivating, harvesting, and storing maize and amaranth; note the use of the digging stick or coa. From Sahagún. LEFT Cross-section of a *chinampa* plot showing how the long narrow plots were constructed with stakes, willows, and a wattle fence, which were then filled with sediment.

MAIZE

Sophisticated hydraulic engineering was required to build these water-courses over broken terrain, and in three locations large embankments were constructed to bridge ravines and saddles. In a number of places the aqueducts are associated with agricultural terracing, most notably in the Tetzcotzingo crescent and vicinity. When the aqueduct system was first investigated in the late 1940s and early 1950s, it was thought to have been primarily a state-sponsored project; but subsequent enquiries have questioned this assumption.[3] Local communities were encouraged and supported but not necessarily coerced by the central administration. Calculations have shown that the flow of water through this system was insufficient to have maintained intensive farming as well as household use for so many people throughout the year. Instead the hydraulic system is now thought mostly to have supplied the towns with household water, with the little left over used for small-scale irrigation during the dry season. The aqueducts effectively permitted permanent year-round settle-ment, while the vast terrace systems were used to create new farmland, whose crops were still largely dependent on seasonal rain.

The role of Tetzcotzingo as a ritual place, as well as a center for hydraulic administration and other concerns of government, has been discussed in Chapter 8. Among the most important cults celebrated at this place were that of Tlaloc, god of rain; Chalchiuhtlicue, groundwater; Tonan, the earth-mother, and Cinteotl and Chicomecoatl, young maize and seed maize. It will be remembered that Tetzcotzingo also enshrined the historical monuments of Netzahualcoyotl himself. The entire system of terraces, aqueducts, towns, and the central agricultural ritual place gave Acolhuacan political, ritual, and administrative cohesion that it might not have acquired otherwise.

We cannot leave the subject of farming and agriculture without mentioning the special experimental botanical gardens and royal pleasances. During the reign of Motecuhzoma I (Ihuilcamina), an old garden that once belonged to "the ancestors" was discovered by the Aztecs in Huaxtepec, in the modern state of Morelos. It was decided that this warm, well-watered place in the shadow of Popocatepetl would be rebuilt, and Motecuhzoma commissioned an overseer named Pinotetl to inspect and restore the fountains, springs, streams, reservoirs, and the irrigation system. At the same time Motecuhzoma dispatched messengers to the tropical coast of Veracruz, with a request to the Lord of Cuetlaxtlan for plants of the vanilla orchid, for cacao trees, and other valuable species. He asked that these be carefully transported to Huaxtepec by native gardeners, who would be capable of replanting them in the proper season and tending them. The treasured plants were duly dug up with their roots encircled in earth, and then wrapped in fine textiles and dispatched to Huaxtepec. Before planting them, the gardeners assembled for a planting rite. They fasted for eight days and, drawing blood from their earlobes, they spattered the plants. Pinotetl supplied incense, paper, and rubber for

112 Wild plants and herbs were cultivated in botanical gardens for food and medicinal purposes. From Sahagún.

burnt offerings, and also many quail, whose blood was spattered over the plants and upon the earth. The success of these ceremonies was apparent before three years had passed, for the transplants began to blossom luxuriantly. The Cuetlaxtla gardeners were amazed to see that the plants could flourish away from their original home. Motecuhzoma took great joy in the successful experiment and gave thanks to the Lord of the Heavens and of the Day and the Night.

The botanical gardens at Huaxtepec, and another established by Netzahualcoyotl at Tetzcotzingo, combined practical considerations, ritual use, and pleasure. Dr Hernandez, the Spanish botanist who visited New Spain between 1570 and 1577 on commission by Philip II, wrote a botanical study of native plants and mentions valuable medicinal trees in the Huaxtepec garden.[4] Netzahualcoyotl's garden at Tetzcotzingo was similarly a source of therapeutic plants.[5]

Pleasure gardens were also a feature of Aztec ruling-class houses. The most detailed description of such a garden was written by Cortés in his second letter to Charles V in 1520. This garden was at Ixtapalapan, where Cortés and his staff were quartered on their way to Tenochtitlan in November 1519.

> Its Lord or Chief has some new houses which, though still unfinished, are as good as the best in Spain; I mean as large and as well constructed, not only in the stonework but also in the woodwork, and all arrangements for every kind of household service, all except the (carved) relief work and other rich details which are used in Spanish houses but are not found here. There are both upper and lower rooms and very refreshing gardens with many trees and sweet-scented flowers, (and) bathing places of fresh water, well constructed and having steps leading down to the bottom. He also has a large orchard near the house, overlooked by a high terrace with many beautiful corridors and rooms. Within the orchard is a great square pool of fresh water, very well constructed, with sides of handsome

masonry, around which runs a walk with a well-laid pavement of tiles, so wide that four persons can walk abreast on it, and 400 paces square, making in all 600 paces. On the other side of the promenade toward the wall of the garden are hedges of lattice work made of cane, behind which are all sorts of plantations of trees and aromatic herbs. The pool contains many fish and different kinds of waterfowl.[6]

The fruits of the earth: Aztec diet

Aztec farmers inherited a knowledge of plants that had developed over thousands of years. Many more varieties of plants were originally domesticated in the Americas than in the Old World, and many of the immensely varied foods and dishes in modern Mexican cuisine today originated long before the Spanish arrived. In ancient Mexico, the dog, turkey, and duck were the only domesticated livestock; sheep, goats, pigs, cattle, and horses were introduced by the Spanish. The basic diet of the Aztecs was therefore vegetarian, supplemented by game animals, fish, turkeys and other birds, and various kinds of insects. Maize was the universal staple, and the basis of the economy. It was prepared as it still is in rural Mexican villages, by cooking the kernels with lime, and then grinding the dough on a stone slab with a long cylindrical grinding-stone. The dough was patted into thin round tortillas, or wrapped in corn-husk *tamales* with a piece of meat or another flavoring; it was a very versatile foodstuff that could be used to create a great variety of dishes. The many species of beans were a principal source of protein. Aztec diet featured a diversity of chiles, with a wide range of flavors and hotness. Chiles are important sources of vitamins A and C, and also serve as condiments and stimulants. Squashes and calabashes (used as containers) were a third important crop. *Huautli* (amaranth) was a very high protein grain that was second in importance only to maize. (Amaranth lost most of its appeal in colonial times, but is now making a comeback.) The Aztecs raised several varieties of onions, as well as red tomatoes, *xictomatl*, and green tomatoes, *tomatl*. Sweet potatoes, *camotli*, were grown as an important root crop. The jícama was also important; this turnip-like root, often eaten raw with salt and chile, was also steamed or stewed with other ingredients in a variety of dishes. Peanuts and popcorn were other significant elements in the diet. The Aztecs chewed gum (chicle), bitumen, and other natural gums to clean their teeth. The public chewing of gum, especially with loud snapping noises, was considered offensive. Squash seeds and many fruits were cultivated, including the mamey, white and black zapotes, chirimoyas, guavas, and custard apples. Other important vegetable crops were nopal cactus paddles (tunafruit), and the maguey agave, whose fermented juice provided *pulque*, and whose leaves provided roofing, roots for roasting, and fiber for unlimited uses. Maguey, and cotton were the principal sources of fiber for weaving.

Among the more well-known spices were chenopodium, coriander and sage. Vanilla, extracted from the pods of a species of orchid, was among the most esteemed flavorings. Chocolate was prepared by grinding roasted cacao beans, sometimes with parched corn, and then mixing the powder with water. This was beaten with a wooden whisk until foamy and flavored with vanilla orchid pods or sweetened with honey. Like tea and coffee, this beverage is rich in caffeine and was much prized in ancient Mesoamerica. The beans are primarily grown in warm, moist tropics – the coastal regions of Tabasco and south Veracruz, and the Pacific slopes of Guatemala. The Codex Mendoza reveals that cacao was the primary tribute from certain regions, and was also used as a form of money. Cacao beans had been a highly valued item of long-distance trade since the time of Teotihuacan, and it is to trade that we shall now turn.

The markets of Tenochtitlan and Tlatelolco

All the principal towns in the Valley of Mexico had flourishing markets located close to the main temple at the center of each community. According to Diego Durán, a law made it obligatory to go to market and bring supplies to town, and he also notes that no one could sell anything on the way to the market, firstly under penalty of law and secondly for fear of angering the market god.

But it must not be imagined that secular and supernatural sanctions were the only stimuli to commerce, for markets were certainly more than mere centers for the exchange of material goods. As Durán says, "The markets are so appetizing and friendly that a great concourse of people come here," and he describes at length the powerful attraction exerted by markets upon the population. Markets were places for meeting people and gathering information and gossip: more than once Aztec women overheard rumors of impending rebellion or attack by neighboring peoples, particularly during the formative years of the empire; and indeed a whole profession of trader-spies was to develop (see below).

The principal market of the Aztec metropolis was at Tlatelolco. Another was located adjacent to the great ceremonial precinct of Tenochtitlan, where the Zócalo of Mexico City lies today. Elsewhere, small markets were scattered throughout the city to serve the various wards. Canoes supplied the markets via the system of main canals and lesser waterways, many of which continued to operate in Spanish colonial times. In this respect the design of the city responded to trade activities. It is probable that the small-scale markets of Tenochtitlan were held on a temporary basis by vendors from around the lakeshore or local peddlers selling goods obtained in the larger markets at Tlatelolco and Tenochtitlan.

The great market at Tlatelolco was described by the conquistador Anónimo as being thronged daily by some 25,000 people. A special market was held every fifth day, when the crowd would increase to about 40,000–50,000. This roughly tallies with Cortés' estimate of 60,000, probably made on an unusually crowded occasion since at the time the Spanish had only been in the city for four days. Not simply the size, but the organization and the variety of goods sold astonished the Spaniards. The scene is described in lively terms by Bernal Diaz:

> When we arrived at the great marketplace, called Tlatelolco, we were astounded at the number of people and the quantity of merchandise that it contained, and at the good order and control that was maintained, for we had never seen such a thing before. The chieftains who accompanied us acted as guides. Each kind of merchandise was kept by itself and had its fixed place marked out. Let us begin with dealers of gold, silver, and precious stones, feathers, mantles, and embroidered goods. Then there were other wares consisting of Indian slaves, both men and women; and I say that they bring as many of them to that great market for sale as the Portuguese bring Negroes from Guinea; and they brought them along tied to long poles, with collars around their necks so that they could not escape, and others they left free. Next there were other traders who sold great pieces of cloth and cotton, and articles of twisted thread, and there were *cacahuateros* who sold cacao. In this way one could see every sort of merchandise that is to be found in the whole of New Spain. There were those who sold cloths of hennequen and ropes and the sandals with which they are shod, which are made from the same plant, and sweet cooked roots, and other tubers which they get from this plant, all were kept in one part of the market in the place assigned to them. In another part there were skins of tigers and lions, of otters and jackals, deer and other animals and badgers and mountain cats, some tanned and others untanned, and other classes of merchandise.
>
> Let us go and speak of those who sold beans and sage and other vegetables and herbs in another part, and to those who sold fowls, cocks with wattles, rabbits, hares, deer, mallards, young dogs and other things of that sort in their part of the market, and let us also mention the fruiterers, and the women who sold cooked food, dough and tripe in their own part of the market; then every sort of pottery made in a thousand different forms from great water jars to little jugs, these also had a place to themselves; then those who sold honey and honey paste and other dainties like nut paste, and those who sold lumber, boards, cradles, beams, blocks and benches, each article by itself, and the vendors of ocote firewood, and other things of a similar nature. But why do I waste so many words in recounting what they sell in that great market? – for I shall never finish if I tell it all in detail. Paper, which in this country is called *amal*, and reeds scented with liquidambar, and full of tobacco, and yellow ointments and things of that sort are

sold by themselves, and much cochineal is sold under the arcades which are in that great market place, and there are many vendors of herbs and other sorts of trades. There are also buildings where three magistrates sit in judgment, and there are executive officers like Alguacils who inspect the merchandise. I am forgetting those who sell salt, and those who make the stone knives, and how they split them off the stone itself; and the fisherwomen and others who sell some small cakes made from a sort of ooze which they get out of the great lake, which curdles, and from this they made a bread having a flavour something like cheese. There are for sale axes of brass and copper and tin, and gourds and gaily painted jars made of wood. I could wish that I had finished telling of all the things which are sold there, but they are so numerous and of such different quality and the great market place with its surrounding arcades was so crowded with people, that one would not have been able to see and inquire about it all in two days.[7]

Cortés noted in his letter to Charles V that everything was sold by counts and measures but not by weight. Sahagún describes the ordering and administration of the marketplace by appointed directors drawn from the ranks of the principal merchants, the *pochteca* (see below). These officials pronounced harsh judgment upon those who cheated the customers. Anyone caught stealing would be sentenced to death, as would a person found to be selling stolen goods. The directors were also responsible for assigning each type of merchandise to a particular section of the plaza, and for the fixing of prices. Barter was at all times a means of effecting exchange. Cacao beans were widely used as money in the market, though they may not have had a standardized value from region to region within the Aztec empire. Other items were also used as currency, such as gold in transparent quills, tropical feathers, or small copper axes and pieces of tin.

Arts and crafts

The range of goods displayed in Aztec markets deeply impressed the Spaniards, both in terms of variety and artistry. These manufactures reflected a long tradition that reached back, in some cases, to the remotest periods of human occupation in the Americas.

Stoneworking

The working of stone had been a fundamental industry since the earliest times, for metallurgy only arrived in Mesoamerica around the 9th century AD and was principally used in the making of jewelry. Obsidian was always ranked as one of the most useful stones. This brittle volcanic glass occurs in gigantic natural deposits in several places in the central highlands, where mines were established in antiquity. During the early centuries AD, Teotihuacan had controlled the prime sources of this valuable material and traded obsidian as far south as Guatemala. Using technologies

Aztec carving

113–116 TOP Mother-of-pearl fish, recovered from the Great Pyramid. ABOVE Parts of an obsidian wand, carved as a rattlesnake, also found at the Great Pyramid. RIGHT Turtle man: one of the many Aztec sculptures devoted to natural species and composite creatures. BELOW Aztec carving of a coyote.

Opposite:
117,118 Two exceptionally fine examples of mosaic work. ABOVE A ritual mask with turquoise inlay crafted by Aztec or Mixtec artisans, thought to have been included in the first shipment of gifts and trophies sent by Cortés to Europe. BELOW Double-headed dragon-like creatures were symbols of the sky in Mesoamerica, and this example from Tenochtitlan was probably worn as a badge of royal or priestly office.

that were essentially developed in Upper Paleolithic times, a multiplicity of cutting and puncturing implements were made from obsidian for specialized purposes. Razor-like blades were flaked off larger blanks of the stone in a sophisticated "unwrapping" process; single-edged and double-edged knives were also made, as were scrapers, v-shaped gougers, dart-points of various dimensions, and heavy striking blades. The refinement achieved in working this natural glass is evident from objects such as polished obsidian mirrors, earspools as delicate and thin as if machined with precision instruments, and even whole vessels such as the famous obsidian monkey-vase now held in the National Museum of Anthropology. Yet the making of such admirable objects, and others of crystal, amethyst, jade, and turquoise, depended on knowledge of how to employ hard stones against softer ones, how to use sand and pumice-powder as an abrasive for cutting with cords or in polishing surfaces, how to use simple hand-held pump-drills, and how to apply the right pressure and where to strike a stone in knapping operations. In Mesoamerica the techniques and skills of stone technology reached their fullest flowering. Other aspects of stonework are seen in the extraordinary mosaic inlaid masks held in the Museum of Mankind in London. These ritual objects are completely covered with a delicate mosaic of the finest craftsmanship, including turquoise, jet, pyrites and several colored shells. It is widely assumed that such masterpieces were manufactured by Mixtec craftsmen residing in Tenochtitlan. The custom of bringing foreign artisans to reside in special sections of cities had its origins in Teotihuacan.

At the other end of the stoneworking scale, Aztec craftsmen were employed by the state to make colossal basalt sculptures. Such figures as the great Coatlicue and the disk of Coyolxauhqui, and the huge dragon-heads that formed balustrade-ends in pyramid stairways, are examples of the Aztec genius for carving in high relief; although sculptures such as the Coatlicue or the Stone of Tizoc were conceived and meant to be viewed as three-dimensional objects, one always senses the weight of the monolith. Aztec sculptors rarely ventured into the realm of "liberating" figures from the block of stone as did the sculptors of Mediterranean antiquity, although works such as the seated Xochipilli or the standing masked Ehecatl show that by the end of the 15th and the beginning of the 16th centuries, master sculptors were increasingly venturing in that direction. The technologies of quarrying, transporting, and working large monoliths were already well developed as far back as Olmec times, c.900 BC, and had reached new levels of achievement in Teotihuacan (during the early centuries AD) where sculptural monuments weighing up to 40 tons were brought from distant quarries (presumably using log rollers) to be set up in the ceremonial center. At Toltec Tula, the "Atlantean" warriors on top of the principal pyramid were assembled in a system of tenoned drums. The Aztecs acquired the tradition of monumental stone carving first from Atzcapotzalco, and later from the Huaxtecs of the Gulf

119 Stone sculptures of standard-bearers, found reclining at the foot of the Great Temple stairway.

120,121 The status of individuals was often reflected by their attire. Peasants went barefoot and dressed in simple cloaks and loincloths (LEFT), while the more important members of society wore sandals and richly decorated clothes (RIGHT).

Coast. Their ability to develop their own expressive style is evident when we compare the primitive sculptural forms and Itzcoatl's pyramid, dating to about 1430, with monuments made between the 1450s and early 16th century.

Basket-making

This was another ancient manufacturing art inherited by the Aztecs. Like methods of making stone tools, basketry had been a feature of hunting-and-gathering cultures. The extensive reedbeds of the highland lakes provided an inexhaustible source of prime material, but other fibers were woven from palmleaf, cane slats, various cacti, and especially from the long broad leaves of the maguey agave. At the market in Tenochtitlan, baskets of many sizes and shapes were used and sold, for carrying produce, storing grains, and as special containers designed for different foods. Fine baskets of very tight weave were intended for personal use, holding valuables such as jewelry or family keepsakes. Larger square or rectangular baskets with lids were used as chests for clothing. Closely related to the basketmakers were the weavers of reed mats – *petlatl* – and the makers of reed seats. In ancient Mexico, furniture was limited to stools, litters, and low small tables. Mats, like Japanese tatami, were an essential item in both royal and humble households where activities took place on or close to the floor. The mat was an old symbol of rulership and one of the names for the *tlatoani* was "he who is seated upon the mat." *Petlatls* are still produced, especially in the Toluca Valley, but they are fast becoming a residual art of what was once a major industry producing mats both coarse and fine for all levels of society.

The art of featherworking

122–124 ABOVE A featherworker dyes and glues feathers; from Sahagún. LEFT Ceremonial shield with feather decoration and gold trim, sent to Europe by Cortés. The coyote in the center represents the Aztec god of fire. BELOW In this page from the Codex Mendoza, high-ranking military officers parade in full ceremonial regalia, carrying elaborate feather shields and banners.

Textiles

The beginnings of the textile arts are unclear in Mesoamerica, because climatic conditions here rarely permit the survival of cloth and clothing. This is unlike the coast of Peru, where splendid textiles have been preserved in the desert environment. Spanish descriptions, pictorial manuscripts, and details of finely sculpted figures show the intricacy and variety of cloth made throughout the empire. Each region had its distinctive designs, woven, embroidered, dyed or painted on the basic male and female garments, for clothing was highly emblematic of place as well as social status and function. At Tenochtitlan and Tetzcoco, sumptuary laws were enforced to regulate the wearing of clothes according to social and official position. Most commonly, cloth was made of maguey or henequen fiber for capes, loincloths, skirts, and *huipiles* (mantles worn by women). This was a stiff and uncomfortable material, but the techniques for weaving such fiber were capable of producing highly flexible and delicate cloth. Cotton had long been cultivated in Mesoamerica, and was raised in warm lowland Morelos since the time of Teotihuacan. Even at the highest levels of Aztec society, men and women wore the same styles of garments as the lower orders – only the materials used and the fineness of weave and ornamentation varied. There was no tradition of tailoring clothes to fit the limbs and body. Pictorial and sculptural sources show that textiles were predominantly decorated with geometric designs, but some were embroidered with patterns reflecting local flora and fauna. Dyes were made from mineral sources such as blue clay and yellow ocher, and vegetal dyes were derived from a multitude of plants. Red color was obtained from cochineal insects which were raised in nopal cactus groves, and violet was obtained by dyeing skeins of cotton thread with a secretion from coastal mollusks.

Feather garments were a specialty of weavers called *amanteca*, whose brilliant products were reserved for the nobility and the highest-ranking officials. Feathers for these most prized garments were gathered by professional hunters who netted birds in the tropical forests, but colorful plumage could also be obtained from birds raised in captivity. The art of feather-working was old in Mesoamerica and consists of tying the stems of feathers into the fabric during weaving. Several Aztec ceremonial shields have survived which demonstrate the bold effects achieved by these artisans, who were not only superb technicians but also unsurpassed colorists and designers. The Spaniards speak of superb featherwork cloaks and elegant *huipiles*, as well as sumptuously ornamented loincloths.

Ceramics

One of the most extensive sections of the Tlatelolco market was assigned to the pottery-sellers. Pottery began in ancient Mexico with the appearance of village agricultural life, and like others before them the Aztecs had their own styles of ceramics. The potter's wheel was not used in the Americas

Ceramics

125–127 ABOVE Highly prized ceramic cup from Cholollan, with polychrome depiction of a feline. LEFT A utilitarian vessel scored for grating tomatoes and peppers. BELOW An incense-burner with a deity figure, from an offering in the Great Pyramid of Tenochtitlan.

before it was introduced by the Spaniards, so vessels and figures were made by hand. Coiling strips of clay and then scraping and paddling to thin down the walls, joining slats of clay, or assembling pieces from molded sections were well-known ways of manufacture. Neither the Aztecs nor their predecessors had developed the technology of vitreous glazes, or of high-fired stoneware and porcelain. Rather, the ancient American traditions were of low-fire earthenware. Yet, as with stoneworking, relatively simple methods produced some of the most remarkable, varied, and beautiful ceramic arts in the world. In the 15th century Aztec pottery was characteristically a thin-walled, finely-proportioned, cream-colored or red-slipped ware, decorated with fine-line geometric designs that have the quality of calligraphy and often exhibit fine draughtsmanship. By the early 16th century, Aztec potters were beginning to favor more naturalistic motifs, depicting flowers, fish and other animals in combination with fine-line designs. Coarser utilitarian vessels were made in a variety of specialized shapes and sizes for cooking, including large flat clay griddles for baking the indispensable tortillas. The most prized ceramics, such as those used in Motecuhzoma's palace, were made in the environs of Cholollan. This was a polychrome earthenware, painted with mineral-colored slips and burnished when "leather-hard" before firing. The lustrous, warm surfaces were covered with designs related to those seen in manuscript illuminations, in another aspect of what has been called the Mixteca-Puebla "international style." Aztec potters also made special wares for their temples, sometimes using techniques and shapes that followed earlier ceramic traditions. A famous pair of blue Tlaloc vases, found in a Great Pyramid offering-cyst, was painted in a fresco medium that recalls the brilliant frescoed pottery of Teotihuacan. This was almost certainly an intentional "quoting" of the ritual arts of that ruined city. Also recovered from the Great Pyramid were a pair of cylindrical vessels carved, while still moist, with detailed reliefs of Aztec deities. These forms also recall an antique tradition combining Classic Maya and Teotihuacan styles and point again to a deliberate historicizing intention. Other forms of ritual ceramics, such as the large standing incense-burners with attached figures of deities, ultimately derive from a long-lasting tradition of Classic Maya origin. These were fashioned in mold-made forms and handbuilt techniques, and were brilliantly painted with colors that illustrate the spectacular costumes worn by Aztec ritual performers. Such items were designed to be seen at a distance in architectural settings. They would not have reached the marketplace, for they were commissioned especially by temple organizations and patrons.

Jewelry and metallurgy

The golden ornaments worn by Aztec officials and nobles were made by Mixtec craftsmen working in Tenochtitlan. The tradition they brought with them had been developing in their Oaxacan homeland since about

128 A tiny silver, belled pendant with the mask of Xipe, found in an obsidian funerary vessel in the Great Pyramid. This was undoubtedly an item of personal jewelry.

the 10th century AD. The famous discovery of a royal Mixtec burial in Monte Albán tomb 38 revealed to the modern world the extraordinary craftsmanship of the Mixtecs, to be seen in rings and cast pendants, ear-danglers and necklaces. The Aztecs coveted this artistry and hence their own jewelry strongly reflected the tradition of Mixtec goldworking. But it must be remembered that the Mixtecs themselves acquired this knowledge from lands farther south. Beginning around 2000 BC, the sophisticated technique of metallurgy had slowly diffused northward from its place of origin in the Andes of South America, eventually reaching Panama and Costa Rica by overland routes and coastal trade. In Mexico the earliest and most developed metalworking centers were on the Pacific side – amongst the Mixtecs, and also at sites in Guerrero and Michoacán. At Zihuatanejo on the Guerrero coast, pieces of slag were archaeologically recovered with hundreds of metal objects, indicating a flourishing smelting operation between AD 900 and 1100. The Tarascan peoples of Michoacán developed a copper-working industry that included such trade items as cast bells for wear on dance costumes, tweezers, needles, copper axes, and small figurines. The manufacture of bronze was also known. Yet the Mixtecs of Oaxaca remained the most celebrated artisans, and it was through them that the art of jewelry was brought to Tenochtitlan. Gold was panned and collected as nuggets from riverbeds, and smelted in furnaces heated by men blowing through tubes onto charcoal embers. Casting was accomplished by the lost-wax method, and methods evolved in South America were used for gilding copper, and mixing copper and gold to produce an alloy known as tumbaga. Jewelers working at Tenochtitlan combined cast and filigree goldwork with other materials such as crystal, turquoise, and jade. Even though most Aztec works were lost in Spanish melting-pots after the Conquest, the few pieces that survive in museums show the trend towards achieving a new and distinctive style, and a quality of workmanship that matches the finest goldwork from elsewhere in the ancient Americas.

These were but some of the many professions and crafts practiced in Aztec cities. The traders and artists contributed not only to the economic and aesthetic affairs of the community but also to the richly developed religious life and pageantry of the metropolitan centers. For each foreign group brought new customs and new deities that were integrated in the cycle of festivals.

Long-distance traders

Not all the merchandise available in markets was produced locally: much of it came from neighboring highland basins, from the most distant confines of the empire, or even from exotic lands beyond. Most of these items were brought by long-distance merchants known as *pochteca*. The *pochteca* handled long-distance trade on behalf of the Aztec nobility, as well as acting as independent traders in their own right. The importance of the *pochteca* in the expansionist policies of the Aztec state, their role within the religious system, their association with the nobility, and their journeys to distant "ports of trade" form a unique and fascinating chapter in the story of the Aztec economy.[8]

The difference between long-distance *pochteca* trade and the predominantly local character of regular market trade is reflected in the fact that regular markets continued to exist throughout the colonial period and up to the present, whereas long-distance trade disappeared within about five years of the Spanish Conquest. This disappearance was due to the fact that the trade network dealt primarily in the importing of luxury items such as the feathers of tropical birds, greenstones, and exotic animal hides, which had high value for the Aztecs but not for the Spaniards.

According to the early colonial historian Alonso de Zorita, the *pochteca* enjoyed a privileged position with the nobility, as they paid tribute to the rulers in the form of merchandise but were not obliged to render personal services; he also writes that theirs was an occupation that could only be inherited.[9] It is probable that the *pochteca* were organized as a *calpultin* kin unit, living on the land owned by their lineage. There were seven merchant wards in Tlatelolco-Tenochtitlan, of which the most famous was named Pochtlan. The other wards with important long-distance trading communities were Tepetitlan, Tzonmolco, Atlauhco, Amachtlan, and Itztotolco. Significantly, these names appear widely dispersed in regions far beyond the Valley of Mexico, and it has been suggested that some of these sites may have been trading centers as far back as Toltec times. Other towns in the Valley of Mexico with notable trading communities were Tetzcoco, Atzcapotzalco, Huitzilopochco, Huexotla, Cuauhtitlan, Coatlinchan, Chalco, Otumba, Xochimilco, and Mixcoac.

The term *pochotl*, from which *pochteca* and Pochtlan derive, was the name for the Bombax ceiba, the towering, sheltering tree of the tropical forests, which was traditionally regarded as a sacred "tree of life." In a figurative sense, *pochotl* means father, mother, governor, chief, or protector. This meaning of the ancient title is important because it suggests that *pochteca* occupied very high positions in Mesoamerican societies before the Aztecs, as we shall see.

The origins of long-distance trading in Tlatelolco and Tenochtitlan probably date to the 1380s. According to Sahagún, the first two merchants sold only red arara macaw feathers and blue and scarlet parrot feathers. But in the early 15th century, cotton garments began to appear, as well as quetzal feathers (not yet the large ones), turquoise, and green chalchihuite stones. By the 1470s the list of imports had grown to include luxury garments, a wider variety of precious feathers, stone jewelry, and cacao. There was a close association between rulers and merchants that continued after the last of the independent Tlatelolcan rulers and the absorption of Tlatelolco into Tenochtitlan (Chapter 6).

There were four types of *pochteca*, each with specific duties and obligations. The highest officials were referred to as *pochtecatlatoque*, commanders of the *pochteca*. These august personages were appointed by the ruler, selected from the oldest, most prestigious of *pochteca*. They were seasoned travelers who now stayed at home to serve in an administrative capacity, advising and admonishing younger traders, and also commissioning outgoing trading groups to exchange goods in the distant centers of trade. Upon the return of the expedition, the gains were shared by both parties. Another duty of these elder merchants was to sit in judgment on miscreant *pochteca* and to deliver the appropriate sentences; the merchants' courts were held separately from those of the state, and no state authorities had the right to intervene. These principal merchant rulers were also assigned the important task of administering the marketplace.

The second group of *pochteca* comprised the slave traders, known as *tlaltlani*, "bather of slaves." This title referred to the ritual bathing of slaves which was required before their use as sacrificial victims. According to Sahagún the slave traders were the richest merchants, and they were also accorded special privileges by the rulers. Slave traders were considered

129 Travel in the Aztec empire was mainly by foot or canoe; here a deity impersonator is borne on a maize-decorated litter. From the Codex Magliabechiano.

particularly devout and played a central role in the annual Panquetzalitzli festival devoted to the deified hero, Huitzilopochtli (see below).

Certain merchants were specially commissioned by the rulers to carry out their personal trade. These were the *tencunenenque*, "royal travelers, passengers." They also served on occasion as tribute-collectors. These royal administrative trade officials may have constituted a special category among *pochteca*, but it is more likely that they were simply particularly able or trustworthy *oztomeca* "vanguard merchants," who carried out the bulk of long-distance trade.

The fourth group were the *naualoztomeca*, or "disguised merchants," trader-spies whose development as a special type of merchant at the service of the state forms a most interesting theme in Aztec trading. *Naualoztomeca* began as ordinary travelers who were obliged to disguise themselves as natives when entering enemy territories in search of rare goods:

> When they entered land under which they were at war, and went among people who were far distant, they became like their enemies in their garments, their hair-dress, their speech, that they might mimic the natives.
>
> And if they came to an evil pass, if they were discovered, then they were slain in ambush and served up with chili sauce. But if any – even one, even two – escaped alive, such a one informed Motecuhzoma.[10]

The gossip of the marketplaces and the network of commercial contacts yielded vital information to the trader-spies. As the empire evolved during the 15th century, the *naualoztomeca* were regularly employed as spies by the state before the initiation of hostilities.

By the reign of Ahuizotl (1486–1502), merchants had attained particular prominence in the Aztec hierarchy. Following their remarkable actions in the conquest of the province of Soconusco, the *pochteca* were publicly acclaimed by the ruler in Tenochtitlan and were awarded special capes and breechcloths (although these items might be worn only on special occasions, since it was the privilege of the nobility always to wear fine capes). The *tlatoani* of Tenochtitlan also gave certain traders the privilege of handling his personal trade. The *pochteca* thus became increasingly involved in the work of the imperial state; new categories of *pochteca* developed; and the *pochteca* in general were brought into close commercial association with the military aristocracy.

Trading centers

By the time of the Spanish Conquest, the *pochteca* were trading almost exclusively in regions beyond the limits of the Aztec empire. Most of what is presently known about this trade concerns the southern Gulf of Mexico region, but it is also probable that Aztec merchants were operating to the northwest, in the ancient mining districts of Hidalgo and Queretaro, and even further north, in Zacatecas and Durango. To the south, the trade routes led down from the central plateau to Tochtepec, where the trail forked. One branch continued into Oaxaca, the Isthmus of Tehuantepec, and Soconusco. The other branch led to the Gulf Coast at Coatzacoalco. Inland from Coatzacoalco was the powerful Nahuatl town of Cimatan, strategically located on the Grijalva river – a major trade route leading into the sierra of Chiapas, which was a source of amber. To the east of Cimatan lay the populous, tropical region known as the Chontalapa, the location of some 25 towns where the Aztec traders kept warehouses and representatives. Just beyond lay Potonchán, above the confluence of the Grijalva and Usumacinta rivers. The Usumacinta River had been a trade artery since Classic Maya times, and gave Potonchán ready communication with the inland forest region known as Acalán and, through a network of trails and waterways, into the dense forests of the Petén in Guatemala and the trading center called Nito on the Gulf of Honduras. However, Potonchán was not frequented by Aztec *pochteca*, for it was controlled by powerful Maya traders. On the other hand, the trading center of Xicallanco, located at the outlet of the Laguna de Términos, was almost certainly a headquarters for Aztec *pochteca*. The rulers of Xicallanco spoke Nahuatl, although the population was Chontal Maya, so it is quite probable that Aztec traders ruled this important town. In this respect they followed the Maya tradition in which traders and rulers were almost one and the same.

Both Potonchán and Xicallanco enjoyed access by trail and canoe to the forests of Acalán in Guatemala and across to the Gulf of Honduras. Traders from Acalán had access to the resources of the Petén forests, and occupied a ward in Nito on the Honduran Gulf. The principal trading center of Acalán was Itzamkanac on the Candelaria River. This thriving center was visited by Cortés on his Honduras march of 1523. Five years later a lieutenant under the command of Francisco de Montejo, the conqueror of Yucatan, arrived at Acalán and reported that although there were some 500 limestone and stucco buildings, the former prosperity had fallen away. This was of course due to the collapse of the *pochteca* system. Itzamkanac was also probably an outlet for trade from the rich cacao-producing valleys of the Sarstoon, Polochic, and Motagua rivers of Belize.

The principal commodities exported by *pochteca* from Tenochtitlan, Tlatelolco, Tetzcoco, and other highland cities were manufactured sumptuary items made from imported raw materials or materials acquired as tribute. These commodities were supplied to the *pochteca* by the nobility or by the *pochteca* network itself. Other trade wares included obsidian, copper bells and ornaments, needles, obsidian ornaments, combs, red ocher, herbs, cochineal, alum, and rabbit-fur skins. Many such items were supplied by commoners, who had purchased them in the marketplaces of the metropolis. Finally, slaves were exported to Cimatan and the Acalán regions, to meet the need for rowers in these aquatic environments, and perhaps to act as laborers in the cacao groves, since cacao is a crop requiring year-round care. In return for these commodities the *pochteca* received feathers of various kinds, valuable stones, animal skins, cacao, gold and related luxury goods. Though cacao was carried by the *pochteca* en route to the trading centers, once there exchanges were performed in kind. Cacao probably served to purchase supplies along the way.

The southern centers of trade do not seem to have had open markets, for transactions took place between *pochteca*, their local representatives, and the native rulers of the region. In the highlands, however, thriving traders' markets existed at Coixtlahuaca, Tochtepec, and Tepeaca, suggesting that the mutually exclusive aspects of long-distance and marketplace trade that were so marked at the time of the Spanish Conquest may not always have applied in every region.

Religious functions of the pochteca
Traders played a central role in the religious life of Tenochtitlan, especially during the annual Panquetzaliztli festival dedicated to the patron deity, Huitzilopochtli.[11] This was celebrated on the fifteenth *veintena* of the *tonalpohualli* cycle. The priesthood began preparing for this most significant festival 40 days in advance, and singing and dancing began on the second day of the *veintena*. Long before this, young traders seeking professional status had begun preparations with a visit to the Atzcapotzalco slave-market, to purchase four slaves to be sacrificed during the culminating ceremonies of the festival. Time and effort were also spent accumulating expensive gifts for the guests – especially for the other merchants and nobles who would be invited to attend a huge banquet. Soon thereafter the young prospective traders made a long ceremonial trip to Tochtepec, where they personally extended invitations to the Aztec merchant elders –

the *pochtecatlatoque* – residing in that town. On the ninth day before the festival the four slaves were ritually bathed with sacred water from the springs at Huitzilopochco and ceremonially dressed. On the eve of the festival the slaves were given a drink of cacao, "to comfort them," and were led by the young initiate traders in a procession to the ward temple in Pochtlan, where ceremonies were conducted in honor of Yacatecuhtli, the traders' patron deity.

Meanwhile, the image of Paynal (or Painalton) had begun a ceremonial circuit of Tenochtitlan-Tlatelolco:

> Paynal was "the delegate," "the substitute," "the deputy;" because he represented Huitzilopochtli when there was a procession. He was named Paynal because he pressed and urged them ahead. And the people followed [the impersonator], jostling, howling, roaring. They made the dust rise, they made the ground to smoke. Like people possessed, they stamped upon the earth. And one man carried the image in his arms.[12]

In touring the city, Paynal was ritually "purifying" the area within the circuit boundaries, rendering it sacred and marking off the crucial, most essentially Aztec space in the empire. On completion of Paynal's circuit the procession arrived before the temple of Huitzilopochtli on the summit of the Great Pyramid. On the twentieth and final day the four slaves were brought to this building and were led around four times, thus duplicating on a smaller scale the symbolism of the larger processional circuit. A vast crowd had now assembled in the plaza and the Aztec ruler himself arrived to witness the conclusion of the festival. First there came many sacrifices of prisoners captured by warriors on conquest campaigns, and finally, as dusk approached, Paynal personally sacrificed the four slaves and cast their bodies down the steps of the pyramid. The young traders, now officially initiated, stored their ceremonial attire in boxes which were to be kept until the end of their lives and would be cremated with them at death. Parts of the body of one of the slaves were taken home to be cooked and ritually eaten with maize and salt as part of a sacramental offering. A great banquet followed, with lavish distribution of gifts to the guests.

A similar ceremony was held by traders of the old city of Chololan during the festival of the patron deity of that city, Quetzalcoatl. Comparison of events here with those at Tenochtitlan suggest that the traders' ritual had a very old history in Mesoamerica, and that at Tenochtitlan it was grafted onto the festivals of Huitzilopochtli. Throughout the empire traders were admitted to office during the special festival celebrating a particular city's patron deity. This was another instance of Aztec syncretism, in which the practices and beliefs of different ethnic groups were integrated into a larger ceremonial system.

It appears, then, that the *pochteca* were far from being a rising mercantile middle class in the Aztec empire. Rather, they formed an ancient institution, coexisting with the new military aristocracy of Aztec cities.

11 · Priests, Warriors, and Kings

The priests: servants of the gods

When the Spanish expedition first came to Tenochtitlan and Cortés and his party were shown the sacred precinct, they were shocked by the sinister appearance of the Aztec priests. Bernal Diaz del Castillo writes:

> They wore black cloaks like cassocks and long gowns reaching to their feet. Some had hoods like those worn by canons, and others had smaller hoods like those of Dominicans, and they wore their hair very long, right down to the waist, and some had it even reaching down to the ankles. Their hair was covered with blood, and so matted together that it could not be separated, and their ears were cut to pieces by way of penance. They stank like sulphur and they had another bad smell like carrion. They were the sons of chiefs and abstained from women. They fasted on certain days and what I saw them eat was the pith of seeds. The nails on their fingers were very long, and we heard it said that these priests were very pious and led good lives.[1]

What Bernal Diaz described were priests engaged in special duties, requiring long penances and behavior "contrary" to normal life, in the course of service to the deities. Behind these bizarre figures there lay an organization that was heir to a tradition of great complexity and sophistication, for religion was a unifying and pervasive force in all manifestations of Aztec life. From birth to death the stages of a person's development were marked by ceremonial activity. Divination charted the course of one's life just as it determined the most auspicious time for the planting of crops. A multitude of deities and cults were honored in the great cycle of public festivals, which were attended by thousands of people and patronized by different professional groups, by the *calputin*, and by other social divisions. The concept of sacrifice was deeply tied to the practice of war, and the *tlatoani* himself was required to make blood offerings upon pyramids and mountaintop shrines. The priesthood that supervised the religious establishment and all its activities also directed Aztec intellectual and artistic life. They governed the schools, they managed the cults, and coordinated and choreographed the public rites and performances.[2]

At the top of the priestly hierarchy was the *tlatoani*, for in Aztec society religion and state could not be separated. The *tlatoani* of Tenochtitlan

130 Priestly duties included burning incense and playing the drums. From the Codex Mendoza.

was invested with a certain measure of divine power at the time of coronation. Although he was not considered a god, his priestly responsibilities included presiding over the annual rites for rain on Mt Tlaloc, and he also made regular appearances in all the most crucial festivals held in the annual cycle. The maintenance and renewal of society was an integral aspect of the ruler's larger responsibility for the annual rain and the renewal of nature. His titles included *yiollo alteptl*, "the heart of the city," and *inan, ita altepetl*, "the mother, the father of the city." He was obliged to perform penances and retreats in caves, and to observe the stars for favorable or inauspicious signs. Various taboos surrounded the *tlatoani*: he was required to eat alone, no one could look him in the eye, and his spiritual power was periodically renewed by means of special sacrificial ceremonies.

As chief priest the *tlatoani* headed a vast organization that reflected the pyramidal, tiered structure of Aztec society. Although priests could come from any social class, even the poorest levels, the highest priests were drawn from the ranks of the *pipiltin* – the hereditary nobility. Immediately under the ruler were two supreme priests whose titles and dual functions reflect a pre-Aztec system of organization. The *Quetzalcoatl totec tlamacazqui* and *Quetzalcoatl tlaloc tlamacazqui* were respectively associated with the cults of Huitzilopochtli and Tlaloc. Quetzalcoatl was an ancient title, and totec was similarly an old cult name from a time before the Aztecs in the Valley of Mexico. Tlamacazqui was simply the term for priest. The second priest's title included the name Tlaloc and was clearly connected to the long and prominent history of that deity in Mesoamerica. The dual high priesthood may find its roots in an old moiety type of social division, in which the cult responsibilities alternated according to the dry and rainy seasons.

The next priestly rank was the *Mexicatl Teohuatzin*, described as a general commander and overseer of ritual, and the superintendent of the *calmecac* school. He was assisted by the *Huitznahua Teohuatzin* and *Tecpan Teohuatzin*, who governed the rest of the priestly orders. The latter were in charge of particular temples and attending to the communal festivals and worship pertaining to the cults of their temple deity. They had important duties in administering the temple lands, *teopantlalli*. They oversaw the selection of deity-impersonators who wore the sacred masks and other regalia in public performances and processions, and they might also on occasion wear the regalia themselves. Certain priests were also warriors, and their duties included carrying the effigies of deities in the vanguard of Aztec armies during campaigns. The warrior-priests also captured enemies, and made the appropriate sacrifices in the field. Women fulfilled priestly duties, especially in connection with the numerous earth-mother cults, and their responsibilities included the instruction of young girls and women in the service and impersonation of these deities and the various maize goddesses.

All such priestly officials were assisted by students from the *calmecac* and by postulants to the priesthood. In the *calmecac*, postulants lived under strict supervision. Meditation and the learning of prayers were accompanied by periods of fasting. Long vigils were kept and marked by periodic offerings and purifying baths; food was usually taken in meager amounts at midday and midnight. Special occasions demanded auto-sacrifice; blood would be drawn by pricking the legs and arms with maguey spines, by cutting the earlobes with obsidian blades, or by running a cord through the tongue or the penis.

As in the monastic orders of Europe, the Aztec priesthood had a place for every kind of talent and interest. Some priests were codex painters and scribes. Specialized knowledge included the reading and interpretation of almanacs in connection with calendrical calculations and the observation of the night sky and the sun's travels from north to south and back again during the course of the year. The progression of the sunrise each day along the eastern horizon was the index to naming the right day for festivals and to attuning the vast apparatus of religious life in Aztec cities to the regular movements of the heavenly bodies. Certain priests engaged in prophesies and the interpretation of visions: these could be induced by psychotropic plants – jimson weed, *Psilocybe* mushrooms, or peyote cactus buttons. Perhaps the most highly esteemed priests were the teachers called *tlamatini*, a term which may be translated as "wise man." Bernardino de Sahagún's informant speaks eloquently of these individuals:

131 Warriors were graded according to the number of captives they took, and each new rank entitled the warrior to wear a more elaborate costume; the highest ranking officers are at the bottom. From the Codex Mendoza.

The wise man [is] exemplary. He possesses writings; he owns books. [He is] the tradition, the road; the leader of men, a mover, a companion, a bearer of responsibility, a guide.

The good wise man [is] a physician, a person of trust, a counsellor; an instructor worthy of confidence, deserving of credibility, deserving of faith; a teacher ... He lights the world for one; he knows of the land of the dead; he is dignified, unreviled.[3]

The warriors

As in the case of the priesthood, the *tlatoani* stood at the top of the military hierarchy. He was the commander-in-chief of the army, and his prowess as a warrior was of critical importance to the Aztec state. His first military task was to conduct a campaign as part of the coronation procedure – a performance regarded as ritually symbolic and a pragmatic demonstration of his abilities. The *tlatoani* was closely advised by the *cihuacoatl*, "Woman serpent;" this office was occupied by Tlacaelel from the reign of Itzcoatl and the Atzcapotzalco war in the 1420s to the reign of Ahuizotl in the 1480s. As adviser to five *tlatoanis*, Tlacaelel must be regarded as one of the most influential thinkers and men of action that shaped the expansion of the Aztec empire.

The structure of the Aztec military hierarchy has been outlined by Ross Hassig.[4] A supreme council of four noblemen governed the army, fulfilling a function roughly analogous to that of a general staff. These high officials were the *tlacochcalcatl*, the *tlaccatecatl*, the *etzhuanhuanco*, and the *tillancalqui*. There is evidence to suggest that the *tlaccatecatl* and *tlacochcalcatl* were titles in use long before the Aztecs and that, like the titles of the two chief priests, they reflect an older system of social organization. At Tenochtitlan the members of the council of four were all brothers or close relatives of the *tlatoani*. One would be heir apparent, usually the *tlaccatecatl*. The Codex Mendoza depicts these officials in regalia of state. The next levels of office were held by warriors either from the nobility or commoners, for although sons of the nobles tended to be more successful in the military by virtue of their education and general privileges, men from the lowest classes could attain all but the highest positions.

The two highest military societies or orders were the *otontin* "otomies" and the *cuauhchique*, "shorn ones." Only the most daring battlefield veterans could be admitted, for it was required to have taken many captives and to have performed at least 20 deeds of exceptional bravery. The highest military commanders such as the *tlaccatecatl* and *tlacochcalcatl* were members of these two orders. All the soldiers in these societies (such as the eagle- and jaguar warriors) were entitled to wear attire appropriate to their rank. Headgear, jewelry, cloaks, and other accessories and emblems were strictly prescribed, and were personally handed to the warriors during special ceremonies held for that purpose, sometimes by the *tlatoani* himself. The war suits given to commoners were of animal skins, while those of the nobility were woven with feathers. The Codex Mendoza depicts warriors capturing one, two, three, and four enemies, and the special attire that was awarded in each case (ill. 131). Even commoners achieving these feats were given special privileges, such as the right to wear cotton clothing and sandals in the royal palaces, to drink pulque in public, to keep concubines, and to dine in the palace. On ritual occasions the warriors ate human flesh taken from the arms or thighs of their sacrificed captives. The great mass of common warriors wore body paint for identification and maguey cloth mantles, a breechcloth, and no sandals.

Military training for young boys began during their schooling. Martial exercises were actually conducted on the premises of the eagle- and jaguar-warriors' meeting-houses, where youths assembled for instruction on the handling of arms, basic drill and maneuvers, and on discipline, military hierarchy, history, and battlefield lore. Although early Spanish colonial histories speak of military houses in the royal palace, archaeological evidence indicates that the *cuauhcalli*, "eagle house," was located in the main ceremonial center. Platform bases with eagle sculptures on the moldings gave access to rooms surrounding two inner patios. Impressive life-size ceramic sculptures of eagle warriors were recovered from this setting, and a low bench running around the wall of one of the inner patios was found to be sculpted in low relief with processions of warriors converging on a sacrificial implement. The motif and style of this processional scene was "quoted" directly from the art of Toltec and late Maya centers. The intention was to evoke the memory of those "ancestral" warrior-nations. The students gradually became adept in managing the obsidian-bladed clubs, stabbing javelins, and round shields with protective leather fringes. Atlatl or spear-throwing also demanded practice: this ancient implement was grooved to hold a dart, and its length gave additional power and accuracy to the throw. While training in the patios of the warriors' meeting-houses, the youths had ample opportunity to see the colorful and impressive regalia of their seniors, and to hear of their battle-exploits. The novices' first experience of campaigning was to carry loads for the warriors. There was much vying by the youths' families to find a warrior of the best possible qualifications for their boy to serve.

There was no standing army as exists in the modern world. Rather, troops were called up for specific campaigns. The organization of the army was in units from local *calpultin*, or towns. In Tenochtitlan, each *calpultin* was required to contribute 400 men. Each unit marched under its own standards and was commanded by its own community leaders. There were probably several subdivisions of 200 to 100 men, much like platoons or squads. The large basic unit of the Aztec army consisted of 8,000 men, roughly like a battalion. Long distance expeditions might involve as many as 25 units, equaling 200,000 warriors, plus porters to carry supplies and equipment. The various divisions were identified by banners or standards strapped on the back of a bearer, who was usually positioned in the middle of a unit. As in modern armies, these standards were objects of great pride to the group, and were as strongly defended as they were aggressively sought by the enemy as trophies.

When the *tlatoani* and the supreme council decided to carry out a campaign, orders were given to collect supplies. Tribute-towns were obliged to send maize cakes, maize meal, toasted maize, beans, chile, pumpkin-seeds, pinolli, and salt. Indiviual warriors also carried as much food as they could to supplement the basic rations. When all was prepared and the conch-shells were sounded, the first units set out. Roads in ancient Mexico were maintained by local towns, but they were barely wide enough for two people to pass. The first to depart were the scouts, followed by warrior-priests carrying sacred effigies, who marched a day ahead of the force. Then came the veteran warriors and members of the prestigious military orders, including the *tlacochcalcatl* and *tlaccatecatl*, and the *tlatoani* himself if he was personally to direct the campaign in the field. The third great contingent of warriors from Tenochtitlan followed, with units spaced out at regular intervals. Then came contingents from Tlatelolco, Tetzcoco, Tlacopan, and other allied cities, again formed in

Eagle warriors

Opposite:

132–135 TOP LEFT The stone head of an eagle warrior, wearing a helmet. RIGHT Aztec sculpture of a warrior carved in an archaic "Toltec" style. Compare with the figure of a warrior from the temple at Tula (ill. 28). CENTER LEFT Detail of the banquette frieze in the Eagle House patio at the Great Pyramid. Its style is distinctively Toltec and reflects the Aztecs' concern to match the military prowess of their predecessors. BOTTOM Patio of the Eagle House, showing the banquette which functioned as a seat of rank and authority.

136 ABOVE This life-sized ceramic sculpture of an eagle warrior was recovered in the excavation of the Eagle House at the Great Pyramid.

long columns stretching for many miles. Hassig has calculated that a basic unit of 8,000 men would stretch as far as 15 miles, or even 20 miles along winding trails. The final units of warriors in the march came from subject towns as a form of tribute-payment. Camp was set up with reed mats for shelter, or tents for the high nobility, while the ordinary warriors slept in the open wrapped in their mantles.

Battlefield practices have been outlined in the chapters on the Spanish Conquest and the Aztec imperial expansion, but no discussion of Aztec warriors can fail to mention the curious military ritual known as *xochiyaotl*, "flower war" (referring to the battlefield where finely-attired warriors would fall like a rain of blossoms). Flower wars were staged by previous mutual agreement between opposing communities for the sole purpose of capturing prisoners for sacrifice. Those formal ritualistic encounters may be another custom transmitted from an ancient past, but precedent has yet to be firmly traced. An early reference says that the conflict between the Tepanec-Mexica and the Chalca began as a *xochiyaotl* in 1376. By the 15th century flower wars were regularly held between the members of the Triple Alliance and Huexotzingo, Atlixco, and other towns in the Valley of Puebla. A generation ago, scholars assumed that they were a unique Mesoamerican phenomenon, but parallels have now been drawn with head-hunting tribal societies elsewhere in the world. Warfare among these peoples was not primarily waged for booty or land. Even among the Aztecs, who conducted regular campaigns to acquire tribute, ritual sacrifice invested their enterprise with a strongly religious character.

Among the Toltecs and the late Maya, ballgames involving human sacrifice were played as a form of jousting and a substitute for armed conflict. The popularity of such games persisted under the Aztecs. Divination may also have been strongly featured in the outcome of such games, as it was in Classic Maya centers where ballgames were held during rites of passage. As Johan Huizinga speculated in his imaginative book, *Homo Ludens: A Study of the Play Element in Culture*, war may find its origins in the sense of play.[5] Waged with limiting game-like rules between equals or antagonists with equal rights, warfare in many early societies was conducted according to a way of thought that was deeply concerned with fate, chance, judgment and contest as different expressions of the sacred. Flower wars may be seen as a type of mock-war with a still unknown past in Mesoamerica, that continued to be practiced intermittently within the larger pattern of Aztec warfare. Although flower wars grew disproportionately to include hundreds, even thousands, of warriors in response to the need for prisoners for display and status, their original intention was to make offerings for the renewal of society and nature.

137,138 LEFT and ABOVE A wooden drum (*panhuehuetl*) from Malinalco, carved with eagles and jaguars dancing and uttering the cry for war. The iconography of these anthropomorphic figures echoes that of the rock-cut temple at Malinalco and is related to Aztec military imagery.

War games

139,140 RIGHT This scene from the Codex Magliabechiano shows a two-man ballcourt. The popular ballgame – dating back to the beginnings of civilization in Mesoamerica – was played for sport and gambling, for resolving disputes, and as a form of divination. The skull markers indicate that the game could be played "to the death." BELOW RIGHT The hips and shoulders were used to hit a solid rubber ball.

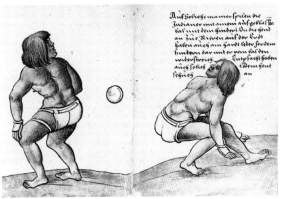

Aztec kingship: a tlatoani takes office

The idea of kingship in Aztec society cannot be understood in political and economic terms alone, for the *tlatoani* was also the focus of religious activities by which the prosperity and continuity of the community were ensured. We have seen that he stood at the summit of the social pyramid, embodying the functions of the chief priest and commander of the armed forces. When a new *tlatoani* was initiated into office, he became the central protagonist of a ritual drama that engaged the whole nation.[6]

The election of a new *tlatoani* at Tenochtitlan was not based on primogeniture. As the old ruler neared the end of his life he would confirm his choice of a successor. In effect this would have already been prearranged, for the man to be *tlatoani* held the office of *tlaccatecatl* in the supreme military council of four. Officially however the appointment depended on the approval of the council; the *cihuacoatl's* advice was also important, and in some cases the rulers of Tetzcoco and Tlacopan were consulted. The candidate always came from a very restricted group of princes. Two pre-imperial *tlatoani* were sons of the rulers, but after Itzcoatl we find a succession of brothers, nephews, and grandsons belonging to an extended family oligarchy. The selection and election process was only the beginning of a rite of passage by which the prince would be transformed into the semi-deified, supreme source of authority in the Aztec state.

The rites of kingship at Tenochtitlan were organized in distinct episodes, featuring elaborate processions, speeches, prayers and performances carefully staged for dramatic effect. The Great Pyramid formed the central stage and point of reference. The building was at once the manifestation of Tlaloc's "mountain of sustenance" and Huitzilopochtli's mythic Coatepetl. Consecrated by a multitude of artifacts and offerings from previous reigns, the building was conceived as a cosmic symbol and a sign of the ancestral past. The royal rites of passage unfolded in a sequence of four phases: (1) separation and retreat; (2) investiture and coronation; (3) the coronation war; and (4) confirmation.

Separation and retreat

During this phase society was in a state of suspension following the death of the previous ruler. The ruler-elect withdrew from all usual social contact as a ritual detachment from his former status and functions. The separation began when he was formally stripped of his finery and all emblems of rank and authority. Wearing only a loincloth, he was led by the rulers of Tetzcoco and Tlacopan to the base of the Great Pyramid stairway. Feigning weakness as a sign of humility, he was supported by two other noblemen on his climb to the Huitzilopochtli shrine. On the high platform he was dressed in a dark green cape with skull and crossbones designs. This attire signaled his withdrawal from ordinary life in order to return to a "primordial" state, a ritual time of the beginning of things. Dressed in the garb of fasting and penitence, and in the company of nobles who were similarly dressed, he burnt incense before Huitzilopochtli's shrine and then descended the stairway. All movements were deliberately slow and solemn, and the assembled crowds were silent. The ruler-elect and his entourage now entered the building known as the Tlacochcalco, a military headquarters and armory in the central precinct. Here began a four-day, four-night retreat, with fasting and penitential observances. Every noon and midnight a silent procession revisited the Huitzilopochtli shrine, where incense was burnt and the ruler offered drops of his royal blood pricked from his calves, arms, and earlobes. The mood was somber and reflective, and afterwards everyone went to bathe in a ceremony of religious purification. During this time of betwixt and between, the prospective ruler contemplated the meaning and burdens of his office and the responsibilities of command. The orations delivered during this period were quiet and struck a tone of humility. The ruler stood bowed while speaking, and the very devout stood naked. One of the most significant speeches was addressed to Tezcatlipoca, whose metaphoric titles "wind," "night," "lord of the near and the nigh," respectively suggested the breath of life, invisibility, and pervasiveness. Tezcatlipoca was a cult of Toltec origin and was especially identified with royalty. By invoking Tezcatlipoca while standing before the Huitzilopochtli effigy, the rulers expressed a bond between the older cult and that of the deified Aztec warrior-hero. For this reason Tezcatlipoca and Huitzilopochtli were sometimes referred to as "brothers."

Investiture and coronation
The brilliant investiture and coronation of the new ruler contrasted with the somber mood of the retreat. This second episode demonstrated the ruler's return to society and the assumption of his new social role. Now the ruler and his entourage processed from the great enclosure to one of the royal palaces. Within the palace he stood surrounded by nobles to be dressed in royal attire by the *tlatoani* of Tetzcoco. This dressing in the regalia of state signaled the taking of command as the first step in reconstituting Aztec society after the dissolution of the retreat.

The tlatoani of Tetzcoco took the crown of green stones, all worked in gold, and placed it upon the new ruler's head, and piercing the septum of his nose he inserted a green emerald as thick as a quill pen, and in his ears two round emerald earplugs in gold settings, and on his arms from elbow to shoulder two very resplendent gold bracelets, and on his ankles, anklets with dangling gold bells, and the [Tetzcocan] King shod him with jaguar-skin sandals all elegantly gilded and clad him with a precious mantle of hennequen-like fiber, very thin and shining, all gilded and painted with elegant pictures; and he put a waistband around him of the same, and taking him by the hand he led him to a throne that they called the *cuauhicpalli*, meaning eagle-seat, also named jaguar-seat, for it was decorated with eagle feathers and jaguar-hides.[7]

This ceremony was at once an investiture, a coronation, and an enthronement. Many speeches were made by members of the nobility, both admonishing and praising the new ruler, who replied to each in turn.[8]

Once crowned, dressed, and seated, the ruler was carried to the Great Pyramid on an eagle and jaguar throne placed upon a litter. This first public appearance, with all the symbols of authority, contrasted markedly with the previous phase of withdrawal. Atop the pyramid, in Huitzilopochtli's shrine, the new ruler was presented with a jaguar's claw for sacrificial bloodletting from his ears and legs. This autosacrifice was followed by more admonishments, prayers, and sermons, and quail were also offered to affirm the bonds between the ruler and the ancestral deity, Huitzilopochtli.

The procession then descended from the pyramid to go to another place, described in some accounts as the location of an "eagle vessel" carved with a receptacle, while other accounts mention a "sun-stone." A magnificent eagle-vessel was recovered during the Great Pyramid excavations, and a fine example of a sun-stone exists in the Philadelphia Museum. Standing before such sculptured monuments (both types may have been displayed together, for the eagle was a solar symbol) the *tlatoani* again offered drops of royal blood from his arms and legs and he also sacrificed quail. Another covenant was thereby made to confirm his rule at the center of the world in the present "sun" or era of creation. From this site the ruler was carried in the royal litter to a building known as the *coateocalli*, the "house of (foreign) gods." There, within a darkened chamber, the captured religious fetishes and paraphernalia of foreign nations were kept. These tokens of Aztec triumphs were also symbolic hostages of the religious identity of tributary peoples. In the *coateocalli* the ruler once again offered blood sacrifices to affirm his obligation to attend to the cycle of religious festivals.

The final station in the ritual enclosure was the earth-temple known as Yopico. The inner chamber had a sunken receptacle in the floor for offerings during the springtime planting festivals of Tlacaxipehualiztli and Tozoztontli. The rites of the deity Xipe Totec housed in this temple were primarily agricultural, but they also assumed a military nature in the confirmation ceremony of young Aztec warriors who had captured prisoners for the springtime sacrifice. Here the connection between war and agriculture was vividly demonstrated. Yopico was a symbolic architectural cave, an entrance to the earth related to the rock-cut Malinalco temple. The circular opening in the floor of the Malinalco temple and the sunken receptacle at Yopico were places for ritual communication with the earth. It was through sacrifice to the earth that the transfer of power to the new *tlatoani* was consecrated and made legal. The idea of transferring power from a deceased ruler to his successor is evident in the Dedication

141 Detail from the Dedication Stone of Tizoc and Ahuizotl. The deceased king Tizoc (left) confronts his successor Ahuizotl (right). Dressed as priests, they draw blood from their earlobes with bone awls: the transfer of power from the dead to the living is legitimized by sacrifice to the sacred earth.

Stone of Tizoc and Ahuitzotl: the centrally positioned mask immediately below their feet represents the earth as a sacred entity and as the land of the Aztecs. Emerging from Yopico after offering his blood, quail, and incense, the *tlatoani* was spiritually "reborn" into his new social role.

Returning to the palace, the new ruler was seated for the ceremony of speeches, which marked the conclusion of the investiture and coronation. In each speech made by the elders, nobles, and chiefs, the new ruler was admonished and encouraged to perform as expected of a person in his office. At one point the ruler was reminded that he now enjoyed sacred status.

> Although the common folk have gladdened thee, and although thy younger brother, thy older brother have put their trust in thee, now thou art deified. Although thou art human, as are we, although thou art our son, our younger brother, no more art thou human, as are we: we do not look upon thee as human. Already thou repentest, thou replacest one. Thou callest out to, thou speakest in a strange tongue to the god, the lord of the near, of the high. And within thee he calleth out to thee; he is within thee; he speaketh forth from they mouth. Thou art his lips, thou art his jaw, thou art his tongue, thou art his eyes, thou art his ears. He hath provided thee thy fangs, thy claws.[9]

We must remember that in Nahuatl the term *teotl* means "something sacred" and does not necessarily imply that the ruler was deified as a god.

In response the *tlatoani* exhorted the population to war and to cultivate the land. Finally, the ceremony of speeches was closed with an address from a representative of the common people, acknowledging the ruler's discourse and showing that his commandments had been understood.

The coronation war

Before the *tlatoani* could be considered fully confirmed as the commander of the Aztec nation, he was required to prove his leadership in battle, to win tribute, and to capture prisoners for sacrifice in the final ceremony of confirmation. The fortunes of Tizoc and his successor-brother Ahuizotl illustrate the importance of this military test. In contrast to Tizoc's unsuccessful coronation war, Ahuizotl's campaign in Xilotepec was a resounding success. His return to the capital was the occasion of a grand triumph, and the booty obtained in the campaign went far to finance the lavish display laid on for his confirmation ceremony.

Confirmation

This was the final step in the rites of kingship. Proclamations were made and invitations sent to allies, administrative officials, and important rulers including those of enemy nations. As the time drew close, all chieftains, traders, and treasurers were expected to send gifts – failure to do so might well lead to loss of rank or even exile. In due time the presents began to arrive. Cloth and clothing, jewelry, bundles of feathers, loads of corn, of cacao, and baskets of fruit, flocks of turkeys, deer, quail, and fish of many kinds were brought across the causeways in astonishing abundance. Within the city, artisans and craftspeople including lapidary workers, jewelers, featherworkers, and potters also made preparations. Masons and plasterers set to work repairing old buildings and constructing new ones.

The feasts that were to follow were offered by the *tlatoani* himself, in a striking expression of his personal control of wealth. The central act of this ceremony was the personal distribution by the new ruler of insignia of rank to every official. This procedure began on the first day, when the allied rulers of Tetzcoco and Tlacopan were formally presented with regalia of office by the new *tlatoani* – thus also making clear to all the supremacy of Tenochtitlan over its two allied cities. The rulers were then dressed and waited to attend a spectacular dance. The singers and musicians began the rhythm on a great *huehuetl* drum in the patio of the palace, and the *tlatoque* of Tetzcoco and Tlacopan led the 2,000 assembled nobles, chieftains, and high-ranking warriors in a stately dance. At a prescribed moment the new *tlatoani* made his triumphal entrance. Enveloped in the smoke of copal incense, the splendidly attired victorious *tlatoani* was encircled by the dancing lords. Standing by the commanding drum, he was converted to a living icon – the heir to Huitzilopochtli – reaffirming his virtue and his warlike purpose at the center of the Aztec world.

Returning to the throne, the new ruler continued his personal distribution of insignia. All high officials including nobles, warriors, and priests, as well as elders from the *calpultin* wards of Tenochtitlan, provincial governors, tax collectors, and chieftains, received gifts and emblems of authority. In the early years of Aztec expansion each town within the empire had had its own internal hierarchy, but few mechanisms existed to establish the rank of one particular community leader in relation to the chief of another or to Aztec officials. The growth of the empire afforded Aztec chiefs increasing authority and it became necessary to create a more general and widespread ranking order. In this respect the function of the confirmation rite, which was originally a validation of the ruler's authority, changed by the end of the 15th century into a demonstration of his absolute superiority within Aztec society, and of Aztec society vis-à-vis the rest of the world. The confirmation events thus symbolically established the reintegration of the social order. The long process that had begun with the death of the former ruler was concluded with the sacrifice of the prisoners taken in the coronation war. With this act the rites of kingship concluded.

In Aztec society the idea of kingship embraced two principal functions. The first was rooted in an ancient chthonic religion and its creation-mythology, personified by the *tlatoani* as a magical rainmaker-king in the annual rites at Mt Tlaloc. In this capacity he was responsible for scheduling and performing the sacrifice for agricultural renewal. The other notion of kingship was linked to this first conception: the *tlatoani* as an invincible warrior, embodying the image of Huitzilopochtli. Both roles may be identified in the kingship rites performed at Tenochtitlan, but the latter was particularly important, because for an island people who had never possessed their own farmlands, war had become the principal means of accruing wealth and power. In this respect the inauguration of a new *tlatoani* reflected the unique history of the original Mexica population.

12 · Epilog

By the time Cortés led the Spaniards and their Tlaxcalan allies across the causeway to meet Motecuhzoma Xocoyotzin, the Aztecs had successfully built the largest empire in Mesoamerican history. The rise of the Aztec nations would have been difficult to foresee 100 years before. Their dynamic expansion in the 15th century belongs to one of those exceptional moments in human history when certain political and economic opportunities are grasped by imaginative, forceful leaders and a vigorous people. In seeking to explain the Aztec achievement, scholars have researched and debated a variety of causes and motivations. It is apparent today that no single dominant cause can be found. Rather, explanations lie in portraying dynamic interactions in the process of social and cultural change.

First to be mentioned is the favorable location of the island of Tenochtitlan: the unclaimed outcrops and reedbeds proved to be a safe haven and a strategic site between powerful neighboring cities. The Mexica were able to establish marketplaces and build their city in comparative safety. Tenochtitlan was never conquered before the Spanish arrived, and its causeways and bridges were easily defensible. Secondly, the idea of empire was learned by the Mexica in service to their Tepanec lords when they participated in the conquest of the Tepanec tribute-domain. They were subsequently allowed to pursue their own course of action until the weakness within the dominant city permitted the Mexica, Acolhua, and a Tepanec faction to take over the empire.

The formation of a firm agricultural base with the intensively farmed *chinampa* system is a third factor behind the Aztec expansion. But the management of this productive zone is not thought to have been the "prime mover" in the rise of the Aztecs, as in the debatable case of the so-called "hydraulic civilizations" in Mesopotamia and China. The Aztec city states were already well established by the time the great agricultural projects were undertaken. The role of individuals is a fourth factor that shaped the events of the 15th century. Itzcoatl, Motecuhzoma I, Netzahualcoyotl, Tlacaelel, and later Ahuizotl were imaginative and energetic rulers who decisively extended Aztec power. They built elaborate tributary networks through the force of arms, they promoted alliances and marriage connections, and they developed a vast system of ritual obligations. Laws were proclaimed that strongly favored the centralized authority of the *tlatoque* and the rule of the state; not even Ahuizotl (who most effectively employed force and terror) could forget that Aztec hegemony was also maintained by extended family bonds and client relationships. Archaeological evidence and the ethnohistoric texts also support the view that Aztec colonization was beginning at Oztoman, Malinalco, Calixtlahuaca, and elsewhere: the Aztecs built monuments at these places to establish the imperial presence and assert the territorial claims of communities resettled from the Valley of Mexico. Although the Aztec empire ultimately rested on the manipulation of force, and the threat of rebellion remained ever-present, it is evident that rulers were taking steps to broaden and strengthen their hold within regions already conquered. It does not appear that the Aztec empire was so overextended and unstable that its collapse was imminent at the time of the Spanish Conquest.

The quest for wealth must be counted as a principal motive for the Aztec expansion. The desire to obtain enormous riches can clearly be seen on the tribute-lists and sumptuous costumes illustrated in the Codex Mendoza. But for the Aztecs the lure of wealth lay not in being able to store it away in the form of bankable riches, as in Renaissance Europe; rather, goods were accumulated in large measure for the purposes of exhibition and distribution during festivals. As a result of the incoming flow of tribute, the lords of Tenochtitlan and Tetzcoco were obliged to assert their rank and authority with ever more lavish patronage. At the highest level, coronations were celebrated with unequaled splendor, and were attended by thousands of guests who had to be housed and fed. The rededication of the Great Pyramid required a similar outlay. Through the expenditure of huge resources on state and ritual occasions, the Aztecs developed an important means of redistributing wealth. This pattern of ceremonial gift-giving, which has been likened to the potlatch of the Northwest Coast, was surely of much older origin, and had the effect of narrowing the economic gap between different families and social groups.[1] The circulation of gifts and the offering of food was an inherent aspect of Aztec culture that found another expression in the practice of making offerings of food and blood to the land and its deities in return for the bounty of nature.

Trade and traders must also be mentioned for their role in the Aztec expansion. The early markets of Tenochtitlan played an essential part in establishing the basic economy, and also functioned as social meeting places where marriages and political alliances were forged. Long-distance traders – the *pochteca* – provided intelligence of conditions in distant places, and were adroitly used by the *tlatoque* and the new military aristocracy as agents for their own commercial interests. But in contrast to the 15th-century merchants of Flanders and Florence who constituted a rising middle class, the *pochteca* were slowly being absorbed into the growing imperial system.

Did the Aztecs have a sense of historical destiny? Their civilization has been characterized as a renascence of the metropolitan culture that had been a legacy of the central highlands since Teotihuacan and Tula.[2] The Aztecs cultivated a strong cultural and historical affinity with the ancient "Toltecs," whom they identified with the idealized past. The adoption of the ways of agricultural peoples long settled in the Valley of Mexico, the learning of the Nahuatl language, the later quoting of symbolic forms derived from monuments in the ruins of Teotihuacan and Tula, and the pervasive aspiration to be like the Toltecs are all testimony to the Aztecs' desire to assimilate themselves to the civilization of antiquity. Mesoamerican notions of cyclical time and the repetition of past events seem to have propelled the Aztecs towards the "recreation of Tula".

Finally, we must reflect on religion in Aztec life, and its role in the growth of the empire. During the 1930s and 1940s, Alfonso Caso viewed Aztec warfare as an eternal quest for sacrificial victims to feed the gods, in repayment for having offered their own blood in the original creation of the world. But while human sacrifice was undeniably a part of Mesoamerican religion, the phenomenal scale of sacrifice practiced in Tenochtitlan must be viewed as an expression of political might and the requirement for warriors to capture victims as a means of recognition and promotion. The growth of the military aristocracy was linked to this basic demand. The cruel spectacles ordered by Ahuizotl were used deliberately to impress both citizens and foreigners with renewed Aztec power and determination following the vacillations of Tizoc and Axayacatl's Tarascan defeat. Were the Aztec armies motivated, like their Islamic contemporaries, to convert the conquered peoples? There is little evidence to suggest so, for the cult of Huitzilopochtli was not widely found beyond Tenochtitlan, and was acknowledged by Tetzcoco and other cities simply as an expression of political alliance.

Ethnohistorian Nigel Davies concludes that two of the principal themes mentioned above were particularly important. The first was Aztec dedication – based on the notion that the present repeated the past – to the task of recreating the former glory of Tula. The second theme was the search for ever-increasing sources of goods for flamboyant celebratory displays, as well as victims for sacrifice.

But to these must be added another, perhaps deeper, motivating force, stemming from the need to define and establish a new social order which was harmonized with the order of the natural world. This was manifested in the preoccupation with the concept of genesis, and the cyclical life, death, and rebirth of nature. Important events and enterprises – both past and present – were marked by genesis imagery, for instance the Chicomoztoc page from the Historia Tolteca-Chichimeca, or the depiction in the Codex Aubin of Netzahualcoyotl's descent from a primitive Acolhua couple within a cave. The authority and responsibilities of Aztec kings were similarly imbued with the idea of genesis and the renewal of nature; indeed, the coronation rites expressed symbolic death and withdrawal followed by social reintegration and rebirth. The annual rites performed at the Temple of Tlaloc, to call forth rain from the womb of the earth, were fundamentally concerned with the cycles of nature at the critical time of change from one season to another.

The principal Aztec sites also expressed this theme of the integration of the cosmological and social order. The Temple of Tlaloc, the Hill of Tetzcotzingo, and the Great Pyramid of Tenochtitlan were visual metaphors of Mother Nature herself and the eternal cycle of life, death, and renewal. On another level, commemorative monuments such as the Calendar Stone and the Stone of Tizoc reflect the organization, function, and history of Aztec society within the larger framework of the cosmos. If the Aztecs sought to recreate the former glories of Tula, surely they also reached further back beyond the beginnings of history, to the moment when the land first rose from primordial waters, when people first emerged from the earth, and when the first order was established. This deeply felt cultural ideal had powerful territorial implications. Transmuted into political and military activity, the imagery of renewal propelled the advance and extension of Aztec empire.

142 Head of the goddess Coyolxauhqui. Carved in greenstone, this sculpture is 0.85 m high.

Annual Ceremonies of the Aztecs

AZTEC "MONTH"	CEREMONY NAME	ENGLISH TRANSLATION	CHRISTIAN CORRELATION	MAIN DEITIES	RITES AND CUSTOMS
I	Atlcaualo Cuauhitleua	Ceasing of Water Raising of Trees	14 FEB–5 MARCH	TLALOC CHALCHIHUTLICUE CHICOMECOATL XILONEN QUETZALCOATL	Poles erected and decorated with ritual banners in temples and homes. Offerings to maize deities. Children sacrificed on mountains, dances.
II	Tlacaxipe-hualiztli	Flaying of Men	6 MARCH–25 MARCH	XIPE TOTEC	Dances, mock skirmishes, young warriors present sacrificial captives at initiation. Gladiatorial sacrifice. Priests wear skins of victims 20 days. Ruler participates in military ceremonies and agricultural dance.
III	Tozoztontli Xochimanaloya	Small Vigil Offering of Flowers	26 MARCH–14 APRIL	TLALOC CHALCHIUHTLICUE CENTEOTL COATLICUE	First rituals in fields, ceremonial planting (probably in *chinampa* zone). Flowers offered. Xipe Totec skins worn by priests from previous festival deposited in Yopico temple "cave."
IV	Huey Tozoztli	Great Vigil	15 APRIL–4 MAY	TLALOC CHALCHIUHTLICUE CENTEOTL CHICOMECOATL XILONEN QUETZALCOATL	Procession of maidens to maize goddess, carrying seed corn to be blessed. Sacrifices of children on Mt Tlaloc and at Pantitlan in Lake Tetzcoco. Participation by the rulers of four cities.
V	Toxcatl	Dryness	5 MAY–22 MAY	TEZCATLIPOCA HUITZILOPOCHTLI MIXCOATL CAMAXTLI	Major renewal festival, sacrifice of youth impersonator of Tezcatlipoca during previous year. Similar sacrifice for Huitzilopochtli, and related ancestral hero–deities in Tlaxcala and Valley of Puebla.
VI	Etzalcualiztli	Eating of Maize and Beans	23 MAY–13 JUNE	TLALOC CHALCHIUHTLICUE QUETZALCOATL	End of the dry season and beginning of rains. Priests fast for rain, the lords dance with maize stalks (from the *chinampas*) and carry pots with maize and beans. Offerings made to agricultural implements. Reeds brought from lake for new mats, seats, and to adorn temples.
VII	Tecuilhuitontli	Small Feast of the Lords	14 JUNE–3 JULY	XOCHIPILLI HUIXTOCIHUATL	Sacrifices to the deity of feasting and vegetation. Salt goddess sacrifices. The lords host commoners at feasts. The ruler dances and distributes gifts.

AZTEC "MONTH"	CEREMONY NAME	ENGLISH TRANSLATION	CHRISTIAN CORRELATION	MAIN DEITIES	RITES AND CUSTOMS
VIII	**Huey Tecuilhuitl**	Great Feast of the Lords	4 JULY – 23 JULY	XILONEN CIHUACOATL	First tender maize festival. Lords again host commoners. The ruler dances, distributes gifts. Young warriors and women dance. Sacrifices made.
IX	**Miccailhuitontli** **Tlaxochimaco**	Little Feast of the Dead Birth of Flowers	24 JULY – 12 AUG	TEZCATLIPOCA HUITZILOPOCHTLI ANCESTORS	Feasts, dances, and offerings in honor of the dead. Sacrifice to Huitzilopochtli, the deified ancestral hero.
X	**Huey Miccail-huitl** **Xocotlhuetzi**	Great Feast of the Dead Great Fall of the Xocotl Fruit (harvest)	13 AUG – 1 SEPT	HUEHUETEOTL XIUHTECUHTLI YACATECUHTLI ANCESTORS	Sacrifices to fire. Pole-climbing ceremony (xocotl tree) competition by boys. Commemoration of ancestors.
XI	Ochpaniztli	Sweeping	2 SEPT – 21 SEPT	TOCI TLAZOLTEOTL TETEOINNAN COATLICUE CINTEOTL CHICOMECOATL	Major harvest season begins. Ceremonies honoring earth goddesses. General cleaning, sweeping, repairing. Ripe corn deity honored, seed corn cast to populace. In preparation for the coming war season, the ruler gives insignia to warriors. Ruler participates in dances. Military ceremonies at borders of traditional enemies in Valley of Puebla. Priests begin 80-day fasts to culminate in Panquetzalitzli festivals, Nov.– Dec.
XII	Teotleco	Arrival of the Deities	22 SEPT – 11 OCT	ALL DEITIES HONORED	Return of the deities to participate in grand harvest festival. Their advent signaled by the appearance at midnight of footprint in a maize-flour bowl in temple. Youngest deity (TLAMAZINCATL) arrives first; oldest (HUEHUETEOTL) last. General feasting, rejoicing, dancing, offering of food.
XIII	Tepeilhuitl	Feast of the Mountains	12 OCT – 31 OCT	TLALOC TLALOQUE TEPICTOTON OCTLI (Pulque deities) XOCHIQUETZAL and MAJOR RAIN MOUNTAINS: POPOCATEPETL IXTACCIHUATL MT TLALOC MATLALCUEYE	Offerings at shrines on major rain mountains. Amaranth-dough effigies and serpent-like branches covered with amaranth paste in rituals and sacrifices. Mat-makers honor NAPPATECUHTLI; fishermen, OPOCHTLI; turpentine-makers, ZAPOTLANTENAN; weavers, embroiderers, and painters, XOCHIQUETZAL.

AZTEC "MONTH"	CEREMONY NAME	ENGLISH TRANSLATION	CHRISTIAN CORRELATION	MAIN DEITIES	RITES AND CUSTOMS
XIV	**Quecholli**	Precious Feather (Roseate spoonbill)	1 NOV – 20 NOV	MIXCOATL CAMAXTLI TLAMATZINCATL	Fasting of warriors. Manufacture of weapons for hunt and war. Commemoration of dead warriors. Ancient tribal hunting rites, communal hunts and prizes to best hunter. Prisoners bound like deer and sacrificed.
XV	**Panquetzaliztli**	Raising of Banners	21 NOV – 10 DEC	HUITZILOPOCHTLI TEZCATLIPOCA	Major military rites celebrating birth of HUITZILOPOCHTLI and his victory over COYOLXAUHQUI, enacted at Great Pyramid of Tenochtitlan. Large sacrifice of prisoners. Great procession from pyramid to Tlatelolco, Chapultepec, Coyoacan, and back to pyramid. Paper flags on fruit trees and houses.
XVI	**Atemoztli**	Descent of Water	11 DEC – 30 DEC	TLALOQUE MOUNTAINS	This period may bring light rains, mountains again honored.
XVII	**Tititl**	Stretching	31 DEC – 19 JAN	CIHUACOATL ILAMATECUHTLI TONANTZIN YACATECUHTLI	Priests dressed as deities, dance. Great feast with lords and priests. Ritual dances in which the ruler participates. Merchants sacrifice slaves in traders' initiation rites. Weavers honor ILAMATECUHTLI (old mother goddess).
XVIII	**Izcalli Huauhquiltamal- cualiztli**	Growth Eating of Tamales Stuffed with Greens	20 JAN – 8 FEB	XIUHTECUHTLI TLALOC CHALCHIUHTLICUE	Amaranth-dough effigy of XIUHTECUHTLI (fire god) honored. Sacrifice of animals to fire, toasting of corn. Rulers participate in ceremonies as this deity is their patron.Tamales with greens eaten. Children pulled by neck to "make them grow." Every four years, special lordly dance, children have ears pierced and are assigned "godparents."
	Nemontemi	Useless Days (considered unlucky)	9 FEB – 13 FEB		No rituals, general abstinence, no business conducted.

Two Special Non-Annual Ceremonies

CEREMONY NAME	ENGLISH TRANSLATION	CHRISTIAN CORRELATION	RITES AND CUSTOMS
Toxiuhmolpilia	Binding of the Years (New Fire rites)	Every 52 years in *2 Acatl*	All fires extinguished, all activities cease. Quietness observed. New Fire rites at Uixachtlan Hill, torches taken by runners to light temple fires in all cities. Renewal of clothing and utensils, old clothing and utensils discarded.
Atamalcualiztli	Eating of Water Tamales	Every 8 years in *Tecpatl*	Seven-day initial fast. Only water-soaked tamales eaten, no condiments, "to give the maize a rest." Dances, ceremonial swallowing of water-snakes and frogs.

Notes to the Text

Introduction (pp. 7–11)
1 Cortés 1971; Diaz 1970.
2 Sahagún 1951–69; Durán 1967 and 1971; Ixtlilxóchitl 1895; Chimalpahin 1965.
3 Leon y Gama 1990.

Chapter 1 (pp. 14–34)
1 Sahagún 1951–69; Book 12, *The Conquest of Mexico*; Prescott 1931; Collis 1954; White 1971.
2 Davies 1982, pp. 257–260.
3 Gillespie 1989, pp. 173–207.
4 Umberger 1981, pp. 10–17.
5 Sahagún 1951–69, Book 12, *The Conquest of Mexico*, p. 42.

Chapter 3 (pp. 44–65)
1 Davies 1977; Healan 1989; Diehl 1983.
2 Davies 1980.
3 Sahagún 1951–69, Book 3, *The Origin of the Gods*, p. 13.
4 Kubler 1962, pp. 176–78; Diehl and Berlo 1989.
5 Dibble 1980, plate 1.
6 Ixtlilxóchitl 1895.
7 Gillespie 1989, pp. xvii–xli.
8 Durán 1967, vol. 2, pp. 217–18.
9 Tezozomoc 1949, p. 23.
10 Kirchhoff 1961.
11 Gillespie 1989, pp. 56–95.
12 Durán 1964, p. 44.

Chapter 4 (pp. 66–72)
1 Durán 1967, pp. 79–80. This well-known passage has been questioned as apocryphal by Nigel Davies (Davies 1987, p. 40), who points out that it suggests the elite might abdicate power to the proletariat – a pattern unknown in Mesoamerican culture. However, it may well be a metaphorical expression, perhaps misconstrued from the original Nahuatl in the Cronica X as a formalized expression of communal solidarity.
2 Ixtlilxóchitl 1895, vol. 1, p. 316.
3 Davies 1982, p. 78.

Chapter 5 (pp. 74–85)
1 Parsons 1976, pp. 233–57.
2 Barlow 1949.
3 Hassig 1988.
4 Offner 1988, pp. 88–95.
5 *Ibid.*, p. 95.
6 *Ibid.*, pp. 106–9.
7 *Ibid.*, p. 104.
8 Zorita 1942, pp. 200–3.
9 Townsend 1982b, pp. 111–40.
10 Barlow 1946.
11 Townsend 1982a.
12 Barlow 1946, pp. 110–27.
13 Offner 1982, pp. 153–155.

Chapter 6 (pp. 86–106)
1 Hassig 1988.

2 Spores 1967 and 1984; Flannery and Marcus 1983.
3 Hassig 1988, pp. 157–175.
4 *Ibid.*, pp. 176–188.
5 Davies 1982.
6 Marquina 1951, pp. 218–220; Seler 1960–61.
7 Payón 1936.
8 Payón 1947.
9 Stanislawski 1947, pp. 45–55.
10 Hassig 1988, pp. 208–213.
11 Moedano 1948.
12 Davies 1982, p. 201.

Chapter 7 (pp. 108–128)
1 Nicholson 1971.
2 Sahagún 1951–69, Book 1, *The Gods*.
3 Nicholson 1971, pp. 397–408.
4 Tedlock 1985.
5 Caso 1958.
6 Sahagún 1951–69, Book 7, *The Sun, The Moon, and the Binding of the Years*, p. 4.
7 *Ibid.*, p. 6.
8 *Ibid.*, p. 7.
9 Nicholson 1971, pp. 400–401.
10 Durán 1971, p. 396.
11 Durán 1971; Sahagún 1951–69.
12 Wilhelm 1950.
13 Tedlock 1985.

Chapter 8 (pp. 129–154)
1 Durán 1971, pp. 154–171.
2 Townsend 1982a, pp. 37–62.
3 Sahagún 1951–69, Book 2, *The Ceremonies*, pp. 59–61, 91–100, 110–117; Durán 1971, pp. 422–425, 436–440.
4 Matos Moctezuma 1987, pp. 186–209; Matos Moctezuma 1988, pp. 109–145.
5 Broda 1987, pp. 211–256.
6 Reed 1991, pp. 260–300.

Chapter 9 (pp. 156–165)
1 Sahagún 1951–69, Book 6, *Rhetoric and Moral Philosophy*, p. 175.
2 Townsend 1979, pp. 23–34.
3 Martínez 1972, pp. 125–135; León-Portilla 1963.
4 Durán 1971, pp. 154–171.
5 Mendieta 1945.
6 Martínez 1972, pp. 101 (translated by Richard Townsend).

Chapter 10 (pp. 166–191)
1 Sanders, Parsons and Santley 1979.
2 Calnek 1972; Parsons 1971.
3 Palerm and Wolf 1971; Palerm 1955.
4 Nuttall 1925, pp. 453–464.
5 *Ibid.*
6 Quoted in Nuttall 1925.
7 Diaz 1970, pp. 215–217.
8 Townsend 1970; Berdan 1978, pp. 187–198; Berdan 1980, pp. 37–41; Berdan 1986.

9 Zorita 1942.
10 Sahagún 1951–69, Book 9, *The Merchants*, p. 22.
11 Sahagún 1951–69, Book 2, *The Ceremonies*, pp. 130–138.
12 Sahagún 1951–69, Book 1, *The Gods*, pp. 1–2.

Chapter 11 (pp. 192–207)
1 Diaz 1956, pp. 104–105.
2 Acosta Saignes 1946, pp. 147–205.
3 Sahagún 1951–69, Book 10, *The People*, p. 29.
4 Hassig 1988, pp. 17–47.

5 Huizinga 1950.
6 Townsend 1987, pp. 371–407.
7 Durán 1967, vol. 2, p. 301.
8 Sahagún 1951–69, Book 10, *Rhetoric and Moral Philosophy*, pp. 47–85.
9 *Ibid.*, p. 52.

Epilog (pp. 208–211)
1 Davies 1982, p. 204.
2 Davies 1987.

Further Reading

A vast number of books have been written about the Aztecs, and only a selection can be listed here. For an introduction to Aztec history, the general reader is referred to Nigel Davies, *The Aztecs: A History*, and Inga Clendinnen's *Aztecs: An Interpretation*. Michael D. Coe's *Mexico* provides a good summary of the history of Mexico as a whole. Two useful surveys of Aztec life and history can be found in Warwick Bray's *Everyday Life of the Aztecs* and Jacques Soustelle, *Daily Life of the Aztecs on the Eve of the Spanish Conquest*. For those interested in the art of this period, see Esther Pasztory's finely illustrated *Aztec Art* and Mary Ellen Miller's *Art of Mesoamerica*. The standard work on Aztec kingship is Susan Gillespie's *The Aztec Kings*, and on warfare, Ross Hassig's *Aztec Warfare*. Finally, Maudslay's translation of Bernal Diaz del Castillo, *The Discovery and Conquest of Mexico* is a vivid eyewitness account of the Conquest itself.

Abbreviations

INAH = Instituto Nacional de Antropología e Historia
UNAM = Universidad Nacional Autónome de México
SEP = Secretaría de Educacion Pública

ACOSTA SAIGNES, MIGUEL. *"Los Teopixque" Revista Mexicana de Estudios Antropológicos* 8, 1946.
ALVARADO TEZOZÓMOC. *Crónica Mexicáyotl.* Imprenta Universitaria, Mexico City, 1949.
ANAWALT, PATRICIA R. *Indian Clothing Before Cortés.* Foreword by Henry Nicholson. University of Oklahoma Press, Norman, 1981.
AVENI, ANTHONY. *Empires of Time: Calendars, Clocks, and Cultures.* I. B. Tauris & Co., London, 1990.
AVENI, ANTHONY and SHARON GIBBS. "On the Orientation of Pre-Columbian Buildings in Central Mexico," *American Antiquity*, vol. 41, 1976.

BARLOW, ROBERT H. "The Titles of Tetzcotzingo" in *Tlalocan* II (2). Mexico City, 1946.
— "The Extent of the Empire of the Culhua-Mexica," in *Ibero-Americana* no. 28. University of California Press, Berkeley, 1949.
BERDAN, FRANCES. "Ports of Trade in Mesoamerica: A Reappraisal," in *Cultural Continuity in Mesoamerica*, ed. D. Browman. Mouton Publishers, The Hague, 1978.
— "Aztec Merchants and Markets: Local Level Economic Activity in a Non-Industrial Empire." *Mexicon 2* (3), 1980.
— "The Economics of Aztec Luxury Trade and Tribute," in *The Aztec Templo Mayor*, ed. Elizabeth Boone. Dumbarton Oaks, Washington, D.C., 1986.
BRAY, WARWICK. *Everyday Life of the Aztecs.* B.T. Batsford, London, G. P. Putnam's Sons, New York, 1968.
BRODA, JOHANNA. "The Provenance of the Offerings: Tribute and Cosmovision," in *The Aztec Templo Mayor*, ed. Elizabeth Boone. Dumbarton Oaks, Washington, D.C., 1987.
CALNEK, EDWARD E. "Settlement Patterns and Chinampa Agriculture in Tenochtitlan," in *American Antiquity*, vol. 37, no. 1, 1972.
— "The Internal Structure of Tenochtitlan," in *The Valley of Mexico: Studies in Pre-Hispanic Ecology and Society*, ed. E. Wolf. A School of American Research Book, University of New Mexico Press, Albuquerque, 1976.
CARMICHAEL, ELIZABETH. *Turquoise Mosaics from Mexico.* Trustees of the British Museum, London. 1970.
CARRASCO, DAVID (ed.). *To Change Place: Aztec Ceremonial Landscapes.* The University of Colorado Press, Boulder, 1991.
CARRASCO, PEDRO. "Social Organization of Ancient Mexico," *Handbook of Middle American Indians*, vol. 10, *Archaeology of Northern Mesoamerica.* University of Texas Press, Austin, 1971.
CASO, ALFONSO. *The Aztecs: People of the Sun.* Translated by Lowell Dunham. The University of Oklahoma Press, Norman, 1958.

CHIMALPAHÍN, DOMINGO FRANCISCO DE SAN ANTON MUÑON. *Relaciones originales de Chalco Amequemecan.* Edited by S. Rendón. UNAM, Mexico City, 1965.

CLENDINNEN, INGA. *Aztecs: An Interpretation.* Cambridge University Press, Cambridge and New York, 1991.

CODEX BORBONICUS. Bibliothèque de l'Assemblée Nationale. Paris, 1974.

CODEX BORGIA. Commentaries by Eduard Seler. Fondo de Cultura Económica, Mexico, 1963.

CODEX MAGLIABECHIANO. Biblioteca Nazionale Centrale di Firenze, 1970.

CODEX MENDOZA. Edited and translated by James Cooper Clark. Waterlow & Sons, London, 1938.

COE, MICHAEL D. "Religion and the Rise of Mesoamerican States," in *The Transition to Statehood in the New World,* ed. Grant D. Jones and Robert R. Kautz. Cambridge University Press, Cambridge, 1981.

— *Mexico.* Thames and Hudson, London and New York, 1984.

COLLIS, MAURICE. *Cortés and Montezuma.* Faber and Faber, London, 1954.

CORTÉS, HERNÁN. *Letters from Mexico.* Translated by A. R. Pagden. Orion Press, New York, 1971.

DAVIES, NIGEL. *The Toltecs until the Fall of Tula.* University of Oklahoma Press, Norman, 1977.

— *The Toltec Heritage from the Fall of Tula to the Rise of Tenochtitlan.* University of Oklahoma Press, Norman, 1980.

— *The Aztecs: A History.* University of Oklahoma Press, Norman, 1982.

— *The Aztec Empire: The Toltec Resurgence.* University of Oklahoma Press, Norman, 1987.

DIAZ DEL CASTILLO, BERNAL. *The Discovery and Conquest of Mexico.* Translated by A. P. Maudslay. Farrar, Straus, and Cudahy, New York, 1956.

DIBBLE, CHARLES E. *Codíce Xolotl,* vol. 2.

DIEHL, RICHARD A. *Tula: The Toltec Capital of Ancient Mexico.* Thames and Hudson, London and New York, 1983.

DIEHL, RICHARD and JANET BERLO. *Mesoamerica after the Decline of Teotihuacan AD 700–900.* Dumbarton Oaks, Washington, D.C., 1989.

DURÁN, DIEGO. *The Aztecs: The History of the Indies of New Spain (1581).* Translated by Doris Heyden and Fernando Horcasitas. New York, Gordon Press, 1964.

— *Historia de las Indias de Nueva España e Islas de Tierra Firme.* 2 vols. Edited by Angel M. Garibay K. Editorial Porrúa, Mexico City, 1967.

— *Book of the Gods and Rites and the Ancient Calendar.* Translated by Doris Heyden and Fernando Horcasitas. University of Oklahoma Press, Norman, 1971.

ELLWOOD, ROBERT. *The Feast of Kingship.* Sophia University Press, Tokyo, 1978.

FERNÁNDEZ, JUSTINO. *Coatlicue, estética del arte indígena antigua.* Prologue by Samuel Ramos. Centro de Estudios Filosóficos, Mexico City, 1959.

FLANNERY, KENT V. and JOYCE MARCUS (eds.). *The Cloud People.* Academic Press, New York, 1983.

FRANKFORT, HENRI. *Kingship and the Gods.* University of Chicago Press, Chicago, 1948.

GIBSON, CHARLES. *"Structure of the Aztec Empire,"* in *Handbook of Middle American Indians,* vol. 10. University of Texas Press, Austin, 1971.

GILLESPIE, SUSAN. *The Aztec Kings.* University of Arizona Press, Tucson, 1989.

GILLMOR, FRANCES. *Flute of the Smoking Mirror: a Portrait of Nezahualcoyotl, Poet-King of the Aztecs.* University of New Mexico Press, Albuquerque, 1949.

HASSIG, ROSS. *Aztec Warfare.* University of Oklahoma Press, Norman, 1988.

HEALAN, DAN M. (ed.). *Tula of the Toltecs.* University of Iowa Press, Iowa City, 1989.

HEYDEN, DORIS. "Los Ritos de Paso en las Cuevas," *Boletin INAH* II, vol. 19, 1976.

— "Caves, Gods and Myths: world-view and planning in Teotihuacan," in *Mesoamerican sites and world views,* ed. Elizabeth P. Benson. Dumbarton Oaks, Washington, D.C., 1981.

HOCART, A. M. *Kingship.* Oxford University Press, London, 1927.

HUIZINGA, JOHAN. *Homo Ludens: A Study of the Play Element in Culture.* Beacon Press, Boston, 1950.

HVIDTFELDT, ARILD. *Teotl and Ixiptlatli: Some Central Conceptions in Ancient Mexican Religion, with a General Introduction on Cult and Myth.* Munksgaard, Copenhagen, 1958.

IXTLILXÓCHITL, FERNANDO DE ALVA. *Obras Históricas.* Editorial Chavero, Mexico City, 1895.

KELLEY, JOYCE. *The Complete Visitor's Guide to Mesoamerican Ruins.* University of Oklahoma Press, Norman, 1982.

KIRCHHOFF, PAUL. "Land tenure in ancient Mexico," *Revista Mexicana de Estudios Antropológicos,* vol. 14, pt. 1, 1954–55.

— "Se puede localizar Aztlán?" in *Anuario de Historia,* año 1. UNAM, Facultad de Filosofia y Letras, Mexico City, 1961.

KIRCHHOFF, PAUL, LINA ODENA GUEMAS, and LUIS REYES GARCIA. *Historia Tolteca-Chichimeca.* CISINAH, Mexico City, 1976.

KLEIN, CECELIA F. "Who was Tlaloc?" *Journal of Latin American Lore* 6:2. University of California Press, Los Angeles, 1980.

KUBLER, GEORGE. *The Art and Architecture of Ancient America.* Penguin Books, Harmondsworth and Baltimore, 1962.

LEON Y GAMA, ANTONIO. *Descripción histórica y cronológica de las dos piedras ...* Mexico, 1832. (Reprinted INAH, Mexico City, 1990.)

LEÓN-PORTILLA, MIGUEL. *Aztec Thought and Culture.* Translated by Jack Emory Davis. University of Oklahoma Press, Norman, 1963.

MAPA QUINATZIN. Edited by J. M. A. Aubin. Published in *Anales del Museo Nacional de México,* pt. 1, vol. 3, 1886.

MAPA TLOTZIN. Edited by J. M. A. Aubin. Published in *Anales del Museo Nacional de México,* pt. 1, vol. 3, 1886.

MARQUINA, IGNACIO. *Arquitectura prehispánica.* INAH, Mexico City, 1951.

MARTÍNEZ, JOSÉ LUIS. *Nezahualcoyotl: vida y obra.* México City, Fondo de Cultura Económica, 1972.

MATOS MOCTEZUMA, EDUARDO. "Symbolism of the Templo Mayor," in *The Aztec Templo Mayor,* ed. Elizabeth Boone. Dumbarton Oaks, Washington, D.C., 1987.

— *The Great Temple of the Aztecs.* Thames and Hudson, London and New York, 1988.

MAUDSLAY, ALFRED P. "Plano hecho en papel de maguey que se conserva en el Museo Nacional de Mexico," in *Anales del Museo Nacional de México,* 1909.

MENDIETA, GERÓNIMO DE. *Historia Eclesiástica Indiana.* Editorial Chavez Hayhoe, Mexico City, 1945.

MILLER, MARY ELLEN. *The Art of Mesoamerica: From Olmec*

to Aztec. Thames and Hudson, London and New York, 1986.

MOEDANO, H. "Oztotitlan," in *El Occidente de Mexico*. Sociedad Mexicana de Antropologia, 4. Mexico City, 1948.

NICHOLSON, HENRY. "Religion in Pre-Hispanic Central Mexico," in *Handbook of Middle American Indians*, vol. 10. University of Mexico Press, Austin, 1971.

NICHOLSON, H. B. and ELOISE QUIÑONES KEBER. *Art of Aztec Mexico; Treasures of Tenochtitlan*. National Gallery of Art, Washington, D.C., 1983.

NUTTALL, ZELIA. "The Gardens of Ancient Mexico," in *Annual Report of the Smithsonian Institution 1923*. U.S. Government Printing Office, Washington, D.C., 1925.

OFFNER, JEROME. "Aztec Legal Process: The Case of Texcoco," in *The Art and Iconography of Late Post-Classic Central Mexico*, ed. Elizabeth Boone. Dumbarton Oaks, Washington, D.C., 1982.

— *Law and Politics in Aztec Texcoco*. Cambridge University Press, Cambridge, 1988.

PALERM, ANGEL. "La base agrícola de la civilización urbana de Mesoamerica," in *Las civilizaciones antigues del viejo mundo y de América*. Unión Panamericana, Washington, D.C., 1955.

PALERM, ANGEL and ERIC R. WOLF. "El desarrollo del area clave de imperio Texcocano," in *Agricultura y Civilizacion en Mesoamérica*, 32. SEP, Mexico City, 1971.

PARSONS, JEFFREY. *Prehistoric Settlement Patterns in the Texcoco Region, Mexico*. Memoirs of the Museum of Anthropology, no. 3. University of Michigan, Ann Arbor, 1971.

— "The Role of Chinampa Agriculture in the Food Supply of Tenochtitlan," in *Cultural Change and Continuity*, ed. Charles E. Cleland. Academic Press, Albuquerque, 1976.

PASZTORY, ESTHER. *The Aztec Tlaloc: God of water and antiquity*. Paper presented at the 43rd International Congress of Americanists, Vancouver, 1979.

— *Aztec Art*. Harry Abrams, New York, 1983.

PAYÓN, JOSÉ GARCÍA. *La zona arqueológica de Tecaxic-Calixtlahuaca y los Matlazinca*. Talleres Gráficos de la Nación, Mexico City, 1936.

— *Los monumentos arqueológicos de Malinalco*. Talleres Gráficos de la Nación, Mexico City, 1947.

POMAR, JUAN BAUTISTA. "Relación de Texcoco," in *Nueva colección de documentos para la historia de México*, vol. 3, ed. Icazbalceta. Editorial Porrúa, Mexico City, 1891.

PRESCOTT, WILLIAM H. *History of the Conquest of Mexico*. Random House, New York, 1931.

RANDS, R. "Artistic connections between the Chichén Itzá Toltec and the Classic Maya," *American Antiquity*, vol. 19, 1954.

REED, KAY. *Binding Reeds and Burning Hearts: Mexica-Tenochca Concepts of Time and Sacrifice*. PhD dissertation, University of Chicago, 1991.

RICARD, ROBERT. *The Spiritual Conquest of Mexico*. Translated by Lesley Byrd Simpson. University of California Press, Berkeley, 1966.

ROBERTSON, DONALD. *Mexican Manuscript Painting of the Early Colonial Period*. Yale University Press, New Haven, 1959.

SAHAGÚN, BERNARDINO DE. *Florentine Codex: General History of the Things of New Spain*. 12 vols. Translated by Arthur J. O. Anderson and Charles Dibble. The School of American Research, Santa Fe, 1951–69.

SANDERS, WILLIAM T., JEFFREY R. PARSONS and ROBERT S. SANTLEY. *The Basin of Mexico: Ecological Processes in the Evolution of a Civilization*. Academic Press, New York, 1979.

SELER, EDUARD. *The Temple of Tepoxtlan*. Bureau of American Ethnology, 28. U.S. Government Printing Office, Washington, D.C., 1960–61.

SPORES, RONALD. *The Mixtec Kings and their People*. University of Oklahoma Press, Norman, 1967.

— *The Mixtecs in Ancient and Colonial Times*. University of Oklahoma Press, Norman, 1984.

SOUSTELLE, JACQUES. *Daily Life of the Aztecs on the Eve of the Spanish Conquest*. Stanford University Press, Palo Alto, 1961.

STANISLAWSKI, DAN. "Tarascan Political Geography," *American Anthropologist*, vol. 49, 1947.

SULLIVAN, THELMA. "Tlaloc: A New Etymological Interpretation of His Name and What it Reveals of His Essence and Nature," *Proceedings of the 40th International Congress of Americanists*, vol. 2. Rome, 1974.

TEDLOCK, DENNIS (trans.). *Popol Vuh*. Simon and Schuster, New York, 1985.

TEZOZOMOC, HERNANDO ALVARADO. *Crónica Mexicana*. Reprinted by Editorial Leyenda, Mexico City, 1944.

— *Crónica Mexicáyotl*. Palcography and Spanish version by Adrián León. Imprenta Universitaria, Mexico City, 1949.

TOWNSEND, RICHARD. "Trade on the Aztec Horizon." Unpublished ms, Tozzer Library, Peabody Museum of Archaeology and Ethnology, Harvard University, 1970.

— *State and Cosmos in the Art of Tenochtitlan*. Dumbarton Oaks, Washington, D.C., 1979.

— "Pyramid and Sacred Mountain," in *Archaeoastronomy and Ethnoastronomy in the American Tropics*. ed. Anthony Aveni and Gary Urton. New York Academy of Sciences, vol. 385. New York, 1982a.

— "Malinalco and the Lords of Tenochtitlan," in *The Art and Iconography of Late Post-Classic Central Mexico*, ed. Elizabeth Boone. Dumbarton Oaks, Washington, D.C., 1982b.

— "Coronation at Tenochtitlan" in *The Aztec Templo Mayor*. Edited by Elizabeth Boone. Dumbarton Oaks, Washington, D.C., 1987.

TURNER, VICTOR. *The Forest of Symbols*. Cornell University Press, Ithaca, New York and London, 1967.

UMBERGER, EMILY. "The Structure of Aztec History," *Archaeoastronomy* vol. IV, no. 4, 1981.

VAN GENNEP, ARNOLD. *The Rites of Passage*. University of Chicago Press, Chicago, 1960.

WHITE, JON MANCHIP. *Cortés and the Downfall of the Aztec Empire*. Carroll and Graf, New York, 1971.

WICKE, C. *Once more around the Tizoc stone: A reconsideration*. Paper presented at 41st International Congress of Americanists, Mexico City, 1976.

WILHELM, RICHARD (trans.). *I Ching or Book of Changes*. Rendered into English by Cary F. Baynes. Bollingen Series XIX, Princeton, 1950.

ZANTWIJK, RUDOLF VAN. "Aztec Hymns as the Expression of the Mexican Philosophy of Life," *Internationales Archiv fur Etnographie*, vol. 48, no. 1, 1957.

— "Principios Organizadores de los Mexicas: Una Introducción al Estudio del Sistema Interno del Régimen Azteca," in *Estudios de Cultura Náhuatl*. vol. 4, 1963.

ZORITA, ALONSO DE. *Breve y sumaria relación de los señores de la Nueva España*. UNAM, Mexico City, 1942.

Sources of Illustrations

Abbreviations
MNA = Museo Nacional de Antropología, Mexico
INAH = Instituto Nacional de Antropología e Historia

Frontispiece: MNA; photo Irmgard Groth-Kimball. *King List* p. 12: drawn by Annick Petersen after Codex Mendoza and Codex Matritense. **1** Drawn by Annick Petersen. **2** From Codex Mendoza; Bodleian Library, Oxford. **3–5** From Sahagún. **6** INAH. **7** After Palacios 1929, fig. 1. **8** Drawn by Annick Petersen. **9** Drawn by Annick Petersen. **10** MNA; photo Richard Townsend. **11** From La Preclara Narratione di Ferdinando Cortese, 1524. **12** Drawn by Annick Petersen. **13** From Codex Matritense; courtesy E. Matos Moctezuma, from *The Great Temple of the Aztecs*, 1988. **14** Reconstruction by Marquina; after Hardoy 1968, fig. 36. **16** From Lienzo de Tlaxcala; courtesy American Museum of Natural History, New York. **17** Courtesy Great Temple Project; photo Salvador Guilliem Arroyo. **18,19** After Lienzo de Tlaxcala; courtesy E. Matos Moctezuma, from *The Great Temple of the Aztecs*, 1988. **20** From Lienzo de Tlaxcala. **21,22** Courtesy Great Temple Project; photo Salvador Guilliem Arroyo. **23** Photo Warwick Bray. **24** Chichén Itzá chacmool. **25** Photo Michael D. Coe. **26** MNA. **27–29** Photos Michael D. Coe. **30** Acosta 1941. **31** From Mapa Quinatzin. **32** After Codex Boturini. Courtesy E. Matos Moctezuma, from *The Great Temple of the Aztecs*, 1988. **33** From Historia Tolteca-Chichimeca; Bibliothèque Nationale, Paris. **34** MNA; photo Irmgard Groth-Kimball. **35** After Palacios 1929, fig. 2. **36** Codex Mendoza, Bodleian Library, Oxford. **37** From Codex Ixtlilxóchitl; Bibliothèque Nationale, Paris. **38** Photo courtesy DETENAL, Mexico City. **39** From Plano en Papel de Maguey. **40** Photo Richard Townsend. **41** From Codex Mendoza; Bodleian Library, Oxford. **42** From Codex Mendoza; Bodleian Library, Oxford. **43** From Pasztory, *Aztec Art*, 1983, plate 152. **44** From Pasztory, *Aztec Art*, 1983; redrawn after Barlow 1950, pls. 1 and 2. **45** Drawn by Annick Petersen. **46** From Codex Mendoza; Bodleian Library, Oxford. **47** From Codex Mendoza; Bodleian Library, Oxford. **48** From Codex Magliabechiano; Biblioteca Nazionale Centrale, Florence. Photo Nicholas J. Saunders. **49** MNA. **50** After Orozco y Berra 1877. **51** From Codex Magliabechiano; Biblioteca Nazionale Centrale, Florence. **52** Photo Michael D. Coe. **53** MNA; photo Irmgard Groth-Kimball. **54** From Durán. **55** Photo Richard Townsend. **56** Photo Richard Townsend. **57** After Marquina. **58** Photo Richard Townsend. **59** From Codex Borgia. **60** Photo Richard Townsend. **61** INAH. **62** Courtesy Great Temple Project; photo Salvador Guilliem Arroyo. **63** MNA. **64** Photo Richard Townsend. **65** From Codex Ixtlilxóchitl; Bibliothèque Nationale, Paris. **66,67** From Codex Borbonicus; Bibliothèque de l'Assemblée Nationale, Paris. **68** Photo courtesy The Art Institute of Chicago.

69 From Codex Borbonicus; Bibliothèque de l'Assemblée Nationale, Paris. **70** Adapted from M. Coe in A. Aveni (ed.), *Archaeoastronomy in Pre-Columbian America* (University of Texas Press, 1975). **71** MNA. **72** From Coe 1984; drawing Dr Patrick Gallagher. **73** From Codex Fejervary-Mayer. **74** From Codex Magliabechiano; Biblioteca Nazionale Centrale, Florence. **75** From Codex Telleriano-Remensis. **76** Bibliothèque de l'Assemblée Nationale, Paris. **77** Richard Townsend. **78** Photo Richard Townsend. **79** From Codex Borgia. **80** Photo Richard Townsend. **81** Photo Richard Townsend. **82** Photo Richard Townsend. **83** Drawing Annick Petersen; after Matthew Pietryka. **84** Photo courtesy Dumbarton Oaks Center for Pre-Columbian Studies. **85** From Codex Borbonicus; Bibliothèque de l'Assemblée Nationale, Paris. **86** MNA. **87** Photo Richard Townsend. **88** MNA. **89** From Codex Borbonicus; Bibliothèque de l'Assemblée Nationale, Paris. **90** Reconstruction model by Marquina. **91** After Matos Moctezuma and Rangel, *El Templo Mayor de Tenochtitlan: Planos, Cortes y Perspectivas* (INAH, 1982). **92** From Matos Moctezuma 1988. **93** Courtesy Great Temple Project; photo Salvador Guilliem Arroyo. **94** After Heyden 1984. **95** Courtesy Great Temple Project; photo Salvador Guilliem Arroyo. **96** Photo Richard Townsend. **97** From Codex Ixtlilxóchitl; Bibliothèque Nationale, Paris. **98** After Coe 1984; drawing by David Kiphuth. **99–102** Courtesy Great Temple Project; photo Salvador Guilliem Arroyo. **103** From Codex Mendoza; Bodleian Library, Oxford. **104,105** Photo courtesy The Art Institute of Chicago. **106** From Codex Tovar; courtesy Carter Brown Memorial Library, Brown University, Providence, Rhode Island. **107** MNA. **108** INAH. **109** From Codex Mendoza; Bodleian Library, Oxford. **110** After Coe; drawing ML Design. **111** From Sahagún. **112** From Sahagún. **113,114** Courtesy Great Temple Project; photo Salvador Guilliem Arroyo. **115** INAH. **116** MNA. **117, 118** Museum of Mankind, London. **119** Courtesy Great Temple Project; photo Salvador Guilliem Arroyo. **120** From Codex Vaticanus; Vatican Library. **121** From Sahagún. **122** Courtesy Museum für Völkerkunde, Vienna. **123** From Sahagún; Biblioteca Mediceo-Laurenziana, Florence. **124** From Codex Mendoza; Bodleian Library, Oxford. **125** Metropolitan Museum of Art, New York. **126** University Museum of Archaeology and Ethnology, Cambridge. **127,128** Courtesy Great Temple Project; photo Salvador Guilliem Arroyo. **129** From Codex Magliabechiano; Biblioteca Nazionale Centrale, Florence. **130** From Codex Mendoza; Bodleian Library, Oxford. **131** From Codex Mendoza; Bodleian Library, Oxford. **132** INAH. **133** Photo Richard Townsend. **134** MNA, INAH. **135** Photo Richard Townsend. **136** Courtesy Great Temple Project; photo Salvador Guilliem Arroyo. **137** INAH. **138** After Marquina 1964, fig. 15. **139** From Codex Magliabechiano; Biblioteca Nazionale Centrale, Florence. **140** Sketch by Karl Weiditz, 1528. **141** After Seler, II, 1904, fig. 47. **142** MNA.

Index